ABOUT THIS PUBLICATION

FOR SERVICE ASSISTANCE

Please call Customer Service Department At:
1.704.921.9271

North Carolina General Statues is published by The Muliti-Media Group of Greater Charlotte in Charlotte, North Carolina. Copyright 2015 by the Multi-Media Group of Greater Charlotte. This book or parts thereof may not be reproduced in any form, stored in a retrieval system, or transmitted in any form by any means—electronic, mechanical, photocopy, recording or otherwise—without prior written permission of the publisher, except as provided by United States of America copyright law. All persons in Pen-Pal Magazine are over the age of 18.

The records required by U.S. Code 2257(a) through (c) and the pertinent regulations 28 C.F.R. Cli. 1, Part 75 with respect to this publication and all materials associated with such records are maintained by The Multi-Media Group of Greater Charlotte, Publisher and available for review by Attorney General.

www.visionbooks.org

Copyright © 2015 by MMGGC
All rights reserved!

TID: 5061561
ISBN (10) digit: 1502914093
ISBN (13) digit: 978-1502914095

123-4-56789-01239-Paperback
123-4-56789-01239-Hardback

First Edition

090520140547

Printed in the United States of America

2015 EDITION

North Carolina Criminal Law And Procedure-Pamphlet # 43

Printed In conjunction with the Administration of the Courts

North Carolina Criminal Law and Procedure
Pamphlet Reference Guide

Chapters	Pamphlet
Chapter 1 Civil Procedure	1
Chapter 1 Civil Procedure (Continue)	2
Chapter 1A Rules of Civil Procedure	2
Chapter 1B Contribution.	2
Chapter 1C Enforcement of Judgments.	2
Chapter 1D Punitive Damages.	2
Chapter 1E Eastern Band of Cherokee Indians.	2
Chapter 1F North Carolina Uniform Interstate Depositions and Discovery Act.	2
Chapter 2 - Clerk of Superior Court [Repealed and Transferred.]	3
Chapter 3 - Commissioners of Affidavits and Deeds [Repealed.]	3
Chapter 4 - Common Law	3
Chapter 5 - Contempt [Repealed.]	3
Chapter 5A - Contempt	3
Chapter 6 - Liability for Court Costs	3
Chapter 7 - Courts [Repealed and Transferred.]	3
Chapter 7A – Judicial Department	3
Chapter 7A – Continuation (Judicial Department)	4
Chapter 7A – Continuation (Judicial Department)	5
Chapter 7B - Juvenile Code	5
Chapter 8 - Evidence	6
Chapter 8A - Interpreters for Deaf Persons [Recodified.]	6
Chapter 8B - Interpreters for Deaf Persons	6
Chapter 8C - Evidence Code	6
Chapter 9 - Jurors	6
Chapter 10 - Notaries [Repealed.]	6
Chapter 10A - Notaries [Recodified.]	6
Chapter 10B - Notaries	6
Chapter 11 - Oaths	6
Chapter 12 - Statutory Construction	6
Chapter 13 - Citizenship Restored	6
Chapter 14 - Criminal Law	7
Chapter 14 –Criminal Law (Continuation)	8
Chapter 15 - Criminal Procedure	9
Chapter 15A - Criminal Procedure Act (Continuation)	10
Chapter 15A - Criminal Procedure Act (Continuation)	11
Chapter 15B - Victims Compensation	11
Chapter 15C - Address Confidentiality Program	11
Chapter 16 - Gaming Contracts and Futures	11
Chapter 17 - Habeas Corpus	11

Chapter 17A - Law-Enforcement Officers [Recodified.]	11
Chapter 17B - North Carolina Criminal Justice Education and Training System [Recodified.] Chapter 17C - North Carolina Criminal Justice Education and Training Standards Commission	11 11
Chapter 17D - North Carolina Justice Academy	11
Chapter 17E - North Carolina Sheriffs' Education and Training Standards Commission	11
Chapter 18 - Regulation of Intoxicating Liquors [Repealed.]	12
Chapter 18A - Regulation of Intoxicating Liquors [Repealed.]	12
Chapter 18B - Regulation of Alcoholic Beverages	12
Chapter 18C - North Carolina State Lottery	12
Chapter 19 - Offenses against Public Morals	12
Chapter 19A - Protection of Animals	12
Chapter 20 - Motor Vehicles	13
Chapter 20 - Motor Vehicles (Continuation)	14
Chapter 20 - Motor Vehicles (Continuation)	15
Chapter 20 - Motor Vehicles (Continuation)	16
Chapter 21 - Bills of Lading	17
Chapter 22 - Contracts Requiring Writing	17
Chapter 22A - Signatures	17
Chapter 22B - Contracts Against Public Policy	17
Chapter 22C - Payments to Subcontractors	17
Chapter 23 - Debtor and Creditor. r 24 - Interest	17
Chapter 24 – Interest	17
Chapter 25 – Uniform Commercial Code	18
Chapter 25 – Uniform Commercial Code (Continuation)	19
Chapter 25A – Retail Installment Sales Act	20
Chapter 25B - Credit	20
Chapter 25C - Sales of Artwork	20
Chapter 26 - Suretyship	20
Chapter 27 - Warehouse Receipts [Repealed.]	20
Chapter 28 - Administration [Repealed.]	20
Chapter 28A - Administration of Decedents' Estates	20
Chapter 28B - Estates of Absentees in Military Service	20
Chapter 28C - Estates of Missing Persons	20
Chapter 29 - Intestate Succession	21
Chapter 30 - Surviving Spouses	21
Chapter 31 - Wills	21
Chapter 31A - Acts Barring Property Rights	21
Chapter 31B - Renunciation of Property and Renunciation of Fiduciary Powers Act	21
Chapter 31C - Uniform Disposition of Community Property Rights at Death Act	21
Chapter 32 - Fiduciaries	21
Chapter 32A - Powers of Attorney	21
Chapter 33 - Guardian and Ward [Repealed and Recodified.]	21

Chapter 33A - North Carolina Uniform Transfers to Minors Act	21
Chapter 33B - North Carolina Uniform Custodial Trust Act	21
Chapter 34 - Veterans' Guardianship Act	22
Chapter 35 - Sterilization Procedures	22
Chapter 35A - Incompetency and Guardianship	22
Chapter 36 - Trusts and Trustees [Repealed.]	22
Chapter 36A - Trusts and Trustees	22
Chapter 36B - Uniform Management of Institutional Funds Act [Repealed.]	22
Chapter 36C - North Carolina Uniform Trust Code	22
Chapter 36D - North Carolina Community Third Party Trusts, Pooled Trusts	23
Chapter 36E - Uniform Prudent Management of Institutional Funds Act	23
Chapter 37 - Allocation of Principal and Income [Repealed.]	23
Chapter 37A - Uniform Principal and Income Act	23
Chapter 38 - Boundaries	23
Chapter 38A - Landowner Liability	23
Chapter 39 - Conveyances	23
Chapter 39A - Transfer Fee Covenants Prohibited	23
Chapter 40 - Eminent Domain [Repealed.]	23
Chapter 40A - Eminent Domain	23
Chapter 41 - Estates	23
Chapter 41A - State Fair Housing Act	23
Chapter 42 - Landlord and Tenant	23
Chapter 42A - Vacation Rental Act	23
Chapter 43 - Land Registration	23
Chapter 44 - Liens	24
Chapter 44A - Statutory Liens and Charges	24
Chapter 45 - Mortgages and Deeds of Trust	24
Chapter 45A - Good Funds Settlement Act	24
Chapter 46 - Partition	24
Chapter 47 - Probate and Registration	25
Chapter 47A - Unit Ownership	25
Chapter 47B - Real Property Marketable Title Act	25
Chapter 47C - North Carolina Condominium Act	25
Chapter 47D - Notice of Settlement Act [Expired.]	25
Chapter 47E - Residential Property Disclosure Act	25
Chapter 47F - North Carolina Planned Community Act	25
Chapter 47G - Option to Purchase Contracts	25
Chapter 47H - Contracts for Deed	25
Chapter 48 - Adoptions +	26
Chapter 48A - Minors	26
Chapter 49 - Bastardy	26
Chapter 49A - Rights of Children	26
Chapter 50 - Divorce and Alimony	26
Chapter 50A - Uniform Child-Custody Jurisdiction and	

Enforcement Act	26
Chapter 50B - Domestic Violence	26
Chapter 50C - Civil No-Contact Orders	26
Chapter 51 - Marriage	26
Chapter 52 - Powers and Liabilities of Married Persons	27
Chapter 52A - Uniform Reciprocal Enforcement of Support Act [Repealed.]	27
Chapter 52B - Uniform Premarital Agreement Act	27
Chapter 52C - Uniform Interstate Family Support Act	27
Chapter 53 - Banks	27
Chapter 53A - Business Development Corporations and North Carolina Capital Resource Corporations	28
Chapter 53B - Financial Privacy Act	28
Chapter 54 - Cooperative Organizations	28
Chapter 54A - Capital Stock Savings and Loan Associations [Repealed.]	28
Chapter 54B - Savings and Loan Associations	29
Chapter 54C - Savings Banks	29
Chapter 55 - North Carolina Business Corporation Act	30
Chapter 55A - North Carolina Nonprofit Corporation Act	31
Chapter 55B - Professional Corporation Act	31
Chapter 55C - Foreign Trade Zones	31
Chapter 55D - Filings, Names, and Registered Agents for Corporations, Nonprofit Corporations, and Partnerships	31
Chapter 56 - Electric, Telegraph and Power Companies [Repealed.]	31
Chapter 57 - Hospital, Medical and Dental Service Corporations [Recodified.]	31
Chapter 57A - Health Maintenance Organization Act [Recodified.]	31
Chapter 57B - Health Maintenance Organization Act [Recodified.]	31
Chapter 57C - North Carolina Limited Liability Company Act.	31
Chapter 58 - Insurance.	32
Chapter 58 - Insurance (Continuation)	33
Chapter 58 - Insurance (Continuation)	34
Chapter 58 - Insurance (Continuation)	35
Chapter 58 - Insurance (Continuation)	36
Chapter 58 - Insurance (Continuation)	37
Chapter 58 - Insurance (Continuation)	38
Chapter 58A - North Carolina Health Insurance Trust Commission [Recodified.]	38
Chapter 59 - Partnership.	39
Chapter 59B - Uniform Unincorporated Nonprofit Association Act.	39
Chapter 60 - Railroads and Other Carriers [Repealed and Transferred.]	39
Chapter 61 - Religious Societies	39
Chapter 62 - Public Utilities	39

Chapter 62 - Public Utilities (Continuation)	40
Chapter 62A - Public Safety Telephone Service And Wireless Telephone Service	40
Chapter 63 - Aeronautics	40
Chapter 63A - North Carolina Global TransPark Authority	40
Chapter 64 - Aliens	40
Chapter 65 – Cemeteries	40
Chapter 66 - Commerce and Business	41
Chapter 67 - Dogs	41
Chapter 68 - Fences and Stock Law	41
Chapter 69 - Fire Protection	41
Chapter 70 - Indian Antiquities, Archaeological Resources and Unmarked Human Skeletal Remains Protection	42
Chapter 71 - Indians [Repealed.]	42
Chapter 71A - Indians	42
Chapter 72 - Inns, Hotels and Restaurants	42
Chapter 73 - Mills	42
Chapter 74 - Mines and Quarries	42
Chapter 74A - Company Police [Repealed.]	42
Chapter 74B - Private Protective Services Act [Repealed.]	42
Chapter 74C - Private Protective Services	42
Chapter 74D - Alarm Systems	42
Chapter 74E - Company Police Act	42
Chapter 74F - Locksmith Licensing Act	42
Chapter 74G - Campus Police Act	42
Chapter 75 - Monopolies, Trusts and Consumer Protection	42
Chapter 75A - Boating and Water Safety	43
Chapter 75B - Discrimination in Business	43
Chapter 75C - Motion Picture Fair Competition Act	43
Chapter 75D - Racketeer Influenced and Corrupt Organizations	43
Chapter 75E - Unlawful Activities in Connection With Certain Corporate Transactions	43
Chapter 76 - Navigation	43
Chapter 76A - Navigation and Pilotage Commissions	43
Chapter 77 - Rivers, Creeks, and Coastal Waters	43
Chapter 78 - Securities Law [Repealed.]	43
Chapter 78A - North Carolina Securities Act	43
Chapter 78B - Tender Offer Disclosure Act [Repealed.]	43
Chapter 78C - Investment Advisers	43
Chapter 78D - Commodities Act	43
Chapter 79 - Strays [Repealed.]	43
Chapter 80 - Trademarks, Brands, etc.	44
Chapter 81 - Weights and Measures [Recodified.]	44
Chapter 81A - Weights and Measures Act of 1975.	44
Chapter 82 - Wrecks [Repealed.]	44
Chapter 83 - Architects [Recodified.]	44

Chapter 83A - Architects	44
Chapter 84 - Attorneys-at-Law	44
Chapter 84A - Foreign Legal Consultants	44
Chapter 85 - Auctions and Auctioneers [Repealed.]	44
Chapter 85A - Bail Bondsmen and Runners [Recodified.]	44
Chapter 85B - Auctions and Auctioneers	44
Chapter 85C - Bail Bondsmen and Runners [Recodified.]	44
Chapter 86 - Barbers [Recodified.]	44
Chapter 86A - Barbers	44
Chapter 87 - Contractors	44
Chapter 88 - Cosmetic Art [Repealed.]	44
Chapter 88A - Electrolysis Practice Act	44
Chapter 88B - Cosmetic Art	45
Chapter 89 - Engineering and Land Surveying [Recodified.]	45
Chapter 89A - Landscape Architects	45
Chapter 89B - Foresters	45
Chapter 89C - Engineering and Land Surveying	45
Chapter 89D - Landscape Contractors	45
Chapter 89E - Geologists Licensing Act	45
Chapter 89F - North Carolina Soil Scientist Licensing Act	45
Chapter 89G - Irrigation Contractors	45
Chapter 90 - Medicine and Allied Occupations	45
Chapter 90 - Medicine and Allied Occupations (Continuation)	46
Chapter 90 - Medicine and Allied Occupations (Continuation)	47
Chapter 90 - Medicine and Allied Occupations (Continuation)	48
Chapter 90A - Sanitarians and Water and Wastewater Treatment Facility Operators	48
Chapter 90B - Social Worker Certification and Licensure Act	48
Chapter 90C - North Carolina Recreational Therapy Licensure Act	48
Chapter 90D - Interpreters and Transliterators	48
Chapter 91 - Pawnbrokers [Repealed.]	48
Chapter 91A - Pawnbrokers Modernization Act of 1989	48
Chapter 92 - Photographers [Deleted.]	48
Chapter 93 - Certified Public Accountants	48
Chapter 93A - Real Estate License Law	49
Chapter 93B - Occupational Licensing Boards	49
Chapter 93C - Watchmakers [Repealed.]	49
Chapter 93D - North Carolina State Hearing Aid Dealers and Fitters Board.	49
Chapter 93E - North Carolina Appraisers Act	49
Chapter 94 - Apprenticeship	49
Chapter 95 - Department of Labor and Labor Regulations	49
Chapter 95 - Department of Labor and Labor Regulations (Continuation)	50
Chapter 96 - Employment Security	50
Chapter 97 - Workers' Compensation Act	50
Chapter 97 - Workers' Compensation Act (Continuation)	51

Chapter 98 - Burnt and Lost Records	51
Chapter 99 - Libel and Slander	51
Chapter 99A - Civil Remedies for Criminal Actions	51
Chapter 99B - Products Liability	51
Chapter 99C - Actions Relating to Winter Sports Safety and Accidents	51
Chapter 99D - Civil Rights	51
Chapter 99E - Special Liability Provisions	51
Chapter 100 - Monuments, Memorials and Parks	51
Chapter 101 - Names of Persons	51
Chapter 102 - Official Survey Base	51
Chapter 103 - Sundays, Holidays and Special Days	51
Chapter 104 - United States Lands	51
Chapter 104A - Degrees of Kinship	51
Chapter 104B - Hurricanes or Other Acts of Nature	51
Chapter 104C - Atomic Energy, Radioactivity and Ionizing Radiation [Repealed and Recodified.]	51
Chapter 104D - Southern States Energy Compact	51
Chapter 104E - North Carolina Radiation Protection Act	51
Chapter 104F - Southeast Interstate Low-Level Radioactive Waste Management Compact [Repealed]	51
Chapter 104G - North Carolina Low-Level Radioactive Waste Management Authority Act of 1987 [Repealed]	51
Chapter 105 - Taxation	51
Chapter 105 - Taxation (Continuation)	52
Chapter 105 - Taxation (Continuation)	53
Chapter 105 - Taxation (Continuation)	54
Chapter 105A - Setoff Debt Collection Act	55
Chapter 105B - Defaulted Student Loan Recovery Act	55
Chapter 106 - Agriculture	55
Chapter 106 - Agriculture (Continue)	56
Chapter 106 - Agriculture (Continue)	57
Chapter 107 - Agricultural Development Districts [Repealed.]	57
Chapter 108 - Social Services [Repealed and Recodified.]	57
Chapter 108A - Social Services	57
Chapter 108B - Community Action Programs	58
Chapter 108C Medicaid and Health Choice Provider Requirements.	58
Chapter 108D Medicaid Managed Care for Behavioral Health Services.	58
Chapter 109 - Bonds [Recodified.]	58
Chapter 110 - Child Welfare	58
Chapter 111 - Aid to the Blind	58
Chapter 112 - Confederate Homes and Pensions [Repealed.]	58
Chapter 113 - Conservation and Development	58
Chapter 113 - Conservation and Development (Continuation)	59

Chapter 113A - Pollution Control and Environment	59
Chapter 113A - Pollution Control and Environment (Continuation)	60
Chapter 113B - North Carolina Energy Policy Act of 1975	60
Chapter 114 - Department of Justice	60
Chapter 115 - Elementary and Secondary Education [Repealed.]	60
Chapter 115A - Community Colleges, Technical Institutes, and Industrial Education Centers [Repealed.]	60
Chapter 115B - Tuition and Fee Waivers	60
Chapter 115C - Elementary and Secondary Education	60
Chapter 115C - Elementary and Secondary Education (Continuation)	61
Chapter 115C - Elementary and Secondary Education (Continuation)	62
Chapter 115C - Elementary and Secondary Education (Continuation)	63
Chapter 115D - Community Colleges	63
Chapter 115E - Private Educational Facilities Finance Act [Recodified]	63
Chapter 116 - Higher Education	63
Chapter 116 - Higher Education (Continuation)	63
Chapter 116A - Escheats and Abandoned Property [Repealed.]	64
Chapter 116B - Escheats and Abandoned Property	64
Chapter 116C - Continuum of Education Programs	64
Chapter 116D - Higher Education Bonds	64
Chapter 117 - Electrification	64
Chapter 118 - Firemen's and Rescue Squad Workers' Relief and Pension Funds [Recodified.]	64
Chapter 118A - Firemen's Death Benefit Act [Repealed.]	64
Chapter 118B - Members of a Rescue Squad Death Benefit Act [Repealed.]	64
Chapter 119 - Gasoline and Oil Inspection and Regulation	64
Chapter 120 - General Assembly	65
Chapter 120 - General Assembly (Continuation)	66
Chapter 120 - General Assembly (Continuation)	67
Chapter 120C - Lobbying	67
Chapter 121 - Archives and History	67
Chapter 122 - Hospitals for the Mentally Disordered [Repealed.]	67
Chapter 122A - North Carolina Housing Finance Agency	67
Chapter 122B - North Carolina Agricultural Facilities Finance Act [Repealed.]	67
Chapter 122C - Mental Health, Developmental Disabilities, and Substance Abuse Act of 1985	67
Chapter 122C - Mental Health, Developmental Disabilities, and Substance Abuse Act of 1985 (Continuation)	68
Chapter 122D - North Carolina Agricultural Finance Act	68

Chapter 122E - North Carolina Housing Trust and Oil Overcharge Act	68
Chapter 123 - Impeachment	69
Chapter 123A - Industrial Development [Repealed.]	69
Chapter 124 - Internal Improvements	69
Chapter 125 - Libraries	69
Chapter 126 - State Personnel System	69
Chapter 127 - Militia [Repealed.]	69
Chapter 127A - Militia	69
Chapter 127B - Military Affairs	69
Chapter 127C - Advisory Commission on Military Affairs	69
Chapter 128 - Offices and Public Officers	69
Chapter 128 - Offices and Public Officers (Continuation)	70
Chapter 129 - Public Buildings and Grounds	70
Chapter 130 - Public Health [Repealed.]	70
Chapter 130A - Public Health	70
Chapter 130A - Public Health (Continuation)	71
Chapter 130A - Public Health (Continuation)	72
Chapter 130B - Hazardous Waste Management Commission [Repealed.]	72
Chapter 131 - Public Hospitals [Repealed.]	72
Chapter 131A - Health Care Facilities Finance Act	72
Chapter 131B - Licensing of Ambulatory Surgical Facilities [Repealed.]	72
Chapter 131C - Charitable Solicitation Licensure Act [Repealed.]	72
Chapter 131D - Inspection and Licensing of Facilities	72
Chapter 131E - Health Care Facilities and Services	72
Chapter 131E - Health Care Facilities and Services (Continuation)	73
Chapter 131F - Solicitation of Contributions	73
Chapter 132 - Public Records	73
Chapter 133 - Public Works	74
Chapter 134 - Youth Development [Recodified.]	74
Chapter 134A - Youth Services [Repealed.]	74
Chapter 135 - Retirement System for Teachers and State Employees; Social Security; Health Insurance Program for Children	74
Chapter 135 - Retirement System for Teachers and State Employees; Social Security; Health Insurance Program for Children	75
Chapter 136 - Transportation	75
Chapter 136 - Transportation (Continuation)	76
Chapter 137 - Rural Rehabilitation [Repealed.]	76
Chapter 138 - Salaries, Fees and Allowances	76
Chapter 138A - State Government Ethics Act	76
Chapter 139 - Soil and Water Conservation Districts	76

Chapter 140 - State Art Museum; Symphony and Art Societies	76
Chapter 140A - State Awards System	76
Chapter 141 - State Boundaries	76
Chapter 142 - State Debt	76
Chapter 143 - State Departments, Institutions, and Commissions	77
Chapter 143 - State Departments, Institutions, and Commissions (Continuation)	78
Chapter 143 - State Departments, Institutions, and Commissions (Continuation)	79
Chapter 143 - State Departments, Institutions, and Commissions (Continuation)	80
Chapter 143A - State Government Reorganization	80
Chapter 143B - Executive Organization Act of 1973	80
Chapter 143B - Executive Organization Act of 1973 (Continuation)	81
Chapter 143B - Executive Organization Act of 1973 (Continuation)	82
Chapter 143C - State Budget Act	83
Chapter 143D - The State Governmental Accountability and Internal Control Act	83
Chapter 144 - State Flag, Official Governmental Flags, Motto, and Colors	83
Chapter 145 - State Symbols and Other Official Adoptions.	83
Chapter 146 - State Lands	83
Chapter 147 - State Officers	83
Chapter 148 - State Prison System	84
Chapter 149 - State Song and Toast	84
Chapter 150 - Uniform Revocation of Licenses [Repealed.]	84
Chapter 150A - Administrative Procedure Act [Recodified.]	84
Chapter 150B - Administrative Procedure Act	84
Chapter 151 - Constables [Repealed.]	84
Chapter 152 - Coroners	84
Chapter 152A - County Medical Examiner [Repealed.]	84
Chapter 152A - County Medical Examiner [Repealed.] (Continuation)	85
Chapter 153 - Counties and County Commissioners [Repealed.]	85
Chapter 153A - Counties	85
Chapter 153B - Mountain Resources Planning Act	85
Chapter 153C - Uwharrie Regional Resources Act	85
Chapter 154 - County Surveyor [Repealed.]	85
Chapter 155 - County Treasurer [Repealed.]	85
Chapter 156 - Drainage	85
Chapter 156 – Drainage (Continuation)	86

Chapter 157 - Housing Authorities and Projects	86
Chapter 157A - Historic Properties Commissions [Transferred.]	86
Chapter 158 - Local Development	86
Chapter 159 - Local Government Finance	86
Chapter 159 - Local Government Finance (Continuation)	87
Chapter 159A - Pollution Abatement and Industrial Facilities Financing Act [Unconstitutional.]	87
Chapter 159B - Joint Municipal Electric Power and Energy Act	87
Chapter 159C - Industrial and Pollution Control Facilities Financing Act	87
Chapter 159D - The North Carolina Capital Facilities Financing Act	87
Chapter 159E - Registered Public Obligations Act	87
Chapter 159F - North Carolina Energy Development Authority [Repealed.]	87
Chapter 159G - Water Infrastructure	87
Chapter 159H - [Reserved.]	87
Chapter 159I - Solid Waste Management Loan Program and Local Government Special Obligation Bonds	87
Chapter 160 - Municipal Corporations [Repealed And Transferred.]	87
Chapter 160A - Cities and Towns	88
Chapter 160A - Cities and Towns (Continuation)	89
Chapter 160B - Consolidated City-County Act	89
Chapter 160C - Baseball Park Districts [Repealed.]	90
Chapter 161 - Register of Deeds	90
Chapter 162 - Sheriff	90
Chapter 162A - Water and Sewer Systems	90
Chapter 162B Continuity of Local Government in Emergency.	90
Chapter 163 Elections and Election Laws.	90
Chapter 163 Elections and Election Laws. (Continuation)	91
Chapter 164 Concerning the General Statutes of North Carolina.	92
Chapter 165 Veterans.	92
Chapter 166 Civil Preparedness Agencies [Repealed.]	92
Chapter 166A North Carolina Emergency Management Act.	92
Chapter 167 State Civil Air Patrol [Repealed.]	92
Chapter 168 Persons with Disabilities.	92
Chapter 168A Persons With Disabilities Protection Act.	92

Chapter 75A

Boating and Water Safety.

Article 1.

Boating Safety Act.

§ 75A-1. Declaration of policy.

It is the policy of this State to promote safety for persons and property in and connected with the use, operation, and equipment of vessels, and to promote uniformity of laws relating thereto. (1959, c. 1064, s. 1.)

§ 75A-2. Definitions.

As used in this Chapter, unless the context clearly requires a different meaning:

(1) "Abandoned vessel" means a vessel that has been relinquished, left, or given up by the lawful owner without the intention to later resume any right or interest in the vessel. The term does not include a vessel that is left by an owner or agent of the owner with any person or business for the purpose of storage, maintenance, or repair and that is not subsequently reclaimed.

(1a) "Certificate of number" means the document and permanent identification number issued by the Wildlife Resources Commission for the purpose of registering a vessel in this State.

(1b) "Commission" means the Wildlife Resources Commission.

(1c) "Director" means the Executive Director of the Wildlife Resources Commission.

(1d) "Electric generating facility" means any plant facilities and equipment used for the purposes of producing, generating, transmitting, delivering, or furnishing electricity for the production of power.

(1e) "Motorboat" means any vessel equipped with propulsion machinery of any type, whether or not the machinery is the principal source of propulsion:

Provided, that "propulsion machinery" as used in this section shall not include an electric motor when used as the only means of mechanical propulsion of any vessel.

(1f) "No-wake speed" means idle speed or slow speed creating no appreciable wake.

(2) "Operate" means to navigate or otherwise use or occupy any motorboat or vessel that is afloat.

(3) "Owner" means a person, other than a lienholder, having the property in or title to a vessel. The term includes a person entitled to the use or possession of a vessel subject to an interest in another person, reserved or created by agreement and securing payment or performance of an obligation, but the term excludes a lessee under a lease not intended as security.

(4) "Person" means an individual, partnership, firm, corporation, association, or other entity.

(4a) "Underway" means a vessel that is not at anchor, or made fast to the shore, or aground.

(5) "Vessel" means every description of watercraft or structure, other than a seaplane on the water, used or capable of being used as a means of transportation or habitation on the water.

(6) "Waters of this State" means any waters within the territorial limits of this State, and the marginal sea adjacent to this State and the high seas when navigated as a part of a journey or ride to or from the shore of this State, but does not include private ponds as defined in G.S. 113-129.

(7) Redesignated as subdivision (1d). (1959, c. 1064, s. 2; 1965, c. 634, s. 1; 1969, c. 87; 1975, c. 340, s. 1; 1983, c. 446, s. 1; 1993 (Reg. Sess., 1994), c. 753, s. 2; 2006-185, s. 1.)

§ 75A-3. Wildlife Resources Commission to administer Chapter; Boating Safety Committee; funds for administration.

(a) The Commission shall enforce and administer the provisions of this Chapter.

(b) The chair of the Commission shall designate from among the members of the Commission three members who shall serve as the Boating Safety Committee of the Commission, and who shall, in their activities with the Commission, place special emphasis on the administration and enforcement of this Chapter.

(c) The Boating Account is established within the Wildlife Resources Fund created under G.S. 143-250. Interest and other investment income earned by the Account accrues to the Account. All moneys collected pursuant to the numbering and titling provisions of this Chapter shall be credited to this Account. Motor fuel excise tax revenue is credited to the Account under G.S. 105-449.126. The Commission shall use revenue in the Account, subject to the Executive Budget Act and the Personnel Act, for the administration and enforcement of this Chapter; for activities relating to boating and water safety including education and waterway marking and improvement; and for boating access area acquisition, development, and maintenance. The Commission shall use at least three dollars ($3.00) of each one-year certificate of number fee and at least nine dollars ($9.00) of each three-year certificate of number fee collected under the numbering provisions of G.S. 75A-5 for boating access area acquisition, development, and maintenance. The Commission shall transfer on a quarterly basis fifty percent (50%) of each one-year certificate of number fee and fifty percent (50%) of each three-year certificate of number fee collected under the numbering provisions of G.S. 75A-5 to the Shallow Draft Navigation Channel and Lake Dredging Fund established by G.S. 143-215.73F. (1959, c. 1064, s. 3; 1961, c. 644; 1963, c. 1003; 1981 (Reg. Sess., 1982), c. 1182, s. 2; 1993, c. 422, s. 1; 1995, c. 390, s. 13; 1999-392, s. 5; 2006-185, s. 1; 2007-485, s. 4.1; 2013-360, s. 14.22(a); 2013-380, s. 3.)

§ 75A-4. Identification numbers required.

Every vessel on the waters of this State shall be numbered, except those vessels exempted from numbering under G.S. 75A-7. No person shall operate or give permission for the operation of any vessel on the waters of this State unless all of the following conditions are met:

(1) The vessel is numbered in accordance with this Chapter, or in accordance with applicable federal law, or in accordance with a federally approved numbering system of another state.

(2) The certificate of number awarded to the vessel is in full force and effect.

(3) The identification number set forth in the certificate of number is displayed on each side of the bow of the vessel. (1959, c. 1064, s. 4; 1983, c. 446, s. 1; 1999-392, s. 1; 2006-185, s. 1.)

§ 75A-5. Application for certificate of number; fees; reciprocity; change of ownership; conformity with federal regulations; records; award of certificates; renewal of certificates; transfer of partial interest; destroyed or junked vessels; abandonment; change of address; duplicate certificates; display.

(a) Application for Certificate of Number. - The owner of each vessel requiring numbering by this State shall file an application for a certificate of number with the Commission. The Commission shall furnish application forms and shall prescribe the information contained in the application form. The application shall be signed by the owner of the vessel or the owner's agent and shall be accompanied by a fee, as set out in subsection (a1) of this section. The fee does not apply to vessels owned and operated by nonprofit rescue squads if they are operated exclusively for rescue purposes, including rescue training. The owner shall have the option of selecting a one-year numbering period or a three-year numbering period. Upon receipt of the application in approved form, the Commission shall enter the application in its records and issue the owner a certificate of number stating the identification number awarded to the vessel and the name and address of the owner, and a validation decal indicating the expiration date of the certificate of number. The owner shall paint on or attach to each side of the bow of the vessel the identification number in such manner as may be prescribed by rules of the Commission in order that it may be clearly visible. The identification number shall be maintained in legible condition. The validation decal shall be displayed on the starboard bow of the vessel immediately following the number. The certificate of number shall be pocket size and shall be available for inspection on the vessel for which the certificate is issued at all times the vessel is in operation. Any person charged with failing to so carry a certificate of number shall not be convicted if the person produces in court a certificate of number previously issued to the owner that was valid at the time of the alleged violation.

(a1)   Fees. - The fees for certificates of number are as set out in this subsection:

(1)   The fee for a certificate of number for a one-year period is:

a.   Thirty dollars ($30.00) for a vessel that is less than 26 feet in length.

b.   Fifty dollars ($50.00) for a vessel that is 26 feet or more in length.

(2)   The fee for a certificate of number for a three-year period is:

a.   Ninety dollars ($90.00) for a vessel that is less than 26 feet in length.

b.   One hundred fifty dollars ($150.00) for a vessel that is 26 feet or more in length.

(b)   Reciprocity. - The owner of any vessel already covered by a number in full force and effect pursuant to federal law or a federally approved numbering system of another state shall record the identification number prior to operating the vessel on the waters of this State in excess of the 90-day reciprocity period provided for in G.S. 75A-7(a)(1). The recordation shall be made pursuant to subsection (a) of this section, except that no additional or substitute identification number shall be issued.

(c)   Change of Ownership. - Should the ownership of a vessel change, a new application form with a fee in the amount set in subsection (a) of this section shall be filed with the Commission and a new certificate bearing the same identification number shall be awarded to the new owner in the same manner as an original certificate of number. Possession of the certificate shall in cases involving prosecution for violation of any provision of this Chapter be prima facie evidence that the person whose name appears on the certificate is the owner of the vessel referred to on the certificate.

(d)   Conformity With Federal Regulations. - In the event that an agency of the federal government shall have in force an over-all system of identification numbering for vessels within the United States, the numbering system employed pursuant to this Chapter by the Commission shall be in conformity therewith.

(e) Repealed by Session Laws 2006-185, s. 1.

(f) Records. - All records of the Commission made or kept pursuant to this section shall be public records.

(g) Award of Certificates. - Each certificate of number awarded pursuant to this Chapter, unless sooner terminated or discontinued in accordance with the provisions of this Chapter, shall continue in full force and effect to and including the last day of the month during which the certificate was awarded after the lapse of one year in the case of a one-year certificate or three years in the case of a three-year certificate. No person shall willfully remove a validation decal from any vessel during the continuance of its validity or alter, counterfeit, or otherwise tamper with a validation decal attached to any vessel for the purpose of changing or obscuring the indicated date of expiration of the certificate of number of the vessel.

(h) Renewal of Certificates. - An owner of a vessel awarded a certificate of number pursuant to this Chapter shall renew the certificate on or before the first day of the month after which the certificate expires; otherwise, the certificate shall lapse and be void until such time as it may thereafter be renewed. Application for renewal shall be submitted on a form approved by the Commission and shall be accompanied by a fee in the amount set in subsection (a1) of this section.

(i) Transfer of Partial Interest. - The owner shall furnish the Commission notice of the transfer of any part of the owner's interest other than the creation of a security interest in a vessel numbered in this State pursuant to subsections (a) and (b) of this section within 15 days of the transfer. A transfer of partial interest in a vessel shall not affect the owner's right to operate the vessel, nor shall a transfer of partial interest in a vessel terminate the certificate of number.

(i1) Destroyed or Junked Vessels. - The owner of any destroyed or junked vessel shall furnish the Commission notice of the destruction or junking of that vessel within 15 days of its occurrence. Destruction or junking terminates the certificate of number and renders the hull identification number invalid for that vessel.

(i2) Abandonment. - A person may acquire ownership of an abandoned vessel by providing proof to the Commission that the lawful owner has actually abandoned the vessel. The Commission shall adopt rules by which a person seeking to acquire ownership may demonstrate that the vessel is actually abandoned. At a minimum, the rules shall provide for a reasonable attempt to locate the lawful owner and, if the owner is located, notice by the claimant of an intention to claim ownership of the vessel.

(j) Change of Address. - Whenever any person, after applying for or obtaining the certificate of number of a vessel, moves from the address shown in the application or upon the certificate of number, that person shall notify the Commission of the change of address within 30 days of moving in a form acceptable to the Commission.

(j1) Duplicate Certificates. - The Commission shall issue a duplicate certificate of number for a vessel upon application by the person entitled to hold the certificate, if the Commission is satisfied that the original certificate of number has been lost, stolen, mutilated, or destroyed, or has become illegible. The Commission shall charge a fee of five dollars ($5.00) for issuance of each duplicate certificate.

(k) Display. - No number other than the identification number set forth in the certificate of number or granted reciprocity pursuant to this Chapter shall be painted, attached, or otherwise displayed on either side of the bow of a vessel, except the validation decal required by subsection (a) of this section.

(l) Repealed by Session Laws 2006-185, s. 1. (1959, c. 1064, s. 5; 1961, c. 469, s. 1; 1963, c. 470; 1975, c. 483, ss. 1, 2; 1977, c. 566; 1979, c. 761, ss. 1-7; 1981, c. 161; 1983, c. 194; c. 446, ss. 1, 2; 1987, c. 827, s. 4; 1993, c. 422, ss. 2-4; c. 539, ss. 563, 564; 1994, Ex. Sess., c. 24, s. 14(c); 1998-225, s. 4.1; 1999-248, ss. 1, 2; 1999-392, ss. 2-4; 2006-185, s. 1; 2007-485, ss. 4.2, 4.3, 4.4; 2013-360, s. 14.22(b).)

§ 75A-5.1: Repealed by Session Laws 2013-360, s. 14.22(c), effective October 1, 2013.

§ 75A-5.2. Vessel agents.

(a) In order to facilitate the convenience of the public, the efficiency of administration, the need to keep statistics and records affecting the conservation of wildlife resources, boating, water safety, and other matters within the jurisdiction of the Commission, and to facilitate vessel transactions, the Commission may conduct vessel transactions through any of the following:

(1)   Vessel agents.

(2)   The Commission's headquarters.

(3)   Employees of the Commission.

(4)   Two or more of those sources simultaneously.

(b)   When there are substantial reasons for differing treatment, the Commission may conduct vessel transactions by one method in one locality and by another method in another locality.

(c)   As compensation for services rendered to the Commission and to the general public, vessel agents shall receive the surcharge listed below. The surcharge shall be added to the fee for each certificate issued.

(1)   Renewal of certificate of number - $3.00.

(2)   Transfer of ownership and certificate of number - $5.00.

(3)   Issuance of new certificate of number - $5.00.

(4)   Issuance of duplicate certificate of number - $3.00.

(5)   Issuance or transfer of certificate of title - $5.00.

(d)   When certificates of number are to be issued by vessel agents as provided by subsection (a) of this section, the Commission may adopt rules to provide for any of the following:

(1)   Qualifications of the vessel agents.

(2)   Duties of the vessel agents.

(3)   Methods and procedures to ensure accountability and security for proceeds and unissued certificates of number.

(4) Types and amounts of evidence that a vessel agent must submit to relieve the agent of responsibility for losses due to occurrences beyond the control of the agent.

(5) Any other reasonable requirement or condition that the Commission deems necessary to expedite and control the issuance of certificates of number by vessel agents.

(e) The Commission may adopt rules to authorize the Director to take any of the following actions related to vessel agents:

(1) Select and appoint vessel agents in the areas most convenient to the boating public.

(2) Limit the number of vessel agents in any one area if necessary for efficiency of operation.

(3) Require prompt and accurate reporting and remittance of public funds or documents by vessel agents.

(4) Conduct periodic and special audits of accounts.

(5) Suspend or terminate the authorization of any vessel agent found to be noncompliant with rules adopted by the Commission or when State funds or property are reasonably believed to be in jeopardy.

(6) Require the immediate surrender of all equipment, forms, supplies, records, and State funds and property issued by or belonging to the Commission, in the event of the termination of a license agent.

(f) The Commission is exempt from the contested case provisions of Chapter 150B of the General Statutes with respect to determinations of whether to authorize or terminate the authority of a person to conduct vessel transactions as a vessel agent of the Commission.

(g) If any check or bank account draft of any vessel agent for the issuance of certificates of number shall be returned by the banking facility upon which the same is drawn for lack of funds, the vessel agent shall be liable to the Commission for a penalty of five percent (5%) of the amount of the check or bank account draft, but in no event shall the penalty be less than five dollars ($5.00) or more than two hundred dollars ($200.00). Vessel agents shall be assessed a penalty of twenty-five percent (25%) of their issuing fee on all remittances to the Commission after the fifteenth day of the month immediately following the month of sale.

(h) It is a Class 1 misdemeanor for a vessel agent to do any of the following:

(1) Withhold or misappropriate funds generated from vessel transactions.

(2) Falsify records of vessel transactions.

(3) Willfully and knowingly assist or allow a person to obtain a certificate of number or certificate of title for which the person is ineligible.

(4) Willfully issue a backdated certificate of number or certificate of title.

(5) Willfully include false information or omit material information on vessel transaction forms and records regarding either:

a. A person's entitlement to a particular certificate of number or certificate of title.

b. The applicability or term of a particular certificate of number.

(6) Charge or accept any fee, remuneration, or other item of value that exceeds the fee amounts provided by statute.

(7) Charge or accept any additional fee, remuneration, or other item of value in association with any activity set out in subdivisions (1) through (5) of this subsection. (2006-185, s. 1; 2013-283, s. 17.)

§ 75A-6. Classification; rules.

(a) Vessels subject to the provisions of this Chapter shall be divided into five categories as follows:

(1) Class A. Less than 16 feet in length.

(2) Class 1. Sixteen feet or over and less than 26 feet in length.

(3)   Class 2. Twenty-six feet or over and less than 40 feet in length.

(4)   Class 3. Forty feet or over and not more than 65 feet in length.

(5)   Class 4. More than 65 feet in length.

(b)   through (e) Repealed by Session Laws 1993, c. 361, s. 2.

(f)   through (j) Repealed by Session Laws 2006-185, s. 1.

(k)   Repealed by Session Laws 1993, c. 361, s. 2.

(l)   No person shall operate or give permission for the operation of a vessel that is not equipped as required by this section.

(m)   The Commission may adopt rules to conform to the Federal Boat Safety Act of 1971 and the federal regulations adopted pursuant thereto.

(n)   All vessels propelled by machinery of 10 hp or less that are operated on the public waters of this State shall carry at least one personal flotation device, life belt, ring buoy, or other device of the sort prescribed by rules of the Commission for each person on board, and from one-half hour after sunset to one-half hour before sunrise shall carry a white light in the stern or shall have on board a hand flashlight in good working condition, which light shall be ready at hand and shall be temporarily displayed in sufficient time to prevent collision.

(o)   The Commission for Public Health shall adopt rules establishing standards for sewage treatment devices and holding tanks for marine toilets installed in vessels operating on the inland fishing waters of the State as designated by the Commission and the inland lake waters of the State. The Commission shall not issue a certificate of number for any vessel operating on the inland fishing waters of the State as designated by the Commission and the inland lake waters of this State that is equipped with a marine toilet unless the vessel is provided with a sewage treatment device or holding tank approved by the Commission for Public Health. All vessels operating on the inland fishing waters of the State as designated by the Commission and the inland lake waters of the State that are equipped with a marine toilet shall provide a sewage treatment device or holding tank approved by the Commission for Public Health. Wildlife protectors may inspect vessels on the inland fishing waters of the State as designated by the Commission and the inland lake waters to determine if approved treatment devices or holding tanks are properly installed and if they are operating in a satisfactory manner. A vessel registered, documented, or otherwise licensed in another state and equipped with a marine toilet not prohibited in such state may be operated on the inland fishing waters of the State as designated by the Commission, without regard to the provisions of this subsection while making an interstate trip. (1959, c. 1064, s. 6; 1963, c. 396; 1965, c. 634, s. 2; 1967, cc. 230, 1075; 1971, c. 296, ss. 1, 2; 1973, c. 476, s. 128; 1975, c. 340, s. 2; c. 483, s. 3; 1989 (Reg. Sess., 1990), c. 1004, s. 55; 1993, c. 361, s. 2; 2006-185, s. 1; 2007-182, s. 2.)

§ 75A-6.1. Navigation rules.

(a) Every vessel operated on the waters of this State that is required to obtain an identification number pursuant to this Chapter, has a valid marine document issued by the federal Bureau of Customs or any federal agency successor to it, or issued pursuant to a federally approved numbering system of another state shall comply with the navigation rules, including requirements for navigational lights, sound-signaling devices, and other equipment, contained in the Inland Navigational Rules Act of 1980, codified as amended at 33 U.S.C. §§ 2001-2038, 2071-2073 (1993) and rules adopted pursuant thereto, see 33 C.F.R. Part 84 (1992).

(b) The Commission is responsible for the enforcement of the rules specified in subsection (a) of this section. The rules specified in subsection (a) of this section are also enforceable by all peace officers with general subject matter jurisdiction.

(c) Violation of any rule governing navigational lighting adopted by the Commission shall constitute an infraction as provided in G.S. 14-3.1. (1993, c. 361, s. 1; 1994, Ex. Sess., c. 14, s. 44; 2006-185, s. 1; 2013-360, s. 18B.15(a); 2013-380, s. 4.)

§ 75A-7. Exemption from numbering requirements.

(a) A vessel shall not be required to be numbered under this Chapter if it is:

(1) A vessel that is required to be awarded an identification number pursuant to federal law or a federally approved numbering system of another state, and for which an identification number has been so awarded: Provided, that any such vessel shall not have been within this State for a period in excess of 90 consecutive days.

(2) A vessel from a country other than the United States temporarily using the waters of this State.

(3) A vessel whose owner is the United States, a state or a subdivision thereof.

(4) A ship's lifeboat.

(5) Repealed by Session Laws 2013-360, s. 14.22(d), effective October 1, 2013.

(6) A sailboat of not more than 14 feet on the load water line (LWL).

(7) A vessel with no means of propulsion other than drifting or manual paddling, poling, or rowing.

(b) The Commission is hereby empowered to permit the voluntary numbering of vessels owned by the United States, a state or a subdivision thereof.

(c) Those vessels owned by the United States, a state or a subdivision thereof and those owned by nonprofit rescue squads may be assigned a certificate of number bearing no expiration date but which shall be stamped with the word "permanent" and shall not be renewable so long as the vessel remains the property of the governmental entity or nonprofit rescue squad. If the ownership of any such vessel is transferred from one governmental entity to another or to a nonprofit rescue squad or if a vessel owned by a nonprofit rescue squad is transferred to another nonprofit rescue squad or governmental entity, the Commission shall issue a new permanent certificate of number, displaying the same identification number, without charge to the successor entity. When any such vessel is sold to a private owner or is otherwise transferred to private ownership, the applicable certificate of number shall be deemed to have expired immediately prior to the transfer. Prior to further use on the waters of this State, the new owner shall obtain a certificate of number pursuant to the provisions of this Chapter. The provisions of this subsection applicable to a vessel owned by a nonprofit rescue squad apply only to a vessel operated exclusively for rescue purposes, including rescue training. (1959, c. 1064, s. 7; 1981, c. 162; 1983, c. 446, ss. 1-3; 2006-185, s. 1; 2013-360, s. 14.22(d).)

§ 75A-8. Vessel liveries.

An owner of a vessel livery shall not rent a vessel to any person unless the provisions of this Chapter have been complied with. An owner of a vessel livery shall equip all vessels rented as required by this Chapter. (1959, c. 1064, s. 8; 1975, c. 340, s. 3; 1983, c. 446, s. 1; 2006-185, s. 1.)

§ 75A-9. Muffling devices.

(a) Every internal combustion engine used on a vessel shall have effective muffling equipment installed and used on the exhaust to muffle the noise in a reasonable manner. The use of cutouts is prohibited.

(b) Every internal combustion engine with an open-air exhaust that is used on a vessel that has a capacity of operating at more than 4,000 revolutions per minute shall have effective muffling equipment installed and used on each exhaust manifold stack. This subsection shall not apply to a licensed commercial fishing vessel.

(c) This section shall not apply to vessels competing in a regatta or race approved by the United States Coast Guard, for such vessels while on trial runs during a period not to exceed 48 hours immediately preceding the regatta or race, and for such vessels while competing in official trials for speed records during a period not to exceed 48 hours immediately following the regatta or race. (1959, c. 1064, s. 9; 2006-185, s. 1.)

§ 75A-9.1: Repealed by Session Laws 2006-185, s. 1, effective January 1, 2007, and applicable to offenses committed on or after January 1, 2007.

§ 75A-10. Operating vessel or manipulating water skis, etc., in reckless manner; operating, etc., while intoxicated, etc.; depositing or discharging litter, etc.

(a) No person shall operate any motorboat or vessel, or manipulate any water skis, surfboard, or similar device on the waters of this State in a reckless or negligent manner so as to endanger the life, limb, or property of any person.

(b) No person shall manipulate any water skis, surfboard, nonmotorized vessel, or similar device on the waters of this State while under the influence of an impairing substance.

(b1) No person shall operate any vessel while underway on the waters of this State:

(1) While under the influence of an impairing substance, or

(2) After having consumed sufficient alcohol that the person has, at any relevant time after the boating, an alcohol concentration of 0.08 or more.

(b2) The fact that a person charged with violating this subsection is or has been legally entitled to use alcohol or a drug is not a defense to a charge under subsections (b) and (b1) of this section. The relevant definitions contained in G.S. 20-4.01 shall apply to subsections (b), (b1), and (b2) of this section.

(b3) A person who violates a provision of subsection (a) or (b) of this section is guilty of a Class 2 misdemeanor.

(b4) A person who violates subsection (b1) of this section is guilty of a Class 2 misdemeanor, punishable by a fine of not less than two hundred fifty dollars ($250.00).

(c) No person shall place, throw, deposit, or discharge or cause to be placed, thrown, deposited, or discharged on the waters of this State or into the inland lake waters of this State, any litter, raw sewage, bottles, cans, papers, or other liquid or solid materials which render the waters unsightly, noxious, or otherwise unwholesome so as to be detrimental to the public health or welfare or to the enjoyment and safety of the water for recreational purposes.

(d)   No person shall place, throw, deposit, or discharge or cause to be placed, thrown, deposited, or discharged on the waters of this State or into the inland lake waters of this State any medical waste as defined by G.S. 130A-290 which renders the waters unsightly, noxious, or otherwise unwholesome so as to be detrimental to the public health or welfare or to the enjoyment and safety of the water for recreational purposes.

(e)   A person who willfully violates subsection (d) of this section is guilty of a Class 1 misdemeanor. A person who willfully violates subsection (d) of this section and in so doing releases medical waste that creates a substantial risk of physical injury to any person who is not a participant in the offense is guilty of a Class F felony which may include a fine not to exceed fifty thousand dollars ($50,000) per day of violation. (1959, c. 1064, s. 10; 1965, c. 634, s. 3; 1985, c. 615, ss. 1-5; 1989, c. 742, s. 1; 1995, c. 506, s. 14; 2006-185, s. 1; 2013-380, s. 5.)

§ 75A-10.1. Family purpose doctrine applicable.

The family purpose doctrine, as applicable in this State to tort cases arising from the operation of motor vehicles, shall apply to tort cases arising from the operation of motorboats and vessels as those terms are defined in this Chapter. (1971, c. 450, s. 1.)

§ 75A-10.2. Proof of ownership of a vessel.

(a)   In all actions to recover damages for injury to the person or to property or for the death of a person, arising out of an accident or collision involving a vessel, proof of ownership of such vessel at the time of the accident or collision shall be prima facie evidence that the vessel was being operated and used with the authority, consent and knowledge of the owner in the very transaction out of which the injury or cause of action arose.

(b)   Proof of the certificate of number stating the identification number awarded to the vessel in the name of any person, firm, or corporation as required by this Chapter, or proof of the licensing, registration, or documentation of the vessel as required by other state or federal law in the name of any person, firm, or corporation, shall for the purpose of any such action, be prima facie evidence of ownership and that the vessel was then being operated by and under the control of a person for whose conduct the owner was legally responsible, for the owner's benefit, and within the course and scope of the operator's employment. (1971, c. 652, s. 1; 2006-185, s. 1.)

§ 75A-11. Duty of operator involved in collision, accident, casualty, or other occurrence.

(a) For the purposes of this section, the term "occurrence" means a collision, accident, casualty, or other similar occurrence involving a vessel. The operator of a vessel involved in an occurrence, so far as the operator is able to do so without serious danger to the operator's vessel, crew, and passengers (if any), shall render persons affected by the occurrence any assistance as may be practicable and necessary in order to save them from or minimize any danger caused by the occurrence, and also to give the operator's name, address, and identification of the operator's vessel in writing to any person injured and to the owner of any property damaged in the occurrence.

(b) If an occurrence results in the death, injury, or disappearance indicating death or injury of a person or damage to a vessel or other property of two thousand dollars ($2,000) or more, or if there is complete loss of any vessel, the operator of the vessel shall file with the Commission a full description of the occurrence, including any information the agency may, by rule, require. If an occurrence results in death, disappearance, or injury, the operator of the vessel shall file the report with the Commission within 48 hours of the occurrence. If the occurrence results in vessel or property damage, or complete loss of any vessel, the operator of the vessel shall file the report with the Commission within 10 days of the occurrence. When the operator of the vessel cannot submit the report, the owner of the vessel shall submit the report. Reports filed pursuant to this subsection shall not be admissible as evidence.

(c) When, as a result of an occurrence that involves a vessel or its equipment, a person dies or disappears from a vessel, the operator of the vessel shall, without delay and by the most expeditious means available, notify the nearest law enforcement agency of all of the following:

(1) The date, time, and exact location of the occurrence.

(2) The name of each person who died or disappeared.

(3)   The certificate of number and name of the vessel.

(4)   The name and address of the vessel owner or owners and the vessel operator.

(d)   If the operator of the vessel cannot give notice required by this section, each person on board the vessel shall notify the law enforcement agency or determine that notice has been given. Upon receiving notice under this section, a law enforcement agency shall immediately provide the Commission and the United States Coast Guard with the information required by this section. (1959, c. 1064, s. 11; 1999-248, s. 3; 2006-185, s. 1.)

§ 75A-12. Furnishing information to agency of United States.

In accordance with any request duly made by an authorized official or agency of the United States, any information compiled or otherwise available to the Commission pursuant to G.S. 75A-11(b) shall be transmitted to the requesting official or agency of the United States. (1959, c. 1064, s. 12; 2006-185, s. 1.)

§ 75A-13. Water skis, surfboards, etc.

(a)   No person shall operate a vessel on any water of this State for towing a person or persons on water skis, a surfboard, or similar device unless at least one of the following conditions is met:

(1)   There is in the vessel a person, in addition to the operator, in a position to observe the progress of the person or persons being towed.

(2)   The persons being towed wear a personal flotation device.

(3)   The vessel is equipped with a rear view mirror.

(b)   No person shall operate a vessel on any water of this State towing a person or persons on water skis, a surfboard, or similar device, nor shall any person engage in water skiing, surfboarding, or similar activity at any time between the hours from one hour after sunset to one hour before sunrise.

(c) The provisions of subsections (a) and (b) of this section do not apply to a performer engaged in a professional exhibition.

(d) No person shall operate or manipulate any vessel, tow rope, or other device by which the direction or location of water skis, a surfboard, or similar device may be affected or controlled in such a way as to cause the water skis, surfboard, or similar device, or any person thereon to collide with any object or person. (1959, c. 1064, s. 13; 2006-185, s. 1.)

§ 75A-13.1. Skin and scuba divers.

(a) No person shall engage in skin diving or scuba diving in the waters of this State that are open to boating, or assist in such diving, without displaying a diver's flag from a mast, buoy, or other structure at the place of diving; and no person shall display such flag except when diving operations are under way or in preparation.

(b) The diver's flag shall be square, not less than 12 inches on a side, and shall be of red background with a diagonal white stripe, of a width equal to one fifth of the flag's height, running from the upper corner adjacent to the mast downward to the opposite outside corner.

(c) No operator of a vessel under way in the waters of this State shall permit the vessel to approach closer than 50 feet to any structure from which a diver's flag is then being displayed, except where the flag is so positioned as to constitute an unreasonable obstruction to navigation; and no person shall engage in skin diving or scuba diving or display a diver's flag in any locality that will unreasonably obstruct vessels from making legitimate navigational use of the water.

(d) A person who violates a provision of this section is responsible for an infraction as provided in G.S. 14-3.1. (1969, c. 97, s. 1; 2006-185, s. 1; 2013-360, s. 18B.15(b); 2013-380, s. 6.)

§ 75A-13.2: Repealed by Session Laws 1999-447, s. 3.

§ 75A-13.3. Personal watercraft.

(a) No person shall operate a personal watercraft on the waters of this State at any time between sunset and sunrise. For purposes of this section, "personal watercraft" means a small vessel that uses an outboard or propeller-driven motor, or an inboard motor powering a water jet pump, as its primary source of motive power and which is designed to be operated by a person sitting, standing, or kneeling on, or being towed behind the vessel, rather than in the conventional manner of sitting or standing inside the vessel.

(a1) No person shall operate a personal watercraft on the waters of this State at greater than no-wake speed within 100 feet of an anchored or moored vessel, a dock, pier, swim float, marked swimming area, swimmers, surfers, persons engaged in angling, or any manually operated propelled vessel, unless the personal watercraft is operating in a narrow channel. No person shall operate a personal watercraft in a narrow channel at greater than no-wake speed within 50 feet of an anchored or moored vessel, a dock, pier, swim float, marked swimming area, swimmers, surfers, persons engaged in angling, or any manually operated propelled vessel.

(b) Except as otherwise provided in this subsection, no person under 16 years of age shall operate a personal watercraft on the waters of this State, and it is unlawful for the owner of a personal watercraft or a person who has temporary or permanent responsibility for a person under the age of 16 to knowingly allow that person to operate a personal watercraft. A person of at least 14 years of age but under 16 years of age may operate a personal watercraft on the waters of this State if:

(1) The person is accompanied by a person of at least 18 years of age who physically occupies the watercraft and who is in compliance with G.S. 75A-16.2; or

(2) The person (i) possesses on his or her person while operating the watercraft, identification showing proof of age and a boating safety certification card issued by the Commission, proof of other satisfactory completion of a boating safety education course approved by the National Association of State Boating Law Administrators (NASBLA), or proof of other boating safety education in compliance with G.S. 75A-16.2; and (ii) produces that identification

and proof upon the request of an officer of the Commission or local law enforcement agency.

(b1)   A person who is the lawful owner of a personal watercraft or a person having control of a personal watercraft who knowingly allows a person under 16 years of age to operate a personal watercraft in violation of the provisions of subsection (b) of this section is responsible for an infraction as provided in G.S. 14-3.1.

(c)   No livery shall lease, hire, or rent a personal watercraft to or for operation by a person under 16 years of age, except as provided in subsection (b) of this section.

(c1)   No person, firm, or corporation shall engage in the business of renting personal watercraft to the public for operation by the rentee unless the person, firm, or corporation has secured insurance for the liability of the person, firm, or corporation and that of the rentee, in such an amount as is hereinafter provided, from an insurance company duly authorized to sell liability insurance in this State. Each personal watercraft rented must be covered by a policy of liability insurance insuring the owner and rentee and their agents and employees while in the performance of their duties against loss from any liability imposed by law for damages including damages for care and loss of services because of bodily injury to or death of any person and injury to or destruction of property caused by accident arising out of the operation of such personal watercraft, subject to the following minimum limits: three hundred thousand dollars ($300,000) per occurrence.

(c2)   A vessel livery that fails to carry liability insurance in violation of subsection (c1) of this section is guilty of a Class 2 misdemeanor and shall only be subject to a fine not to exceed one thousand dollars ($1,000).

(c3)   A vessel livery shall provide the operator of a leased personal watercraft with basic safety instruction prior to allowing the operation of the leased personal watercraft. "Basic safety instruction" shall include direction on how to safely operate the personal watercraft and a review of the safety provisions of this section. A vessel livery that fails to provide basic safety instruction is responsible for an infraction as provided in G.S. 14-3.1.

(d)   No person shall operate a personal watercraft on the waters of this State, nor shall the owner of a personal watercraft knowingly allow another person to operate that personal watercraft on the waters of this State, unless:

(1)   Each person riding on or being towed behind the vessel is wearing a type I, type II, type III, or type V personal flotation device approved by the United States Coast Guard. Inflatable personal flotation devices do not satisfy this requirement; and

(2)   In the case of a personal watercraft equipped by the manufacturer with a lanyard-type engine cut-off switch, the lanyard is securely attached to the person, clothing, or flotation device of the operator at all times while the personal watercraft is being operated in such a manner to turn off the engine if the operator dismounts while the watercraft is in operation.

(d1)   No person shall operate a personal watercraft towing another person on water skis, a surfboard, or similar device unless:

(1)   The personal watercraft has on board, in addition to the operator, an observer who shall monitor the progress of the person or persons being towed, or the personal watercraft is equipped with a rearview mirror; and

(2)   The total number of persons operating, observing, and being towed does not exceed the number of passengers identified by the manufacturer as the maximum safe load for the vessel.

(e)   A personal watercraft must at all times be operated in a reasonable and prudent manner. Maneuvers that endanger life, limb, or property shall constitute reckless operation of a vessel as provided in G.S. 75A-10, and include any of the following:

(1)   Unreasonably or unnecessarily weaving through congested vessel traffic.

(2)   Jumping the wake of another vessel within 100 feet of the other vessel or when visibility around the other vessel is obstructed.

(3)   Intentionally approaching another vessel in order to swerve at the last possible moment to avoid collision.

(4)   Repealed by Session Laws 2000-52, s. 2.

(5)   Operating contrary to the "rules of the road" or following too closely to another vessel, including another personal watercraft. For purposes of this

subdivision, "following too closely" means proceeding in the same direction and operating at a speed in excess of 10 miles per hour when approaching within 100 feet to the rear or 50 feet to the side of another vessel that is underway unless that vessel is operating in a narrow channel, in which case a personal watercraft may operate at the speed and flow of other vessel traffic.

(f) The provisions of this section do not apply to a performer engaged in a professional exhibition, a person or persons engaged in an activity authorized under G.S. 75A-14, or a person attempting to rescue another person who is in danger of losing life or limb.

(f1) For purposes of this section, "narrow channel" means a segment of the waters of the State 300 feet or less in width.

(g) Repealed by Session Laws 1999-447, s. 1.

(h) Nothing in this section prohibits units of local government, marine commissions, or local lake authorities from regulating personal watercraft pursuant to the provisions of G.S. 160A-176.2 or any other law authorizing such regulation, provided that the regulations are more restrictive than the provisions of this section or regulate aspects of personal watercraft operation that are not covered by this section. Whenever a unit of local government, marine commission, or local lake authority regulates personal watercraft pursuant to this subsection, it shall conspicuously post signs that are reasonably calculated to provide notice to personal watercraft users of the stricter regulations. (1997-129, s. 1; 1999-447, s. 1; 2000-52, ss. 1-4; 2005-161, s. 1; 2006-185, s. 1; 2009-282, s. 2; 2013-360, s. 18B.15(c); 2013-380, ss. 7, 8.)

§ 75A-14: Repealed by Session Laws 1999-248, s. 4.

§ 75A-14.1. Lake Norman No-Wake Zone.

It is unlawful to operate a vessel at greater than no-wake speed within 50 yards of a vessel launching area, bridge, dock, pier, marina, vessel storage structure, or vessel service area on the waters of Lake Norman. (1997-129, s. 4; 1997-257, s. 10; 1998-217, s. 49; 2006-185, s. 1.)

§ 75A-14.2. Temporary waiver of enforcement of no-wake zones.

The Wildlife Resources Commission may temporarily and conditionally waive enforcement of a no-wake zone upon petition by a unit of local government that encompasses or abuts the no-wake zone if, after investigation of the reasons given for the temporary and conditional waiver, the Commission determines that public safety and the public welfare will not be significantly compromised by the waiver. (2007-46, s. 1.)

§ 75A-15. Rules on water safety; adoption of the United States Aids to Navigation System.

(a)   In accordance with subsection (b) of this section, the Commission is empowered to adopt rules, for the local water in question, as to:

(1)   Operation of vessels, including restrictions concerning speed zones, and type of activity conducted.

(2)   Promotion of boating and water safety generally by occupants of vessels, swimmers, fishermen, and others using the water.

(3)   Placement and maintenance of navigation aids and markers, in conformity with governing provisions of law.

Prior to the adoption of any rules, the Commission shall investigate the water recreation and safety needs of the local water in question. In conducting the investigation, the Commission in its discretion may hold public hearings on the rules proposed and the general needs of the local water in question. After completion of the investigation and application of standards, the Commission may in its discretion adopt the rules requested, adopt them in an amended form, or refuse to adopt them. After adoption, the Commission may amend or repeal the rules after first holding a public hearing.

(b)   Any subdivision of this State may, but only after public notice, make formal application to the Commission for rules on waters within the subdivision's territorial limits as to the matters listed in subsection (a) of this section. The Commission may adopt rules applicable to local areas of water defined by the Commission that are found to be heavily used for water recreation purposes by persons from other areas of the State and as to which there is not coordinated local interest in regulation.

(b1)   The Commission may adopt rules to prohibit entry of vessels into public swimming areas and to establish speed zones at public vessel launching ramps, marinas, or vessel service areas and on other congested water areas where there are demonstrated water safety hazards. Enforcement of rules adopted pursuant to this subsection shall be dependent upon placement and maintenance of regulatory markers in accordance with the United States Aids to Navigation System by the Commission or an agency designated by the Commission.

(c)   The United States Aids to Navigation System, as established by 33 Code of Federal Regulations Part 62 (July 1, 2005 edition), is hereby adopted for use on the waters of North Carolina. The Commission is authorized to adopt rules implementing the marking system and may:

(1)   Modify provisions as necessary to meet the special water recreational and safety needs of this State, provided that the modifications do not depart in any essential manner from the uniform standards being adopted in other states.

(2)   Modify provisions as necessary to conform with amendments to the marking system that may be proposed for adoption by the states.

(3)   Enact supplementary standards regarding design, construction, placement, and maintenance of markers.

(4)   Enact clarifying rules as to matters not covered with precision in the United States Aids to Navigation System.

(5)   Enact implementing rules as to matters left to State discretion in the United States Aids to Navigation System.

(6)   Enact rules forbidding or restricting the placement of markers either throughout the State or in certain classes or areas of waters without prior permission having been obtained from the Commission or some agency or official designated by the Commission.

(c1)   It is unlawful to place or maintain any marker of the sort covered by the marking system in the waters of North Carolina that does not conform to or is in violation of the marking system and the implementing rules of the Commission.

(d) Rules enacted under the authority of subsections (a), (b), and (b1) of this section shall supersede all local rules in conflict or incompatible with such rules. As used in this subsection, "local rules" shall include provisions relating to boating, water safety, or other recreational use of local waters in special local, or private acts, in ordinances or rules of local governing bodies, or in ordinances or rules of local water authorities. Except as may be authorized in subsections (a), (b), and (b1) of this section, no local rules may be made respecting the United States Aids to Navigation System and its implementation or respecting supplemental safety equipment on vessels.

(e) The Commission may adopt rules prohibiting entry or use by vessels or swimmers of waters of the State immediately surrounding impoundment structures and powerhouses associated with electric generating facilities that are found to pose a hazard to water safety. This subsection shall not apply to the Person-Caswell Lake Authority, Carolina Power and Light Company Lake (Hyco). (1959, c. 1064, s. 15; 1965, c. 394; 1969, c. 1093, s. 4; 1977, c. 424; 1983 (Reg. Sess., 1984), c. 1082, ss. 4, 5; 1987, c. 827, s. 5; 1993 (Reg. Sess., 1994), c. 753, s. 3; 2006-185, s. 1.)

§ 75A-16. Repealed by Session Laws 1979, c. 830, s. 9, effective July 1, 1980.

§ 75A-16.1. Boating safety course.

(a) The Commission shall institute and coordinate a statewide course of instruction in boating safety, and in so doing may cooperate with any political subdivision of the State or with any reputable organization having as one of its objectives the promotion of boating safety.

(b) The Commission shall designate those persons or agencies authorized to conduct the course of instruction, and this designation shall be valid until revoked by the Commission. Within 30 days of completion of a course of instruction, a designated person or agency shall submit to the Commission a list of the names of all persons who successfully completed the course of instruction conducted by the designated person or agency.

(c) The Commission may conduct the course in boating safety using Commission personnel or other persons at times or in areas in which competent agencies are unable or unwilling to meet the demand for instruction.

(d) The Commission shall issue a boating safety certification card to each person who successfully completes the course of instruction.

(e) The Commission shall adopt rules to provide for the course of instruction and the issuance of boating safety certification cards consistent with the purposes of this section.

(f) Any person who presents a fictitious boating safety certification card or who attempts to obtain a boating safety certification card through fraud is guilty of a Class 2 misdemeanor. (2006-185, s. 1.)

§ 75A-16.2. Boating safety education required.

(a) No person shall operate a vessel with a motor of 10 horsepower or greater on the public waters of this State unless the operator has met the requirements for boating safety education.

(b) A person shall be considered in compliance with the requirements of boating safety education if the person does one of the following:

(1) Completes and passes the boating safety course instituted by the Wildlife Resources Commission under G.S. 75A-16.1 or another boating safety course that is approved by the National Association of State Boating Law Administrators (NASBLA) and accepted by the Wildlife Resources Commission;

(2) Passes a proctored equivalency examination that tests the knowledge of information included in the curriculum of an approved course;

(3) Possesses a valid or expired license to operate a vessel issued to maritime personnel by the United States Coast Guard;

(4) Possesses a State-approved nonrenewable temporary operator's certificate to operate a vessel for 90 days that was issued with the certificate of number for the vessel, if the boat was new or was sold with a transfer of ownership;

(5) Possesses a rental or lease agreement from a vessel rental or leasing business that lists the person as the authorized operator of the vessel;

(6) Properly displays Commission-issued dealer registration numbers during the demonstration of the vessel;

(7) Operates the vessel under onboard direct supervision of a person who is at least 18 years of age and who meets the requirements of this section;

(8) Demonstrates that he or she is not a resident, is temporarily using the waters of this State for a period not to exceed 90 days, and meets any applicable boating safety education requirements of the state or nation of residency;

(9) Has assumed operation of the vessel due to the illness or physical impairment of the initial operator, and is returning the vessel to shore in order to provide assistance or care for the operator;

(10) Is registered as a commercial fisherman or a person who is under the onboard direct supervision of a commercial fisherman while operating the commercial fisherman's boat; or

(11) Provides proof that he or she was born before January 1, 1988.

Any person who operates a vessel with a motor of 10 horsepower or greater on the waters of this State shall, upon the request of a law enforcement officer, present to the officer a certification card or proof that the person has complied with the provisions of this section.

(c) Any person who violates a provision of this section or a rule adopted pursuant to this section is responsible for an infraction, as provided in G.S. 14-3.1, and shall pay a fine of fifty dollars ($50.00). A person may not be responsible for violating this section if the person produces in court at the adjudicatory hearing a certification card or proof that the person has completed and passed a boating safety course in compliance with subdivision (b)(1) of this section.

(d) No unit of local government shall enact any ordinance or rule relating to boating safety education, and this law preempts all existing ordinances or rules.

(e) An operator of a personal watercraft on the public waters of this State remains subject to any more specific provision of law found in G.S. 75A-13.3. (2009-282, s. 1; 2013-380, s. 9.)

§ 75A-17. Enforcement of Chapter.

(a) Every wildlife protector and every other law-enforcement officer of this State and its subdivisions shall have the authority to enforce the provisions of this Chapter and in the exercise thereof shall have authority to stop any vessel subject to this Chapter. Wildlife protectors or other law enforcement officers of this State, after having identified themselves as law enforcement officers, shall have authority to board and inspect any vessel subject to this Chapter.

(b) In order to secure broader enforcement of the provisions of this Chapter, the Commission is authorized to enter into an agreement with the Department of Environment and Natural Resources whereby the enforcement personnel of the Department shall assume responsibility for enforcing the provisions of this Chapter in the territory and area normally policed by enforcement personnel of the Commission and whereby the Commission shall contribute a share of the expense of such personnel according to a ratio of time and effort expended by them in enforcing the provisions of this Chapter, when the ratio has been agreed upon by both of the contracting agencies. The agreement may be modified from time to time as conditions may warrant.

(c) Law enforcement vessels may use a flashing blue light on the waters of this State whenever they are engaged in law enforcement or public safety activities. The use of a blue light by any other vessel is prohibited. A person other than a law enforcement officer who activates, installs, or operates a flashing blue light on a vessel other than a law enforcement vessel is guilty of a Class 1 misdemeanor.

(d) A siren may not be used on any vessel other than an official law enforcement vessel or other official emergency response vessel.

(e) Vessels operated on the waters of this State shall stop when directed to do so by a law enforcement officer. When stopped, vessels shall remain at idle speed, or shall maneuver in such a way as to permit the officer to come alongside the vessel. Law enforcement officers may direct vessels to stop by using a flashing blue light, a siren, or an oral command by officers in uniform. A person who violates this subsection is guilty of a Class 2 misdemeanor.

(f) Vessels operated on the waters of this State shall slow to a no-wake speed when passing within 100 feet of a law enforcement vessel that is displaying a flashing blue light unless the vessel is in a narrow channel. Vessels operated on the waters of this State in a narrow channel shall slow to a no-wake speed when passing within 50 feet of a law enforcement vessel that is displaying a flashing blue light. A person who violates this subsection is responsible for an infraction as provided in G.S. 14-3.1. (1959, c. 1064, s. 17; 1965, c. 957, s. 9; 1973, c. 1262, ss. 28, 86; 1977, c. 771, s. 4; 1989, c. 727, s. 218(17); 1997-443, s. 11A.119(a); 2006-185, s. 1; 2013-360, s. 18B.15(d).)

§ 75A-18. Penalties.

(a) Except as otherwise provided, a person who violates a provision of this Article is responsible for an infraction as provided in G.S. 14-3.1. This limitation shall not apply in a case where a more severe penalty is prescribed in this Chapter.

(b) through (e) Repealed by Session Laws 2006-185, s. 1.

(f) Except as otherwise provided in this Chapter, a person who violates a rule adopted by the Commission under the authority of this Chapter is responsible for an infraction as provided in G.S. 14-3.1 and shall pay a fine of fifty dollars ($50.00). A person responsible for an infraction under this Chapter shall not be assessed court costs. (1959, c. 1064, s. 18; 1965, c. 634, s. 3; c. 793; 1969, c. 97, s. 2; 1979, c. 761, s. 8; 1985, c. 615, ss. 6, 7; 1989, c. 742, s. 2; 1993, c. 539, ss. 566, 1285; 1994, Ex. Sess., c. 24, s. 14(c); 1997-129, s. 3; 1999-447, s. 2; 2006-185, s. 1; 2013-360, s. 18B.15(e); 2013-380, s. 10.)

§ 75A-19. Operation of vessels by manufacturers, dealers, etc.

Notwithstanding any other provisions of this Chapter, the Commission may adopt rules regarding the operation of vessels by manufacturers, distributors, dealers, and demonstrators as the Commission may deem necessary and proper. (1959, c. 1064, s. 181/2; 2006-185, s. 1.)

Article 2.

Local Water Safety Committees.

§§ 75A-20 through 75A-25. Repealed by Session Laws 1983 (Regular Session, 1984), c. 1082, s. 3, effective July 5, 1984.

§ 75A-26. Local water safety committees.

(a) In order that responsible State and local officials may consult with an advisory body as to the needs and desires of the public in matters of water recreation and safety in various local waters, local authorities may sponsor local water safety committees. When a local government or two or more local governments acting jointly determine that the interests of the public would be served by sponsorship of a local water safety committee, such local government or governments may sponsor a committee. As used in this section, the noun "sponsor" shall include a sponsoring local government or a sponsoring group of local governments acting jointly.

(b) Members of a local committee shall be selected by the sponsor to represent various viewpoints and interests respecting water recreation and safety in the locality concerned. The membership of the committee shall be not less than 15 nor more than 35, and members shall serve at the pleasure of the sponsor. Except where the charter granted by the sponsor may make specific provision, the members of a local committee shall select their officers, determine the need for subcommittees (if any), provide for times and places of regular meetings, and otherwise order the internal organization and administration of the committee. Special meetings may be held:

(1) Upon the call of such officers or members of the local committee as may be specified in the charter from the sponsor or the bylaws enacted by the committee.

(2) Upon the call of three members of the governing body or bodies of the sponsor.

(3) Upon the call of the chairman of the North Carolina Water Safety Committee.

(c) Where the sponsor finds that an existing organization or committee is sufficiently broadly based to represent the various community interests, it may sponsor (and at any time withdraw sponsorship of) the activities of such organization or committee relating to water recreation and safety in lieu of creating a separate local committee. In the event an existing organization or committee is sponsored, the membership restrictions of subsection (b) do not apply. The phrase "local committee" as used in this section shall include such sponsored existing organizations and committees as well as separate committees.

(d) Except as indicated below, members of a local committee shall serve without compensation from the sponsor. Public officers and employees who are acting within the scope and course of their employment, however, may receive such travel and subsistence allowance as authorized by law when attending meetings, whether as members or observers, or otherwise assisting or participating in the affairs of a local committee. Within the bounds set by governing provisions of the law generally, a sponsor may also provide administrative and staff services to a local committee and may underwrite or finance its projects which are carried out to the benefit of water recreation and safety in the area concerned.

(e) At the time of sponsorship, or withdrawal of sponsorship, of a local committee, the sponsor shall notify the following persons of the action taken:

(1) The chairman of the North Carolina Water Safety Committee.

(2) The Executive Director of the North Carolina Wildlife Resources Commission.

(f) All meetings of separately created local committees shall be open to the public. Where an existing organization or committee has received sponsorship, all its meetings devoted to carrying out the advisory functions of a local committee shall be open to the public.

(g) Members of a local committee are under an obligation:

(1) To keep themselves informed as to problems of water recreation and safety in their area.

(2) To study such problems concerning water recreation and safety as may be referred to them by their sponsor or by the chairman of the North Carolina Water Safety Committee.

(3) To make reports from time to time, either on their own motion or in response to a request for a study, on problems of water recreation and safety, and with suggestions for remedies where such are indicated and feasible. Such reports may be made to the sponsor, the chairman of the North Carolina Water Safety Committee, the Executive Director of the North Carolina Wildlife Resources Commission, or any other public or private person, agency, firm, corporation, or organization with the power to effect improvements in the level of water recreation and safety available to the public.

(4) To take part in and, where necessary, to help coordinate programs of public education in the field of water safety. (1969, c. 1093, s. 3.)

Article 3.

Boat Hull Anti-Copying Act.

§ 75A-27 through 75A-31: Repealed by Session Laws 1991, c. 191, s. 1.

Article 4.

Vessel Titling Act.

§ 75A-32. Short title.

This Article shall be known as the Vessel Titling Act. (1989, c. 739, s. 1; 2006-185, s. 2.)

§ 75A-33. Definitions.

The definitions set forth in G.S. 75A-2 shall apply to this Article, unless the context clearly requires a different meaning. (1989, c. 739, s. 1; 2006-185, s. 2.)

§ 75A-34. Who may apply for certificate of title; authority of employees of Commission.

(a) Any owner of a motorized vessel or sailboat 14 feet or longer or any personal watercraft, as defined in G.S. 75A-13.3(a), that is applying for a certificate of number for the first time in this State pursuant to G.S. 75A-5(a), and any new owner of a motorized vessel or sailboat 14 feet or longer or any personal watercraft to whom ownership is being transferred under G.S. 75A-5(c) shall apply to the Commission for a certificate of title for that vessel. Any other vessel may be titled in this State at the owner's option. A vessel may not be titled in this State if it is titled in another state, unless the current title is surrendered along with the application for a certificate of title in this State. The Commission shall issue a certificate of title upon reasonable evidence of ownership, which may be established by affidavit, bill of sale, manufacturer's statement of origin, certificate of title in this State, certificate of number or title from another state, or other document satisfactory to the Commission. Only one certificate of title may be issued for any vessel in this State. A vessel may not be titled in this State if it is documented with the United States Coast Guard, unless the documentation has expired or been deleted by the United States Coast Guard. The Commission shall issue a certificate of title upon receipt of a completed application, along with the appropriate fee and reasonable evidence of ownership. The Commission shall require a manufacturer's statement of origin for all new vessels being issued a certificate of number and a certificate of title for the first time. The Commission may request a pencil tracing of the hull identification number (serial number) for vessels being transferred, in order to positively identify the vessel before issuance of a certificate of title for that vessel.

(b) Employees of the Commission are vested with the power to administer oaths and to take acknowledgements and affidavits incidental to the administration and enforcement of this section. They shall receive no compensation for these services. (1989, c. 739, s. 1; 2006-185, s. 2; 2013-360, s. 14.22(e).)

§ 75A-35. Form and contents of application.

(a) The owner or the owner's attorney shall apply for a certificate of title for a vessel. The application shall contain the name, residence, and mailing address of the owner, the county where the vessel is taxed, proof of ownership, and a statement of all liens or encumbrances upon the vessel in the order of their priority. The application shall also contain the names and addresses of all persons having any interest in the vessel.

(b)   Every application for a certificate of title for a vessel shall contain a brief description of the vessel to be titled, including the name of the manufacturer, certificate of number, hull identification number, length, type, and principal material of construction, model year, and purchase information. It shall also include the name and address of the previous owner or owners from whom the vessel was obtained. If the vessel has an outboard motor of greater than 25 horsepower, the application shall also contain identification of the motor, including the serial number and manufacturer. The application shall be made on forms prescribed and furnished by the Commission and shall contain other information as may be required by the Commission. (1989, c. 739, s. 1; 2006-185, s. 2.)

§ 75A-36. Notice by owner of change of address.

Whenever any person, after applying for or obtaining the certificate of title of a vessel, moves from the address shown on the application or certificate of title, that person shall, within 30 days of moving, notify the Commission of the change of address on a form acceptable to the Commission. (1989, c. 739, s. 1; 2006-185, s. 2.)

§ 75A-37. Certificate of title as evidence; duration; transfer of title.

(a)   A certificate of title is prima facie evidence of the ownership of a vessel. A certificate of title shall remain in force for the life of the vessel.

(b)   Upon the sale, assignment, or transfer of a vessel for which a certificate of title has been issued under this Article, the legal holder of the certificate of title shall deliver it to the purchaser or transferee. The assignment on the certificate must be completed showing transfer of ownership to the purchaser or transferee and settlement of all outstanding liens and encumbrances. The new owner shall submit the assigned certificate of title to the Commission, accompanied by evidence satisfactory to the Commission that all outstanding liens have been released, with the application for transfer of title. The application shall contain all the information required by the Commission for the transfer in order to identify the vessel and the new owner. The application shall show any and all new liens and encumbrances on the vessel, in order of priority, incurred by the owner. The nature of the new liens and encumbrances shall also be given, along with the name and address of all secured parties. (1989, c. 739, s. 1; 2006-185, s. 2.)

§ 75A-38. Commission's records; fees.

(a) The Commission shall maintain a record of any title it issues.

(b) The Commission shall charge a fee of thirty dollars ($30.00) to issue a new or transfer certificate of title. The Commission shall transfer on a quarterly basis at least ten dollars ($10.00) of each new or transfer certificate of title to the Shallow Draft Navigation Channel and Lake Dredging Fund established by G.S. 143-215.73F. The Commission shall charge a fee of ten dollars ($10.00) for each duplicate title it issues and for the recording of a supplemental lien. (1989, c. 739, s. 1; 2006-185, s. 2; 2013-360, s. 14.22(f).)

§ 75A-39. Duplicate certificate of title.

The Commission may issue a duplicate certificate of title plainly marked "duplicate" across its face upon application by the person entitled to hold the certificate if the Commission is satisfied that the original certificate has been lost, stolen, mutilated, destroyed, or has become illegible. Mutilated or illegible certificates shall be returned to the Commission with the application for a duplicate. If a duplicate certificate of title has been issued and the lost or stolen original is recovered, the original shall be promptly surrendered to the Commission. A duplicate certificate of title, not bearing the word "duplicate" across its face, shall be issued for anyone having an address change or name change so long as the original title is surrendered and the appropriate fees paid as provided in G.S. 75A-38(b). If the original certificate of title is not surrendered to the Commission, the duplicate certificate of title shall be plainly marked "duplicate" across its face. (1989, c. 739, s. 1; 2006-185, s. 2.)

§ 75A-40. Certificate to show security interests.

The Commission, after receiving an application for a certificate of title for a vessel, shall, upon issuing the certificate of title to the owner, show upon the face of the certificate of title all security interests in the order of their priority as shown in the application. (1989, c. 739, s. 1; 2006-185, s. 2.)

§ 75A-41. Security interests subsequently created.

Except for security interests in vessels that are inventory held for sale, security interests created in vessels by the voluntary act of the owner after the original issue of title to the owner must be shown on the certificate of title. In such cases, the owner shall file an application with the Commission on a form furnished for that purpose, setting forth all security interests and other information as the Commission requires. The Commission, if satisfied that it is proper that the security interests be recorded, shall upon surrender of the certificate of title covering the vessel, issue a new certificate of title showing any security interests in the order of the priority according to the date of the filing of the application. For the purpose of recording the subsequent security interest, the Commission may require any secured party to deliver the certificate of title to the Commission. The newly issued certificate shall be sent or delivered to the secured party of first priority listed on the certificate of title. (1989, c. 739, s. 1; 2000-169, s. 38; 2006-185, s. 2.)

§ 75A-42. Certificate as notice of security interest.

A certificate of title, when issued by the Commission showing a security interest, shall be deemed adequate notice to the State, creditors, and purchasers that a security interest in the vessel exists. No other recording or filing of the creation or reservation of a security interest in the county or city wherein the purchaser or debtor resides or elsewhere is necessary and shall not be required. Vessels, other than those that are inventory held for sale, for which a certificate of title is currently in effect, shall be exempt from the provisions of G.S. 25-9-309, 25-9-310, 25-9-312, 25-9-320, 25-9-322, 25-9-323, 25-9-324, 25-9-331, 25-9-404, 25-9-405, 25-9-406, and 25-9-501 to 25-9-526 for so long as the certificate of title remains in effect. (1989, c. 739, s.1; 2000-169, s. 39; 2006-185, s. 2.)

§ 75A-43. Security interest may be filed within 30 days after purchase.

If application for the recordation of a security interest to be placed upon a vessel is filed in the principal office of the Commission within 30 days from the date of the applicant's purchase of the vessel, it shall be valid to all persons, including the State, as if the recordation had been done on the day the security interest was acquired. (1989, c. 739, s. 1; 2006-185, s. 2.)

§ 75A-44. Priority of security interests shown on certificates.

Except for security interests in vessels that are inventory held for sale, security interests shown upon the certificates of title issued by the Commission pursuant to applications for certificates shall have priority over any other liens or security interests against the vessel however created and recorded, except for a mechanics lien for repairs, provided that the mechanic furnishes the holder of any recorded lien who may request it with an itemized sworn statement of the work done and materials supplied for which the lien is claimed. (1989, c. 739, s.1; 2000-169, s. 40; 2006-185, s. 2.)

§ 75A-45. Legal holder of certificate of title subject to security interest.

The certificate of title of a vessel shall be delivered to the person holding the security interest having first priority upon the vessel and retained by that person until the entire amount of the security interest is fully paid by the owner of the vessel. The certificate of title shall then be delivered to the secured party next in order of priority and so on, or, if none, then to the owner of the vessel. (1989, c. 739, s. 1; 2006-185, s. 2.)

§ 75A-46. Release of security interest shown on certificate of title.

An owner, upon securing the release of any security interest upon a vessel shown upon the certificate of title issued for the vessel, may exhibit the documents evidencing the release, signed by the person or persons making the release, and the certificate of title to the Commission. When it is impossible to secure the release from the secured party, the owner may exhibit to the Commission any available evidence showing that the debt secured has been satisfied, together with a statement by the owner under oath that the debt has been paid. If the Commission determines that the secured debt has been satisfied in full, the Commission shall issue to the owner either a new certificate of title in proper form or an endorsement or rider showing the release of the security interest which the Commission shall attach to the outstanding certificate of title. (1989, c. 739, s. 1; 2006-185, s. 2.)

§ 75A-47. Surrender of certificate required when security interest paid.

It is unlawful and constitutes a Class 1 misdemeanor for a secured party who holds a certificate of title as provided in this Article to refuse or fail to surrender the certificate of title to the person legally entitled to it within 10 days after the security interest has been paid and satisfied. (1989, c. 739, s. 1; 1993, c. 539, s. 567; 1994, Ex. Sess., c. 24, s. 14(c); 2006-185, s. 2.)

§ 75A-48. Levy of execution, etc.

A levy made by virtue of an execution or other proper court order, upon a vessel for which a certificate of title has been issued by the Commission, shall constitute a lien, subsequent to security interests previously recorded by the Commission and subsequent to security interests in inventory held for sale and perfected as otherwise permitted by law, if and when the officer making the levy reports to the Commission at its principal office, on forms provided by the Commission, that the levy has been made and that the vessel levied upon has been seized by and is in the custody of the officer. Should the lien thereafter be satisfied or should the vessel levied upon and seized thereafter be released by the officer, the officer shall immediately report that fact to the Commission at its principal office. After a levy and seizure by an officer and before the officer reports the levy and seizure to the Commission, any person who fraudulently assigns, transfers, causes the certificate of title to be assigned or transferred, or causes a security interest to be shown upon the certificate of title, is guilty of a Class 1 misdemeanor. (1989, c. 739, s. 1; 1993, c. 539, s. 568; 1994, Ex. Sess., c. 24, s. 14(c); 2006-185, s. 2.)

§ 75A-49. Registration prima facie evidence of ownership; rebuttal.

A valid certificate of number issued under the provisions of this Chapter, or any similar document issued under the jurisdiction of any other state or country, shall be prima facie evidence of ownership of a vessel and entitlement to a certificate of title under the provisions of this Article, but ownership established by such documents shall be subject to rebuttal. (1989, c. 739, s. 1; 2006-185, s. 2.)

Chapter 75B.

Discrimination in Business.

§ 75B-1. Definitions.

The following words and phrases as used in this Chapter shall have the following meaning unless the context clearly requires otherwise:

(1) "Business," the manufacture, processing, sale, purchase, licensing, distribution, provision, or advertising of goods or services, or extension of credit, or issuance of letters of credit, or any other aspect of business;

(2) "Foreign government," all governments and political subdivisions and the instrumentalities thereof, excepting the government, political subdivisions, and instrumentalities of the United States and the states, commonwealths, territories and possessions of the United States, and the District of Columbia;

(3) "Foreign person," any person whose principal place of residence, business or domicile is outside the United States, or any person controlled directly or indirectly by such person or persons; provided, however, that no person shall be deemed a foreign person if after reasonable inquiry and due diligence it cannot be determined that any such person has a principal place of residence, business, or domicile outside the United States or is controlled by such person;

(4) "Foreign trade relationships," the dealing with or in any foreign country of any person, or being listed on a boycott list or compilation of unacceptable persons maintained by a foreign government, foreign person, or international organization;

(5) "International organization," any association or organization, with the exception of labor associations, or organizations of which more than a majority of the membership consists of foreign persons or foreign governments; and

(6) "Persons," one or more of the following or their agents, employees, servants, representatives, directors, officers, partners, members, managers, superintendents, and legal representatives: individuals, corporations, partnerships, joint ventures, associations, labor organizations, educational institutions, mutual companies, joint-stock companies, trusts, unincorporated organizations, trustees, trustees in bankruptcy, receivers, fiduciaries, and all other entities recognized at law by this State. (1977, c. 916, s. 1.)

§ 75B-2. Discrimination in business prohibited.

It shall be unlawful for any person doing business in the State or for the State of North Carolina:

(1) To enter into any agreement, contract, arrangement, combination, or understanding with any foreign government, foreign person, or international organization, which requires such person or the State to refuse, fail, or cease to do business in the State with any other person who is domiciled or has a usual place of business in the State, based upon such other person's race, color, creed, religion, sex, national origin or foreign trade relationships;

(2) To execute in the State any contract with any foreign government, foreign person, or international organization which requires such person or the State to refuse, fail or cease to do business with another person who is domiciled or has a usual place of business in the State, based upon such other person's race, color, creed, religion, sex, national origin, or foreign trade relationships;

(3) To refuse, fail or cease to do business in the State with any other person who is domiciled or has a usual place of business in the State or with the State when such refusal, failure, or cessation results directly or indirectly from an agreement, contract, arrangement, combination, or understanding between the person who refuses, fails or ceases to do business and any foreign government, foreign person, or international organization, and is based upon such other person's race, color, creed, religion, sex, national origin or foreign trade relationships;

(4) To discharge or to fail, refuse or cease to hire, promote or appoint in the State any other person who is domiciled in the State to any position of employment or employment responsibility when such refusal, failure or cessation results from an agreement, contract, arrangement, combination, or understanding with any foreign government, foreign person, or international organization and is based upon such other person's race, color, creed, religion, sex, national origin, or foreign trade relationships;

(5) To willfully and knowingly aid or abet any other person to engage in conduct which is prohibited by this Chapter. (1977, c. 916, s. 1.)

§ 75B-3. Actions not prohibited.

It shall not be unlawful under this Chapter:

(1) To engage in conduct required by or expressly authorized by acts of the United States Congress, a United States treaty, a United States regulation, or a United States executive order;

(2) To enter into any agreement with an international organization entirely composed of member governments or their contracting representatives which requires that a preference or priority be given to the citizens or products of one or more of such member governments;

(3) To enter into any agreement with respect to the insuring, handling, or shipping of goods, or choice of carrier while in international transit. (1977, c. 916, s. 1.)

§ 75B-4. Enforcement.

The Attorney General may institute a civil action to prevent or restrain violations of G.S. 75B-2.

A person injured by a violation of G.S. 75B-2 may maintain an action for damages or for an injunction or both against any person who has committed the violation.

In a proceeding under this section, the court shall determine whether a violation has been committed and enter any judgment or decree necessary to remove the effects of any violation it finds and to prevent continuation or renewal of the violation in the future.

If an application for an injunction is granted, after due notice to all parties, a hearing thereon, and as a disposition on the merits of such application, the complainant may be awarded costs and reasonable attorney's fees.

In an action for damages, if there is a willful violation of G.S. 75B-2 the person injured may be awarded up to three times the amount of actual damages which results from the violation, with costs and reasonable attorney's fees. (1977, c. 916, s. 1.)

§ 75B-5. Remedies cumulative.

The remedies provided in this Chapter are cumulative. (1977, c. 916, s. 1.)

§ 75B-6. Contracts void.

Any provision of any contract or other document or other agreement which violates G.S. 75B-2 or which, if complied with by the person intended to be bound by the provision, would cause a violation of G.S. 75B-2 shall be null and void as being against the public policy of the State. (1977, c. 916, s. 1.)

§ 75B-7. Chapter not exclusive.

This Chapter shall not be deemed to supersede, restrict or otherwise limit the continuing applicability of the antitrust or anti-discrimination laws of the State. (1977, c. 916, s. 1.)

Chapter 75C.

Motion Picture Fair Competition Act.

§ 75C-1. Declaration of policy.

It is the policy of this State to establish fair and open procedures for the bidding and negotiation of motion pictures within the State in order to prevent unfair and deceptive acts or practices and unreasonable restraints of trade in the business of motion picture distribution within the State; promote fair and effective competition in that business; and benefit the movie-going public by holding down admission prices to motion picture theatres, expanding the choice of motion pictures available to the public, and preventing exposure of the public to objectionable or unsuitable motion pictures by insuring that exhibitors have the opportunity to view a picture before committing themselves to exhibiting it. (1979, c. 463, s. 1.)

§ 75C-2. Definitions.

When used in this Chapter, and for the purposes of this Chapter:

(1) The term "bid" means a written or oral offer or proposal by an exhibitor to a distributor, in response to an invitation to bid for the right to exhibit a motion picture, stating the terms under which the exhibitor will agree to exhibit a motion picture.

(2) The term "blind bidding" means the bidding for, negotiating for, or offering or agreeing to terms for the licensing or exhibition of, a motion picture if such first run motion picture has not been trade screened within the State before any such event has occurred.

(3) The term "distributor" means any person engaged in the business of distributing or supplying motion pictures to exhibitors by rental or licensing.

(4) The term "exhibit" or "exhibition" means showing a motion picture to the public for a charge.

(5) The term "exhibitor" means any person engaged in the business of operating one or more theatres.

(6) The term "invitation to bid" means a written or oral solicitation or invitation by a distributor to one or more exhibitors to bid or negotiate for the right to exhibit a first run motion picture.

(7)   The term "license agreement" means any contract, agreement, understanding or condition between a distributor and an exhibitor relating to the licensing or exhibition of a motion picture by the exhibitor.

(8)   The term "person" includes one or more individuals, partnerships, associations, societies, trusts, or corporations.

(9)   The term "run" means the continuous exhibition of a motion picture in a defined geographic area for a specified period of time. A "first run" is the first exhibition of a picture in the designated area, a "second run" is the second exhibition and "subsequent runs" are subsequent exhibitions after the second run.

(10)   The term "theatre" means any establishment in which motion pictures are exhibited to the public regularly for a charge.

(11)   The term "trade screening" means the showing of a motion picture by a distributor within the State which is open to any exhibitor interested in exhibiting the motion picture. (1979, c. 463, s. 1.)

§ 75C-3. Blind bidding prohibited.

(a)   Blind bidding for a first run motion picture is hereby prohibited within the State. No bids shall be returnable, no negotiations for the exhibition or licensing of a first run motion picture shall take place, and no license agreement or any of its terms shall be agreed to for the first run exhibition of any motion picture within the State before the motion picture has been trade screened within the State.

(b)   A distributor shall include in each invitation to bid for the first run exhibition of any motion picture within the State the date, time and place of the trade screening of the motion picture within the State.

(c)   A distributor shall provide reasonable and uniform notice to exhibitors within the State of all trade screenings within the State of motion pictures he is distributing. Such notice may be provided by mail or by publication in a trade magazine or other publication having general circulation among exhibitors within the State.

(d) No exhibitor may bid, negotiate, or offer terms for the licensing or exhibition of a motion picture that has been trade screened in accordance with the provisions of G.S. 75C-3 herein, unless said exhibitor or his agent has attended the trade screening.

The provisions of this subdivision (d) are subject to waiver by the distributor of a motion picture upon notice of such waiver to an exhibitor prior to the trade screening.

(e) Any purported waiver of the requirements of subdivisions (a) through (c) of this section shall be void and unenforceable. (1979, c. 463, s. 1.)

§ 75C-4. Bidding procedures.

When bids are solicited from exhibitors for the licensing of a first run motion picture within the State, then:

(a) The invitation to bid shall specify (i) the number and length of runs for which the bid is being solicited, whether it is a first, second or subsequent run, and the geographic area for each run; (ii) the names of all exhibitors who are being individually solicited; (iii) the date and hour the invitation to bid expires; and (iv) the time and location, including the address, where the bids will be opened, which shall be within the State. The invitation to bid may contain additional terms or conditions not inconsistent with the provisions of this Chapter.

(b) All bids shall be submitted in writing and shall be opened at the same time and in the presence of exhibitors, or their agents, who submitted bids and who are present at such time. Bids may be opened at the scheduled time notwithstanding the absence of exhibitors entitled to appear at such time.

(c) After being opened, bids shall be subject to examination by exhibitors, or their agents, who submitted bids. Within seven business days after a bid is accepted, the distributor shall notify in writing each exhibitor who submitted a bid of the terms of the accepted bid and the name of the winning bidder.

(d) Once bids are solicited and no bids are received or all bids are withdrawn, the distributor shall license the picture by re-bids or negotiation;

provided that nothing in this Chapter shall be interpreted to require any distributor to accept any bid. (1979, c. 463, s. 1.)

§ 75C-5. Enforcement.

Any person who suffers loss or pecuniary damages resulting from a violation of the provisions of this Chapter shall be entitled to bring an individual action to recover damages and reasonable attorney fees. The provisions of this Chapter may be enforced by injunction or any other available equitable or legal remedy. Class actions are not available under this Chapter. (1979, c. 463, s. 1.)

Chapter 75D.

Racketeer Influenced and Corrupt Organizations.

§ 75D-1. Short title.

This Chapter shall be known and may be cited as the North Carolina Racketeer Influenced and Corrupt Organizations Act (RICO). (1985 (Reg. Sess., 1986), c. 999, s. 1.)

§ 75D-2. Findings and intent of General Assembly.

(a) The General Assembly finds that a severe problem is posed in this State by the increasing organization among certain unlawful elements and the increasing extent to which organized unlawful activities and funds acquired as a result of organized unlawful activity are being directed to and against the legitimate economy of the State.

(b) The General Assembly declares that the purpose and intent of this Chapter is: to deter organized unlawful activity by imposing civil equitable sanctions against this subversion of the economy by organized unlawful elements; to prevent the unjust enrichment of those engaged in organized unlawful activity; to restore the general economy of the State all of the proceeds, money, profits, and property, both real and personal of every kind and description which is owned, used or acquired through organized unlawful activity by any person or association of persons whether natural, incorporated or unincorporated in this State; and to provide compensation to private persons injured by organized unlawful activity. It is not the intent of the General Assembly to in any way interfere with the attorney-client relationship.

(c)   It is not the intent of the General Assembly that this Chapter apply to isolated and unrelated incidents of unlawful conduct but only to an interrelated pattern of organized unlawful activity, the purpose or effect of which is to derive pecuniary gain. Further, it is not the intent of the General Assembly that legitimate business organizations doing business in this State, having no connection to, or any relationship or involvement with organized unlawful elements, groups or activities be subject to suit under the provisions of this Chapter. (1985 (Reg. Sess., 1986), c. 999, s. 1; 1989, c. 489, s. 1.)

§ 75D-3. Definitions.

As used in this Chapter, the term:

(a)   "Enterprise" means any person, sole proprietorship, partnership, corporation, business trust, union chartered under the laws of this State, or other legal entity; or any unchartered union, association, or group of individuals associated in fact although not a legal entity; and it includes illicit as well as licit enterprises and governmental as well as other entities.

(b)   "Pattern of racketeering activity" means engaging in at least two incidents of racketeering activity that have the same or similar purposes, results, accomplices, victims, or methods of commission or otherwise are interrelated by distinguishing characteristics and are not isolated and unrelated incidents, provided at least one of such incidents occurred after October 1, 1986, and that at least one other of such incidents occurred within a four-year period of time of the other, excluding any periods of imprisonment, after the commission of a prior incident of racketeering activity.

(c)   (1)   "Racketeering activity" means to commit, to attempt to commit, or to solicit, coerce, or intimidate another person to commit an act or acts which would be chargeable by indictment if such act or acts were accompanied by the necessary mens rea or criminal intent under the following laws of this State:

a. Article 5 of Chapter 90 of the General Statutes of North Carolina relating to controlled substances and counterfeit controlled substances;

b. Chapter 14 of the General Statutes of North Carolina except Articles 9, 22A, 38, 40, 43, 46, 47, 59 thereof; and further excepting G.S. Sections 14-78.1, 14-82, 14-86, 14-145, 14-146, 14-147, 14-177, 14-178, 14-179, 14-183, 14-184, 14-186, 14-190.9, 14-195, 14-197, 14-201, 14-202, 14-247, 14-248, 14-313 thereof.

c. Any conduct involved in a "money laundering" activity; and

(2) "Racketeering activity" also includes the description in Title 18, United States Code, Section 1961(1).

(d) "Documentary material" means any book, paper, document, writing, drawing, graph, chart, photograph, phonocord, magnetic tape, computer printout, other data compilation from which information can be obtained or from which information can be translated into useable form, or other tangible item.

(e) "RICO lien notice" means the notice described in G.S. 75D-13.

(f) "Attorney General" means the Attorney General of North Carolina or any employee of the Department of Justice designated by him in writing. Any district attorney of this State, with his consent, may be designated in writing by the Attorney General to enforce the provisions of this Chapter.

(g) (1) "Beneficial interest" means either of the following:

a. The interest of a person as a beneficiary under any other trust arrangement pursuant to which a trustee holds legal or record title to real property for the benefit of such person; or

b. The interest of a person under any other form of express fiduciary arrangement pursuant to which any other person holds legal or record title to real property for the benefit of such person.

(2) "Beneficial interest" does not include the interest of a stockholder in a corporation or the interest of a partner in either a general partnership or limited partnership. A beneficial interest shall be deemed to be located where the real property owned by the trustee is located.

(h) "Real property" means any real property situated in this State or any interest in such real property, including, but not limited to, any lease of or mortgage upon such real property.

(i) (1) "Trustee" means either of the following:

a. Any person who holds legal or record title to real property for which any other person has a beneficial interest; or

b. Any successor trustee or trustees to any of the foregoing persons.

(2) "Trustee" does not include the following:

a. Any person appointed or acting as a personal representative under Chapter 35A of the General Statutes relating to guardian and ward, or under Chapter 28A of the General Statutes relating to the administration of estates; or

b. Any person appointed or acting as a trustee of any testamentary trust or as trustee of any indenture of trust under which any bonds are to be issued.

(j) "Criminal proceeding" means any criminal action commenced by the State for a violation of any provision of those criminal laws referred to in G.S. 75D-3(c).

(k) "Civil proceeding" means any civil proceeding commenced by the Attorney General or an injured person under any provision of this Chapter. (1985 (Reg. Sess., 1986), c. 999, s. 1; 1987, c. 550, s. 22; 1989, c. 489, s. 1.)

§ 75D-4. Prohibited activities.

(a) No person shall:

(1) Engage in a pattern of racketeering activity or, through a pattern of racketeering activities or through proceeds derived therefrom, acquire or maintain, directly or indirectly, any interest in or control of any enterprise, real property, or personal property of any nature, including money; or

(2) Conduct or participate in, directly or indirectly, any enterprise through a pattern of racketeering activity whether indirectly, or employed by or associated with such enterprise; or

(3) Conspire with another or attempt to violate any of the provisions of subdivision (1) or (2) of this subsection.

(b) Violation of this section is inequitable and constitutes a civil offense only and is not a crime, therefore a mens rea or criminal intent is not an essential element of any of the civil offenses set forth in this section. (1985 (Reg. Sess., 1986), c. 999, s. 1; 1989, c. 489, s. 1.)

§ 75D-5. RICO civil forfeiture proceedings.

(a) All property of every kind used or intended for use in the course of, derived from, or realized through a racketeering activity or pattern of racketeering activity is subject to forfeiture to the State. Forfeiture shall be had by a civil procedure known as a RICO forfeiture proceeding.

(b) A RICO forfeiture proceeding shall be governed by Chapter 1A of the General Statutes of North Carolina except to the extent that special rules of procedure are stated in this Chapter.

(c) A RICO forfeiture proceeding shall be an in rem proceeding against the property.

(d) A RICO forfeiture proceeding shall be instituted by complaint and prosecuted only by the Attorney General of North Carolina or his designated representative. The proceeding may be commenced and a final judgment rendered thereon before or after seizure of the property and before or after any criminal conviction of any person for violation of those laws set forth in G.S. 75D-3(c).

(e) If the complaint is filed before seizure, it shall state what property is sought to be forfeited, that the property is within the jurisdiction of the court, the grounds for forfeiture, and the names of all persons known to have or claim an interest in the property. The court shall determine ex parte whether there is reasonable ground to believe that the property is subject to forfeiture and, if the State so alleges, whether notice to those persons having or claiming an interest in the property prior to seizure would cause the loss or destruction of the property. If the court finds:

(1) That reasonable ground does not exist to believe that the property is subject to forfeiture, it shall dismiss the complaint; or

(2) That reasonable ground does exist to believe the property is subject to forfeiture but there is not reasonable ground to believe that prior notice would result in loss or destruction, it shall order service on all persons known to have or claim an interest in the property prior to a further hearing on whether a writ of seizure should issue; or

(3) That there is reasonable ground to believe that the property is subject to forfeiture and to believe that prior notice would cause loss or destruction, it shall without any further hearing or notice, issue a writ of seizure directing the sheriff of or any other law enforcement officer in the county where the property is found to seize it.

(f) Seizure may be effected by a law enforcement officer authorized to enforce the penal laws of this State prior to the filing of the complaint and without a writ of seizure if the seizure is incident to a lawful arrest, search, or inspection and the officer has probable cause to believe the property is subject to forfeiture and will be lost or destroyed if not seized. Within 24 hours of the time of seizure, the seizure shall be reported by the officer to the district attorney of the prosecutorial district as defined in G.S. 7A-60 in which the seizure is effected who shall immediately report such seizure to the Attorney General. The Attorney General shall, within 30 days after receiving notice of seizure, examine the evidence surrounding such seizure, and if he believes reasonable ground exists for forfeiture under this Chapter, shall file a complaint for forfeiture. The complaint shall state, in addition to the information required in subsection (e) of this section, the date and place of seizure.

(g) After the complaint is filed or the seizure effected, whichever is later, every person known to have or claim an interest in the property, or in the property or enterprise of which the subject property is a part or represents any interest, shall be served, if not previously served, with a copy of the complaint and a notice of seizure in the manner provided by Chapter 1A of the General Statutes of North Carolina. Service by publication may be ordered upon any party whose whereabouts cannot be determined with reasonable diligence within 30 days of filing of the complaint.

(h) (1) Any person claiming an interest in the property, may become a party to the action at any time prior to judgment whether named in the complaint or not. Any party claiming a substantial interest in the property, upon motion may be allowed by the court to take possession of the property upon posting bond with good and sufficient security in double the amount of the property's value conditioned to pay the value of any interest in the property found to be subject to forfeiture or the value of any interest of another not subject to forfeiture.

(2) The court, upon such terms and conditions as it may prescribe, may order that the property be sold by an innocent party who holds a lien on or security interest in the property at anytime during the proceedings. Any proceeds from such sale over and above the amount necessary to satisfy the lien or security interest shall be paid into court pending final judgment in the forfeiture proceeding. No such sale shall be ordered, however, unless the obligation upon which the lien or security interest is based is in default.

(3) Pending final judgment in the forfeiture proceeding, the court may make any other disposition of the property necessary to protect it or in the interest of substantial justice, and which adequately protects the interests of innocent parties.

(i) The interest of an innocent party in the property shall not be subject to forfeiture. An innocent party is one who did not have actual or constructive knowledge that the property was subject to forfeiture. An attorney who is paid a fee for representing any person subject to this act, shall be rebuttably presumed to be an innocent party as to that fee transaction.

(j) Subject to the requirement of protecting the interest of all innocent parties, the court may, after judgment of forfeiture, make any of the following orders for disposition of the property:

(1) Destruction of the property or contraband, the possession of, or use of, which is illegal;

(2) Retention for official use by a law enforcement agency, the State or any political subdivision thereof. When such agency or political subdivision no longer has use for such property, it shall be disposed of by judicial sale as provided in Article 29A of Chapter 1 of the General Statutes of North Carolina, and the proceeds shall be paid to the State Treasurer;

(3) Transfer to the Department of Cultural Resources of property useful for historical or instructional purposes;

(4) Retention of the property by any innocent party having an interest therein, including the right to restrict sale of an interest to outsiders, such as a right of first refusal, upon payment or approval of a plan for payment into court of the value of any forfeited interest in the property. The plan may include, in the case of an innocent party who holds an interest in the property through an estate by the entirety, or an undivided interest in the property, or a lien on or security interest in the property, the sale of the property by the innocent party under such terms and conditions as may be prescribed by the court and the payment into court of any proceeds from such sale over and above the amount necessary to satisfy the divided ownership value of the innocent party's interest or the lien or security interest. Proceeds paid into the court must then be paid to the State Treasurer;

(5) Judicial sale of the property as provided in Article 29A of Chapter 1 of the General Statutes of North Carolina, with the proceeds being paid to the State Treasurer;

(6) Transfer of the property to any innocent party having an interest therein equal to or greater than the value of the property; or

(7) Any other disposition of the property which is in the interest of substantial justice and adequately protects innocent parties, with any proceeds being paid to the State Treasurer.

(k) In addition to the provisions of subsections (c) through (g) relating to in rem actions, the State may bring an in personam action for the forfeiture of any property subject to forfeiture under subsection (a) of this section.

(l) Upon the entry of a final civil judgment of forfeiture in favor of the State:

(1) The title of the State to the forfeited property shall:

a. In the case of real property or beneficial interest, relate back to the date of filing of the RICO lien notice in the official record of the county where the real property or beneficial interest is located and, if no RICO lien notice is filed, then to the date of the filing of any notice of lis pendens in the official records of the county where the real property or beneficial interest is located and, if no RICO lien notice or notice of lis pendens is so filed, then to the date of recording of the final judgment of forfeiture in the official records of the county where the real property or beneficial interest is located; and

b. In the case of personal property, relate back to the date the personal property was seized pursuant to the provisions of this Chapter.

(2) If property subject to forfeiture is conveyed, alienated, disposed of, or otherwise rendered unavailable for forfeiture after the filing of a RICO lien notice or after the filing of a RICO civil proceeding whichever is earlier, the Attorney General may, on behalf of the State, institute in action in an appropriate court against the person named in the RICO lien notice or the defendant in the civil proceeding and the court shall enter final judgment against the person named in the RICO lien notice or the defendant in the civil proceeding in an amount equal to the fair market value of the property, together with investigative costs and attorney's fees incurred by the Attorney General in the action. (1985 (Reg. Sess., 1986), c. 999, s. 1; 1987 (Reg. Sess., 1988), c. 1037, ss. 98, 99; 1989, c. 489, s. 1.)

§ 75D-6. Power to compel examination.

Whenever the Attorney General has reason to believe that any person or enterprise may have information or may be in possession, custody or control of any documentary materials relevant to an activity prohibited under G.S. 75D-4, he may issue in writing, and cause to be served upon such person or upon the appropriate officers, agents, and employees of any such enterprise (other than one employed as an attorney by such person or enterprise), a notice requiring such person or enterprise to submit themselves to examination by him, and produce for his inspection any documentary material relevant to an investigation of activities prohibited by G.S. 75D-4.

The notice shall be served either personally or by registered or certified mail return receipt requested. The notice shall specify the general purpose of the examination, a general description of the documentary material to be produced, and the time and place where such examination will take place. The witness shall be placed under oath or affirmation to testify truthfully. The examination shall be recorded and the witness has the right to a copy upon payment of its cost. The witness has the right to have legal counsel present during the examination.

The Attorney General shall also have the right to apply to any judge of the superior court division, after five days' prior notice of such application served in the same manner as the notice of examination described in this section, for an order requiring such person or enterprise to appear and subject himself or itself to examination, and disobedience of such order shall constitute contempt, and shall be punishable as in other cases of disobedience of a proper order of such court.

No such demand or order of a court shall contain any requirement which would be held to be unreasonable if contained in a civil discovery request or court order issued pursuant to G.S. 1A-1, Rules of Civil Procedure 26-36. Any person or enterprise upon whom a demand is served and who objects to complying with such demand in whole or in part, shall, within five days of service of the demand, serve a written reply upon the Attorney General specifying the nature of the objection.

Such examination shall be held in camera and no one, except the person or enterprise being examined, may release information obtained from the examination prior to a proceeding being instituted under this Chapter by the Attorney General. Such information may be used in any proceeding instituted under this Chapter by the Attorney General. Any person violating the provisions of this paragraph shall be guilty of a Class 1 misdemeanor. If such offending person is a public officer or employee, he shall also be dismissed from such office or employment and shall not hold any public office or employment in this State for a period of five years after conviction. This paragraph does not prohibit disclosure of this information to other employees of the Department of Justice, or to district attorneys designated in writing by the Attorney General as authorized to receive this information. (1985 (Reg. Sess., 1986), c. 999, s. 1; 1989, c 489, s. 1; 1993, c. 539, s. 569; 1994, Ex. Sess., c. 24, s. 14(c).)

§ 75D-7. False testimony.

False testimony as to any material fact by any person examined under the provisions of this Chapter shall constitute perjury and a conviction shall be punishable as in other cases of perjury as a Class F felony. (1985 (Reg. Sess., 1986), c. 999, s. 1; 1993, c. 539, s. 1286; 1994, Ex. Sess., c. 24, s. 14(c).)

§ 75D-8. Available RICO civil remedies.

(a) As part of a final judgment of forfeiture, any judge of the superior court may, after giving reasonable notice to potential innocent claimants, enjoin violations of G.S. 75D-4, by issuing appropriate orders and judgments:

(1) Ordering any defendant to divest himself of any interest in any enterprise, real property, or personal property including property held by the entirety. Where property is held by the entirety and one of the spouses is an innocent person as defined in G.S. 75D-5(i), upon entry of a final judgment of forfeiture of entirety property, the judgment operates, to convert the entirety to a tenancy in common, and only the one-half undivided interest of the offending spouse shall be forfeited according to the provisions of this Chapter;

(2) Imposing reasonable restrictions upon the future activities or investments of any defendant in the same or similar type of endeavor as the enterprise in which he was engaged in violation of G.S. 75D-4;

(3) Ordering the dissolution or reorganization of any enterprise;

(4) Ordering the suspension or revocation of any license, permit, or prior approval granted to any enterprise by any agency of the State;

(5) Ordering the forfeiture of the charter of a corporation organized under the laws of this State or the revocation of a certificate authorizing a foreign corporation to conduct business within this State upon a finding that the board of directors or a managerial agent acting on behalf of the corporation, in conducting affairs of the corporation, has authorized or engaged in conduct in violation of G.S. 75D-4, and that, for the prevention of future unlawful activity, the public interest requires that the charter of the corporation be dissolved or the certificate be revoked;

(6) Appointment of a receiver pursuant to the provisions of Article 38 of Chapter 1 of the General Statutes of North Carolina, to collect, conserve and dispose of all the proceeds, money, profits and property, both real and personal, subject to the provisions of this Chapter in accordance with the provisions hereof as directed by the final judgment of the superior court having jurisdiction over the parties or subject matter of the action; or

(7) Any other equitable remedy appropriate to effect complete forfeiture of property subject to forfeiture, or to prevent future violations of this Chapter.

(b) The State through the Attorney General may institute a proceeding under G.S. 75D-5. In such proceeding, relief shall be granted in conformity with the principles that govern the granting of injunctive relief from threatened loss or damage in other civil cases, provided that no showing of special or irreparable damage to the person shall have to be made and provided further that the State shall not be required to execute any bond before or after obtaining temporary restraining orders or preliminary injunctions.

(c) Any innocent person who is injured or damaged in his business or property by reason of any violation of G.S. 75D-4 involving a pattern of racketeering activity shall have a cause of action for three times the actual damages sustained and reasonable attorneys fees. For purposes of this subsection, "pattern of racketeering activity" shall require that at least one act of racketeering activity be an act of racketeering activity other than (i) an act indictable under 18 U.S.C. § 1341 or U.S.C. § 1343, or (ii) an act which is an offense involving fraud in the sale of securities. Any person filing a private action under this subsection must concurrently notify the Attorney General in writing of the commencement of the action. Thereafter, the Attorney General may file a motion for a protective order in the court where the private action is pending and shall be granted a stay of the private action for a reasonable time if the court finds either:

(1) The bringing of a private action is likely to materially interfere with or impair a public forfeiture action; or

(2) The public interest is so great as to require the Attorney General to investigate and bring a forfeiture action.

(d) Any injured innocent person shall have a right or claim to forfeited property or to the proceeds derived therefrom superior to any right or claim the State has in the same property or proceeds. To enforce such a claim the injured innocent person must intervene in the forfeiture proceeding prior to its final disposition.

(e) A final conviction in any criminal proceeding for a violation of those laws set forth in G.S. 75D-3(c), shall estop the defendant in any subsequent civil action or proceeding under this Chapter as to all matters proved in the criminal proceeding.

(f)   A defendant in an action commenced by the State pursuant to this Chapter whose convictions of two or more criminal offenses of those criminal statutes as set forth in G.S. 75D-3(c) have become final, which offenses have occurred within a four-year period of each other as set forth in G.S. 75D-3(b) shall be deemed to have, per se violated the provisions of G.S. 75D-4(a)(1) or (2) as of the date of the second conviction.

(g)   Any party is entitled to a jury trial in any action brought under this Chapter. (1985 (Reg. Sess., 1986), c. 999, s. 1; 1989, c. 489, s. l.)

§ 75D-9. Period of limitations as to civil proceedings under this Chapter.

Notwithstanding any other provision of law, a civil action or proceeding under this Chapter may be commenced within five years after the conduct in violation of a provision of this Chapter terminates or the claim for relief accrues, whichever is later. If a civil action is brought by the State for forfeiture or to prevent any violation of the Chapter, then the running of this period of limitations with respect to any innocent person's claim for relief which is based upon any matter complained of in such action by the State, shall be suspended during the pendency of the action by the State and for two years thereafter. (1985 (Reg. Sess., 1986), c. 999, s. 1; 1989, c. 489, s. 1.)

§ 75D-10. Civil remedies are supplemental and not mutually exclusive.

The application of one civil remedy under this Chapter shall not preclude the application of any other remedy under this Chapter or any other provision of law. Civil remedies under this Chapter are cumulative, supplemental and not exclusive, and are in addition to the fines, penalties and forfeitures set forth in a final judgment of conviction of a violation of the criminal laws of this State as punishment for violation of the penal laws of this State. (1985 (Reg. Sess., 1986), c. 999, s. 1; 1989, c. 489, s. 1.)

§ 75D-11. Reciprocal agreements with other states.

The Attorney General is authorized to enter into reciprocal agreements with any United States attorney or the attorney general or chief prosecuting attorney of any other state having a civil forfeiture law substantially similar to this Chapter so as to further the purpose of this Chapter. (1985 (Reg. Sess., 1986), c. 999, s. 1; 1989, c. 489, s. 1.)

§ 75D-12. Venue.

In any forfeiture action brought pursuant to this Chapter, the claim for relief shall be considered to have arisen in any county in which an incident of racketeering occurred or in which an interest or control of an enterprise or real or personal property is acquired or maintained. Venue in any private action shall be as provided in Article 7, Chapter 1, of the General Statutes of North Carolina. (1985 (Reg. Sess., 1986), c. 999, s. 1; 1989, c. 489, s. 1.)

§ 75D-13. Filing and attachment of RICO lien notice.

(a)   Upon the institution of any proceeding under this Chapter, the Attorney General then or at any time during the pendency of the proceeding may file in the official records of any one or more counties a RICO lien notice. No filing fee or other charge shall be required as a condition for filing the RICO lien notice. The clerk of the superior court shall, upon the presentation of a RICO lien notice, immediately record it in the official records.

(b)   The RICO lien shall be signed by the Attorney General or his designee or by a designated district attorney. The notice shall be in such form as the Attorney General prescribes and, in addition to a description of the particular property sought to be forfeited, shall set forth the following information:

(1)   If brought in the name of a person, the name of the person against whom the civil proceeding has been brought. In his discretion, the Attorney General may also name in the RICO lien notice any other aliases, names or fictitious names under which the person may be known;

(2)   If known to the Attorney General the present residence and business addresses of the person named in the RICO lien notice and of the other names set forth in the RICO lien notice;

(3) A reference to the civil proceeding stating that a proceeding under this Chapter has been brought against the person named in the RICO lien notice, the name of the county or counties where the proceeding has been brought, and, if known to the Attorney General at the time of filing the RICO lien notice, the case number of the proceeding;

(4) A statement that the notice is being filed pursuant to this Chapter; and

(5) The name and address of the person in the Attorney General's office filing the RICO lien notice and the name of the individual signing the RICO lien notice.

(c) A RICO lien notice shall apply only to one person and, to the extent applicable, any aliases, fictitious names, or other names, including names of corporations, partnerships, or other entities, to the extent permitted in paragraph (1) of subsection (b) of this section. A separate RICO lien notice shall be filed for any other person against whom the Attorney General desires to file a RICO lien notice under this section.

(d) The Attorney General shall, as soon as practicable after the filing of each RICO lien notice, serve, by any method provided for by G.S. 1A-1, Rule 4, upon the person named in the notice and any other person who holds an interest of record, either a copy of the recorded notice or a copy of the notice with a notation thereon of the county or counties in which the notice has been recorded.

(e) The filing of a RICO lien notice creates, from the time of its filing, a lien in favor of the State on the following property of the person named in the notice and against any other names sets forth in the notice:

(1) Any real property situated in the county where the notice is filed then or thereafter owned by the person or under any of the names; and

(2) Any beneficial interest situated in the county where the notice is filed then or thereafter owned by the person or under any of the names.

(f) The lien shall commence and attach as of the time of filing of the RICO lien notice and shall continue thereafter until expiration, termination, or release pursuant to G.S. 75D-14. The lien created in favor of the State shall be superior and prior to the interest of any other person in the real property or beneficial interests if the interest is acquired subsequent to the filing of the notice.

(g) In conjunction with any proceedings pursuant to this Chapter:

(1) The Attorney General may file without prior court order in any county a lis pendens and, in such case, any person acquiring an interest in the subject real property or beneficial interest subsequent to the filing of lis pendens, shall take the interest subject to the civil proceeding and any subsequent judgment of forfeiture; and

(2) If a RICO lien notice has been filed, the Attorney General may name as defendants, in addition to the person named in the notice, any persons acquiring an interest in the real property or beneficial interest subsequent to the filing of the notice. If a judgment of forfeiture is entered in the proceeding in favor of the State, the interest of any person in the property that was acquired subsequent to the filing of the notice shall be subject to the notice and judgment of forfeiture.

(h) (1) A trustee upon whom a RICO lien notice or a RICO civil proceeding has been served shall immediately furnish to the Attorney General the following:

a. The name and addresses, as known to the trustee, of all persons for whose benefit the trustee holds title to the real property; and

b. If requested by the Attorney General's office, a copy of the trust agreement or other instrument pursuant to which the trustee holds legal or record title to the real property.

(2) Any trustee who fails to comply with the provisions of this subsection shall be removed by court order and a substitute trustee shall be named in lieu of the trustee so removed.

(i) The filing of a RICO lien notice shall not affect the use to which real property or a beneficial interest owned by the person named in the RICO lien notice may be put or in the right of the person to receive any avails, rents, or other proceeds resulting from the use and ownership, but not the sale, of the property until a judgment of forfeiture is entered.

(j) All forfeitures or dispositions under this section shall be made with due provision for the rights of innocent persons. (1985 (Reg. Sess., 1986), c. 999, s. 1; 1989, c. 489, s. 1.)

§ 75D-14. Release of lien notice.

The Attorney General filing the RICO lien notice, or the court for good cause shown at anytime, may release in whole or in part any RICO lien notice or may release any specific property or beneficial interest from the RICO lien notice upon such terms and conditions as he may determine. Any release of a RICO lien notice executed by the Attorney General or ordered by the court may be filed in the official records of any county. No charge or fee shall be imposed for the filing of any release of a RICO lien notice. (1985 (Reg. Sess., 1986), c. 999, s. 1; 1989, c. 489, s. 1.)

Chapter 75E.

Unlawful Activities in Connection With Certain Corporate Transactions.

§ 75E-1. Definitions.

The following words and phrases as used in this Chapter shall have the following meanings unless the context clearly requires otherwise:

(1) "Acquiring person statement" has the same meaning as G.S. 55-9A-02.

(2) "Business combination" has the same meaning as G.S. 55-9-01(b)(1).

(3) "Control share acquisition" has the same meaning as G.S. 55-9A-01(b)(3).

(4) "Person" includes "entity" (as that term is defined in G.S. 55-1-40(9)), "individual" (as that term is defined in G.S. 55-1-40(13)) and, without limiting the generality of the foregoing, "other entity" (as that term is defined in G.S. 55-9-01(b)(6)). (1991, c. 440; 1993, c. 553, s. 25.)

§ 75E-2. Unlawful activities in connection with business combinations and control share acquisitions.

It shall be unlawful for any person:

(1) To consummate any business combination in violation of Article 9 of Chapter 55 of the General Statutes.

(2) To make a control share acquisition without complying with the provisions of Article 9A of Chapter 55 of the General Statutes.

(3) To make any untrue statement of a material fact or omit to state any material fact necessary in order to make the statements made, in the light of the circumstances under which they are made, not misleading, or to engage in any fraudulent, deceptive, or manipulative acts or practices, in connection with: (i) the application of Article 9 of Chapter 55 of the General Statutes to any business combination or to the acquisition of beneficial ownership, directly or indirectly, of more than twenty percent (20%) of the voting shares of a corporation within the meaning of Article 9; or (ii) the application of Article 9A of Chapter 55 of the General Statutes to any control share acquisition.

(4) To willfully and knowingly aid or abet any other person to engage in conduct which is prohibited by this Chapter. (1991, c. 440.)

§ 75E-3. Investigative and regulatory powers of the Attorney General.

The Attorney General may conduct such investigations as the Attorney General deems necessary to determine compliance by all persons or entities with the provisions of Articles 9 and 9A of Chapter 55 of the General Statutes; and the Attorney General may exempt from the provisions of Article 9 of Chapter 55 of the General Statutes any business combination that is solely an internal corporate restructuring which does not effect any material change in the ultimate ownership of the corporation and does not affect the ongoing applicability of that Article to the corporation or any other entity. In performing any such investigations, the Attorney General shall have all the powers given him by G.S. 75-10. The provisions of G.S. 75-11 and G.S. 75-12 shall apply to this Chapter. (1991, c. 440, s. 1; 1998-217, s. 24.)

§ 75E-4. Enforcement.

The Attorney General may institute a civil action to prevent or restrain violations of G.S. 75E-2.

A person injured by a violation of G.S. 75E-2 may maintain an action for damages or for an injunction or both against any person who has committed the violation. The holders of the voting shares of a corporation that is the subject of a proposed business combination that is to be consummated in violation of G.S. 75E-2 shall, for purposes of the previous sentence, be deemed to be injured by such violation, notwithstanding the fact that such business combination has not been consummated.

In a proceeding under this section, the court shall determine whether a violation has been committed and enter any judgment or decree necessary to remove the effects of any violation it finds and to prevent continuation or renewal of the violation in the future.

If an application for an injunction is granted, after due notice to all parties, and a hearing thereon, the complainant (including, without limiting the generality hereof, the Attorney General) may be awarded costs and reasonable attorneys' fees.

In an action for damages, if the defendant is found to have willfully violated G.S. 75E-2, the person injured may be awarded up to three times the amount of actual damages which result from the violation, with costs and reasonable attorneys' fees. (1991, c. 440.)

§ 75E-5. Civil penalties.

In any suit instituted by the Attorney General in which the defendant is found to have violated G.S. 75E-2, the court may, in its discretion, impose a civil penalty against the defendant of not more than one hundred thousand dollars ($100,000) for each violation; provided that, if the court shall determine that such violation was willful, it may in its discretion treble such penalty; provided, further, that in either of the foregoing circumstances, the court may in its discretion award to the Attorney General costs and reasonable attorneys' fees. The clear proceeds of any penalty assessed pursuant to this section shall be remitted to the Civil Penalty and Forfeiture Fund in accordance with G.S. 115C-457.2. (1991, c. 440, s. 1; 1998-215, s. 105.)

§ 75E-6. Remedies cumulative.

The remedies provided in this Chapter are cumulative. (1991, c. 440.)

§ 75E-7. Chapter not exclusive.

This Chapter shall not be deemed to supersede, restrict, or otherwise limit any other applicable laws of this State. (1991, c. 440.)

§ 75E-8. Designation of Secretary of State for service.

Every nonresident person who is or is about to become the beneficial owner, directly or indirectly, of more than twenty percent (20%) of the voting shares of a corporation within the meaning of Article 9 of Chapter 55 or to make a control share acquisition, except a foreign corporation which has appointed and keeps a resident agent in this State, shall be deemed to have appointed the Secretary of State as its agent upon whom may be served any lawful process, authorized by this Chapter with the same effect as though served upon the person personally.

Service of process pursuant to this section shall be accomplished by leaving a copy of the process in the office of the Secretary of State, but it shall not be effective unless notice of the service and a copy of the process is sent by certified or registered mail to the nonresident person served, at such person's last known address. (1991, c. 440.)

§ 75E-9. Validity; saving clause.

In the event any provision or application of this Chapter shall be held illegal or invalid for any reason, such holding shall not affect the legality or validity of any other provision or application thereof. (1991, c. 440.)

Chapter 76.

Navigation.

Article 1.

Cape Fear River.

§§ 76-1 through 76-17. Repealed by Session Laws 1981, c. 910, s. 2, effective July 1, 1981.

§ 76-18. Repealed by Session Laws 1975, c. 23, s. 3.

§§ 76-19 through 76-24: Repealed by Session Laws 1981, c. 910, s. 2.

Article 2.

Beaufort Harbor.

§§ 76-25 through 76-34: Repealed by Session Laws 1975, c. 716, s. 4.

Article 3.

Bogue Inlet.

§§ 76-35 through 76-36: Repealed by Session Laws 1975, c. 716, s. 4.

Article 4.

Hatteras and Oracoke.

§§ 76-37 through 76-39: Repealed by Session Laws 1975, c. 716, s. 4.

Article 5.

General Provisions.

§ 76-40. Navigable waters; certain practices regulated.

(a) It shall be unlawful for any person, firm or corporation to place, deposit, leave or cause to be placed, deposited or left, either temporarily or permanently, any trash, refuse, rubbish, garbage, debris, rubble, scrapped vehicle or equipment or other similar waste material in or upon any body of navigable water in this State; "waste material" shall not include spoil materials lawfully dug or dredged from navigable waters and deposited in spoil areas designated by the Department of Environment and Natural Resources; violation of this section shall constitute a Class 2 misdemeanor.

(a1) It shall be unlawful for any person, firm or corporation to place, deposit, leave or cause to be placed, deposited, or left, either temporarily or permanently, any medical waste as defined in G.S. 130A-290 in the open waters of the Atlantic Ocean over which the State has jurisdiction or the navigable waters of this State.

(1) A person who willfully violates this subsection is guilty of a Class 1 misdemeanor.

(2) A person who willfully violates this subsection and in so doing releases medical waste that creates a substantial risk of physical injury to any person who is not a participant in the offense is guilty of a Class F felony which may include a fine not to exceed fifty thousand dollars ($50,000) per day of violation.

(b) No person, firm or corporation shall erect upon the floor of, or in or upon, any body of navigable water in this State, any sign or other structure, without having first secured a permit to do so from the appropriate federal agencies (which would include a permit from the State of North Carolina) or from the

Department of Administration, or from the agency designated by the Department to issue such permit. Provided, however, this subsection shall not apply to commercial fishing nets, fish offal, ramps, boathouses, piers or duck blinds placed in navigable waters. Any person, firm or corporation erecting such sign or other structure without a proper permit or not in accordance with the specification of such permit shall be guilty of a Class 2 misdemeanor. The State may immediately proceed to remove or cause to be removed such unlawful sign or structure after five days' notice to the owner or erector thereof and the cost of such removal by the State shall be payable by the person, firm or corporation who erected or owns the unlawful sign or other structure and the State may bring suit to recover the costs of the removal thereof.

(c) Whenever any structure lawfully erected upon the floor of, or in or upon, any body of navigable water in this State, is abandoned, such structure shall be removed by the owner thereof and the area cleaned up within 30 days of such abandonment; failure to comply with this section shall constitute a Class 2 misdemeanor. The State may, after 10 days' notice to the owner or erector thereof, remove the abandoned structure and have the area cleaned up and the cost of such removal and cleaning up by the State shall be payable by the owner or erector of the abandoned structure and the State may bring suit to recover the costs thereof.

(d) For purposes of this section, the term "navigable waters" shall not include any waters within the boundaries of any reservoir, pond or impoundment used in connection with the generation of electricity, or of any reservoir project owned or operated by the United States.

(e) The provisions of this section, in the coastal waters of this State, shall be enforced by the Department of Environment and Natural Resources. In the inland waters of the State, the provisions of this section shall be enforced by the Wildlife Resources Commission. The Department of Environment and Natural Resources and the Wildlife Resources Commission shall cooperate in the enforcement of this section. (1784, c. 206, s. 11; 1811, c. 839; 1833, c. 146; R.S., c. 88, ss. 23, 24, 45; 1842, c. 65, s. 4; 1846, c. 60, s. 3; R.C., c. 85, ss. 40, 41; Code, ss. 3537, 3538; Rev., s. 3560; C.S., s. 6891; 1969, c. 792; 1973, c. 1262, s. 86; 1977, c. 771, s. 4; 1989, c. 727, ss. 13, 218(18); c. 742, s. 3; 1993, c. 539, ss. 570, 1287; 1994, Ex. Sess., c. 24, s. 14(c); 1997-443, s. 11A.119(a).)

§ 76-41. Obstructing waters of Currituck Sound.

It shall be unlawful for any person to obstruct navigation in the waters of Currituck Sound and tributaries, and all persons, corporations, companies, or clubs, who have heretofore placed or caused to be placed any hedging across the mouth of a bay, creek, strait, or lead of water in Currituck Sound or tributaries, made of iron, wire, or wood or other material, for the purpose of preventing the free passage of boats or vessels of any size or class, or to stop the public use of such bay, creek, strait, or lead of water, are required to forthwith remove the same. Any person, corporation, or club violating any of the provisions of this section shall be guilty of a Class 3 misdemeanor. (1897, c. 277; Rev., s. 3553; C.S., s. 6982; 1993, c. 539, s. 571; 1994, Ex. Sess., c. 24, s. 14(c).)

§ 76-42. Lumbermen to remove obstructions in Albemarle Sound.

If any lumberman shall fail to remove all obstructions placed by him in the waters of Albemarle Sound and its tributaries, as soon as practicable, after they have ceased to use them for the purpose for which they were placed in said waters, from all places where the water is not less than two feet deep, and also from all landing places on both sides, for the space of 60 feet from the shore outward, he shall be guilty of a Class 3 misdemeanor, and only fined not less than one dollar ($1.00) nor more than fifty dollars ($50.00), at the discretion of the court. (1880, c. 37, ss. 1, 2; Code, s. 3303; Rev., s. 3551; C.S., s. 6983; 1993, c. 539, s. 572; 1994, Ex. Sess., c. 24, s. 14(c).)

§ 76-43. Anchorage in range of lighthouses.

If the master of any vessel shall anchor on the range line of any range of lights established by the United States Lighthouse Board, unless such anchorage is unavoidable, he shall be guilty of a Class 3 misdemeanor, and punished only by a fine not to exceed fifty dollars ($50.00). (1883, c. 165, s. 2; Code, s. 3086; Rev., s. 3550; C.S., s. 6984; 1993, c. 539, s. 573; 1994, Ex. Sess., c. 24, s. 14(c).)

§ 76-44. Vessels on inland waterways exempt from pilot laws; proviso as to steam vessels.

All vessels, barges, schooners, or other craft passing through the inland waterway of this State, when bound to a port or ports in this or any other state, be and the same are hereby exempt from the operations of the pilot laws of North Carolina and are not compelled to take a state-licensed pilot: Provided, that steam vessels not having a United States licensed pilot for the waters navigated on board shall be subject to the State pilot laws. (1917, c. 33, s. 2; C.S., s. 6985.)

§ 76-45. Bond of pilot.

Every person, before he obtains a commission or a branch to be a pilot, shall give bond with two sufficient sureties payable to the State of North Carolina, in the sum of five hundred dollars ($500.00), with condition for the due and faithful discharge of his duties, and the duties of his apprentices; and the body appointing such pilot may, from time to time, and as often as they may deem it necessary, enlarge the penalty of the bond, or require new and additional bonds to be given; and every bond taken of a pilot shall be filed with, and preserved by, the said body appointing such pilot in trust for every person that shall be injured by the neglect or misconduct of such pilot, or his apprentices; who may severally bring suit thereon for the damage by each one sustained. (1784, c. 207, s. 3; R.C., c. 85, s. 6; Code, s. 3487; Rev., s. 307; C.S., s. 6986.)

§ 76-46. Pilots to have spyglasses.

Every pilot, within such convenient time as the commissioners may direct, who has control over the waters within which he acts, shall furnish himself with a good telescope or spyglass, under the penalty of fifty dollars ($50.00), to be paid to the commissioners. (1790, c. 320, s. 3; R.C., c. 85, s. 27; Code, s. 3517; Rev., s. 4973; C.S., s. 6987.)

§ 76-47. Acting as pilot without license.

If any person shall act as a pilot, who is not qualified and licensed in the manner prescribed in this Chapter, he shall be guilty of a Class 3 misdemeanor:

Provided, that should there be no licensed pilot in attendance, any person may conduct into port any vessel in danger from stress of weather or in a leaky condition. (1783, c. 194, s. 3; 1784, c. 208, s. 4; R.C., c. 85, s. 29; Code, s. 3519; Rev., s. 4974; C.S., s. 6988; 1933, c. 325; 1993, c. 539, s. 574; 1994, Ex. Sess., c. 24, s. 14(c).)

§ 76-48. Penalty on pilot neglecting to go to vessel having signal set.

When any pilot shall see any vessel on the coast, having a signal for a pilot, or shall hear a gun of distress fired off the coast, and shall neglect or refuse to go to the assistance of such vessel, such pilot shall forfeit and pay one hundred dollars ($100.00), to be recovered in the name of the State, one half to the use of the informer and the other half to the master of the vessel, unless such pilot is then actually in charge of another vessel. (1783, c. 194, s. 6; 1784, c. 207, s. 10; 1790, c. 320, s. 2; R.C., c. 85, s. 31; Code, s. 3521; Rev., s. 4975; C.S., s. 6989.)

§ 76-49. Pilots may be removed.

Unless otherwise provided in the first Article of this Chapter for the Cape Fear River, whenever any pilot appointed, as authorized in this Chapter, shall, on trial, be found incompetent, or shall be guilty of improper conduct by intoxication or otherwise, or of any misbehavior in his office, or shall absent himself from the State for a period of six months, the pilot so offending may be removed from his office by the board of commissioners under whose authority he is acting, by a notice to him in writing; and if after such removal he shall attempt to take charge of any vessel, he shall forfeit and pay two hundred dollars ($200.00) for the use of said board. And it shall be the duty of the board to put up a written notice of the removal, in the public places within the port, or publish it in some convenient newspaper. But no pilot for the navigation of Hatteras Inlet shall be required to surrender or forfeit his branch by reason of absence from the State for a period of less than six months. (1784, c. 207, s. 4; 1800, c. 565; 1819, c. 1025, s. 4; R. S., c. 88, ss. 7, 31, 35; R.C., c. 85, s. 28; 1869-70, c. 235, s. 7; 1876-7, c. 22; 1881, c. 261, ss. 1, 2; Code, ss. 3490, 3518; Rev., s. 4976; C.S., s. 6990.)

§ 76-50. Pilots refused, entitled to pay.

If a branch pilot shall go off to any vessel bound in, and offer to pilot her over the bar, the master or commander of such vessel, if he refuses to take such pilot, shall pay to such pilot, if not previously furnished with one, the same sum as is allowed by law for conducting such vessel in, to be recovered in the district court: Provided, that the first pilot, and no other, who shall speak such vessel so bound in shall be entitled to the pay provided for in this section. (R.C., c. 85, s. 32; 1871-2, c. 117; Code, s. 3522; Rev., s. 4978; C.S., s. 6991; 1973, c. 108, s. 30.)

§ 76-51. Pay of pilots when detained by vessel.

Every master of a vessel who shall detain a pilot at the time appointed, so that he cannot proceed to sea, though wind and weather should permit, shall pay to such pilot three dollars ($3.00) per day during the time of his actual detention. (1858-9, c. 23, s. 7; Code, s. 3495; Rev., s. 4979; C.S., s. 6992.)

§ 76-52. Rates of pilotage annexed to commission.

The commissioners of navigation for the several ports of this State shall annex to the branch or commission, by them given to each pilot, a copy of the fees to which such pilot is entitled. (1784, c. 208, s. 4; 1796, c. 470, s. 5; R.C., c. 85, ss. 9, 38; Code, ss. 3497, 3536; Rev., s. 4980; C.S., s. 6993.)

§ 76-53. Harbor masters; how appointed.

The several boards of commissioners of navigation may appoint a harbor master for their respective ports. They shall appoint a clerk to keep books, in which shall be recorded all their proceedings. (R C., c. 85, s. 35; Code, s. 3525; Rev., s. 4981; C.S., s. 6994.)

§ 76-54. Commissioners of navigation may hold another office.

A commissioner of navigation and pilotage shall be deemed a commissioner for a special purpose within the meaning of Sec. 7 of Article XIV of the Constitution of North Carolina, so as not to be prohibited from holding at the same time with his commissionership another office under the national or State governments. (Ex. Sess., 1913, c. 76; C.S., s. 6995.)

§ 76-55. Commissioners of navigation to designate place for trash.

The several boards of commissioners established by this Chapter may, subject to such regulations as the United States may make, designate the places whereat, within the waters under their several and respective control, may be cast and thrown ballast, trash, stone, and like matter. (1833, c. 146, ss. 1, 2, 3; R.S., c. 88, ss. 23, 24, 45; 1846, c. 60, s. 3; R.C., c. 85, s. 40; Code, s. 3537; Rev., s. 4982; C.S., s. 6996.)

§ 76-56. Harbor master; how appointed where no board of navigation.

Where no board of navigation exists the governing body of any incorporated town, situated on any navigable watercourse, shall have power to appoint a harbor master for the port, who shall have the same power and authority in their respective ports as the harbor master of Wilmington is by this Chapter given for that port, and shall receive like fees and no others.

The board of county commissioners of any county is authorized to appoint a harbor master for any unincorporated community situated on any navigable watercourses in their respective counties. Harbor masters appointed hereunder shall have the same power and authority and shall receive the same fees as set forth in G.S. 76-18. (Rev., s. 4983; C.S., s. 6997; 1953, c. 445.)

§ 76-57. Rafts to exercise care in passing buoys, etc., penalty.

If any person having charge of any raft passing any buoy, beacon, or day mark, shall not exercise due diligence in keeping clear of it, or, if unavoidably fouling it, shall not exercise due diligence in clearing it, without dragging from its position such buoy, beacon, or day mark, he shall be guilty of a Class 3 misdemeanor, and punished only by a fine not to exceed fifty dollars ($50.00). (1883, c. 165, s. 3; Code, s. 3087; Rev., s. 3545; C.S., s. 6998; 1993, c. 539, s. 575; 1994, Ex. Sess., c. 24, s. 14(c).)

§ 76-58. Interfering with buoys, beacons, and day marks.

If any person shall moor any kind of vessel, or any raft or any part of a raft, to any buoy, beacon, or day mark placed in the waters of North Carolina by the authority of the United States Lighthouse Board, or shall in any manner hang on with any vessel or raft, or part of a raft, to any such buoy, beacon, or day mark, or shall willfully remove, damage, or destroy any such buoy, beacon, or day mark, or shall cut down, remove, damage, or destroy any beacon erected on land in this State by the authority of the said United States Lighthouse Board, or through unavoidable accident run down, drag from its position, or in any way injure any buoy, beacon, or day mark, as aforesaid, and shall fail to give notice as soon as practicable of having done so, to the lighthouse inspector of the district in which said buoy, beacon, or day mark may be located, or to the collector of the port, or, if in charge of a pilot, to the collector of the port from which he comes, he shall for every such offense be guilty of a Class 2 misdemeanor. (1858-9, c. 58, ss. 2, 3; 1883, c. 165, s. 1; Code, s. 3085; Rev., s. 3546; C.S., s. 6999; 1993, c. 539, s. 576; 1994, Ex. Sess., c. 24, s. 14(c).)

Article 6.

Morehead City Navigation and Pilotage Commission.

§§ 76-59 through 76-73: Repealed by Session Laws 1981, (Regular Session, 1982), c. 1176, s. 2.

Chapter 76A.

Navigation and Pilotage Commissions.

SUBCHAPTER I. CAPE FEAR RIVER NAVIGATION AND PILOTAGE COMMISSION.

Article 1.

General Provisions.

§ 76A-1. Commission established; powers generally.

In consideration of the requirement for the safe and expeditious movement of waterborne commerce on the navigable waters of the State, it is deemed necessary to establish the Cape Fear Navigation and Pilotage Commission, hereinafter referred to as the Commission. The Commission shall have the exclusive power to license and regulate a group of river pilots familiar with the waters of the Cape Fear River and Bar to best guide vessels within those waters and to exercise authority over navigation in the Cape Fear and Bar and to and from the sea buoy of the port. (1981, c. 910, s. 1; 1983 (Reg. Sess., 1984), c. 1081, s. 1.)

§ 76A-2. Membership.

The Commission shall consist of five voting members, four appointed by the Governor, and the president of the Wilmington-Cape Fear Pilots Association who shall serve as an ex officio voting member. Of the four members appointed by the Governor three shall be from New Hanover County, one shall be from Brunswick County. One member shall represent maritime interests. The Governor shall designate a member to serve at his pleasure as Chairman. With the exception of the ex officio member, licensed pilots and members of their immediate families shall not be allowed to serve on the Commission. (1981, c. 910, s. 1.)

§ 76A-3. Term.

It shall be the duty of the Governor to make initial appointments to the Commission on July 1, 1981. Two of the initial appointees shall serve two-year terms; the other two appointees shall serve four-year terms. All appointees after the initial appointments shall serve four-year terms. Any vacancy in the membership appointed by the Governor shall be filled by the Governor. (1981, c. 910, s. 1.)

§ 76A-4. Quorum.

A simple majority of the Commission shall constitute a quorum and may act in all cases. (1981, c. 910, s. 1.)

§ 76A-5. Duties and authority.

(a)   Rules and Regulations, Pilotage. - The Commission shall make and establish such rules and regulations as necessary and desirable respecting the qualifications, arrangements and station of pilots and for the control of navigation within the Cape Fear River and from and to the Cape Fear Bar and the sea buoys. In the development of such rules and regulations, the Commission should request the advice of the United States Coast Guard, the U.S. Corps of Engineers, the Pilots Association, other maritime interests and any other party that the Commission might deem beneficial.

(b)   Examination and Licensing. - The Commission may examine such persons who hold a federal pilot's license as may offer themselves to be a pilot on the Cape Fear River and Bar. The examination shall consist of, but not be limited to: a personal interview before the Commission; contact by the Commission with personal references; and a physical examination by a licensed physician based on a standard established by the Commission. Licenses shall be granted for a one-year period.

(c)   License Renewal. - Each license shall be renewed annually provided during the preceding year the holder thereof shall have complied with the provisions of this act and the reasonable rules and regulations as prescribed by the Commission under authority hereof. The Commission may for special considerations validate a license for less than a one-year period. Each license renewal submittal shall be accompanied with a physical examination comparable to the standards set in G.S. 76A-5(b).

(d)   Fine, License Suspension and Cancellation. - The Commission shall have the power to fine or call in and suspend or cancel the license of any pilot found to be derelict of duty, in violation of the reasonable rules and regulations as set out by the Commission or for other just cause. Grounds for suspension or cancellation shall include but not be limited to: citation by the United States Coast Guard and/or Commission for careless or neglectful duty resulting in damage to property or personal harm; absence, neglect of duty, absence from duty for a period longer than four weeks without written submission to and written approval from the Commission chairman; other violations of regulations or in actions found by the Commission to be unduly disruptive of the pilotage and service and/or harmful to person or property.

The clear proceeds of fines levied pursuant to this subsection shall be remitted to the Civil Penalty and Forfeiture Fund in accordance with G.S. 115C-457.2.

(e)   Pilots to Give Bond. - The Commission shall require of each pilot prior to granting his commission a bond with surety acceptable to the Commission in an amount not to exceed ten thousand dollars ($10,000). Every bond taken of a pilot shall be filed with and preserved by the Commission in trust for every person, firm or corporation, who shall be injured by the neglect or misconduct of such pilots, and any person, firm or corporation, so injured may severally bring suit for the damage by each one sustained.

(f)   Jurisdiction over Disputes as to Pilotage. - Disputes between pilots may be voluntarily appealed by one of the pilots to the Commission for resolution. If a resolution is not reached or the Commission decision is unacceptable to either party, normal legal recourse is available to resolve the dispute. (1981, c. 910, s. 1; 1983 (Reg. Sess., 1984), c. 1081, s. 2; 1998-215, s. 137(a); 2011-183, s. 127(b).)

§ 76A-6. Classes of licenses.

The Commission shall have general authority to issue the following classes of licenses:

(1)   Limited. - Limited licenses may be issued to those who pass requirements established by the Commission to entitle such person to a limited license.

(2)   Full. - A license to pilot any vessel. Provided there is a vacancy in the number of pilot positions established pursuant to G.S. 76A-14, a full license shall be issued to the holder of a limited license who has in the opinion of the Commission satisfactorily served at least one year under a limited license. Additionally the Commission may issue a full license to any one who in the Commission's judgment has sufficient credentials as established under G.S. 76A-5(b) to perform the pilotage task associated with a full license.

(3)   Apprentice. - A license to engage in a program, approved by the Commission, as apprentice pilot under the terms of G.S. 76A-12. (1981, c. 910, s. 1; 1983 (Reg. Sess., 1984), c. 1081, s. 3; 1985, c. 631, ss. 1, 2; c. 689, s. 26.)

§§ 76A-7 through 76A-11. Reserved for future codification purposes.

Article 2.

Pilots.

§ 76A-12. Apprentices.

The Commission when it deems necessary for the best interest of the State is hereby authorized to appoint in its discretion apprentices, none of whom shall be less than 21 years of age, and to make and enforce reasonable rules and regulations relating thereto. Apprentices shall serve for a minimum of one year but no longer than three years in order to be eligible for a limited license. The Commission shall adopt rules and regulations to monitor the progress of apprentices on a regular basis to assure the progressive development of knowledge and skill necessary to obtain a limited license. (1981, c. 910, s. 1; 1987, c. 475.)

§ 76A-13. Pilotage association.

In consideration that a mutual association for pilots has been formed, is operational and is expedient for effective management, the Commission shall recognize such a proper pilot association formed for the smooth business transactions in the provision of services. However, the Commission may prescribe such reasonable rules and regulations for the governance of such associations in its direct relationship with the Commission as it deems necessary. Any licensed pilot refusing to become a member of such association shall be subject to suspension or have his license revoked, at the discretion of the Commission. (1981, c. 910, s. 1.)

§ 76A-14. Number of pilots.

The Commission shall govern the number of pilots necessary to maintain an efficient pilotage service. Present active pilots shall continue to serve with the Commission's power of reduction to be effective only in the case of natural attrition except as provided in G.S. 76A-15. At no time shall the number of active licensed pilots exceed 15. Docking masters shall not be deemed pilots for this section or any other section in this Chapter. (1981, c. 910, s. 1.)

§ 76A-15. Pilot retirement.

The Commission shall have and is hereby given authority in its discretion and under such reasonable rules and regulations as it may prescribe to retire from active service any pilot who shall become physically or mentally unfit to perform a pilot's duties. Provided, however, that no pilot shall be retired, except with his consent for physical or mental disability unless and until such pilots shall have first been examined by the public health officer or county physician of his respective county of residence and such public health officer or physician shall have certified to the board the fact of such physical or mental disability. (1981, c. 910, s. 1.)

§ 76A-16. Compulsory use of pilots.

Every foreign vessel and every U.S. vessel sailing under register, including such vessels towing or being towed when underway in the Cape Fear River and Bar and over 60 gross tons, shall employ and take a State-licensed pilot, except when maneuvering during berthing or unberthing operations, shifting within the confine of ports or terminals, passing through bridges, with tug assistance and with a docking master aboard the vessel. Any master of a vessel violating this section shall be guilty of a Class 1 misdemeanor except as provided for in G.S. 76A-18. (1981, c. 910, s. 1; 1993, c. 539, s. 577; 1994, Ex. Sess., c. 24, s. 14(c).)

§ 76A-17. Pilotage rates.

The Commission shall set charges for pilotage services on a published tariff basis to be reviewed and revised annually as necessary. The initial publication of rates and subsequent revisions shall be preceded by public notice at least 30 days prior to publication. The rates may be based on the method chosen by the Commission and may be varied on a geographic or other basis which the Commission deems appropriate. In establishing pilotage rates the Commission shall consider but not be limited to factors such as vessels' lengths, vessels' drafts, general design of vessels, distances for which pilotage services are to be provided, nature of waters to be traversed and the rates for comparable pilotage services in other ports. (1981, c. 910, s. 1.)

§ 76A-18. Vessels not liable for pilotage.

Any vessel coming in from sea for harborage without the assistance of a pilot the wind and weather being such that such assistance or service could not have been reasonably given, shall not be liable for pilotage inward from sea. (1981, c. 910, s. 1.)

§§ 76A-19 through 76A-23. Reserved for future codification purposes.

Article 3.

Commission Funds.

§ 76A-24. Expenses of the Commission.

The pilots association shall pay to the Commission according to rules prescribed by the Commission a percentage of pilotage fees not to exceed two percent (2%) per annum for the purpose of providing funds to defray the necessary expense of the Commission. The appropriate percentage shall be set on an annual basis by the Commission. The fees paid shall be deposited to a special account with the State Treasurer in the name of the Commission and shall be administered by the Secretary of Commerce. Surpluses in the account in excess of three thousand dollars ($3,000) at the end of the fiscal year shall be returned to the pilot association on a prorated basis determined and distributed by the

Commission. The Commission, in carrying out its duties, may incur necessary legal and auditing expenses and expenses for its travel and investigation which in addition to the one hundred dollars ($100.00) per meeting fee and other allowances provided by law shall be paid from the foregoing funds. (1981, c. 910, s. 1; 1983 (Reg. Sess., 1984), c. 1081, s. 4.)

§ 76A-25. Widows and Orphans Fund.

The Widows and Orphans Fund established by Chapter 76, Section 7 of the General Statutes shall be dissolved at the earliest possible date under a method to be determined by the Commission. The method of dissolution should be equitable to all current recipients of benefits from the fund and should attempt to make reasonable provision for their future needs in lieu of on-going payments from the fund. Should the Commission determine that the assets of the fund are in excess of those needed to provide for the recipients, it may determine that a portion of the fund may be retained by the Commission and deposited in its operating fund. In such an event the requirement for payment referred to in G.S. 76A-24 shall be suspended until the balance of the operating fund is reduced to three thousand dollars ($3,000) as prescribed in G.S. 76A-24. (1981, c. 910, s. 1.)

§§ 76A-26 through 76-30. Reserved for future codification purposes.

SUBCHAPTER II. MOREHEAD CITY NAVIGATION AND PILOTAGE COMMISSION.

Article 4.

General Provisions.

§ 76A-31. Morehead City Navigation and Pilotage Commission.

In consideration of the requirement for the safe and expeditious movement of waterborne commerce on the navigable waters of the State, it is deemed necessary to establish the Morehead City Navigation and Pilotage Commission, herein called Commission. The Commission shall have the exclusive power to license and regulate pilots familiar with the waters of Morehead City Harbor and Beaufort Bar and the water route from Morehead City to Aurora, North Carolina (to include from Morehead City through the Inland or Intracoastal Waterway North, through Adams Creek, the Neuse River, the Bay River, the Hobuken Canal, the Pamlico River, and South Creek to Aurora or from the Neuse River around Brant Island Shoal through the Pamlico River and South Creek to Aurora), referred to herein as the regulated area, to best guide vessels within those waters and to exercise authority over navigation in Morehead City Harbor and Beaufort Bar and to and from the sea buoy of the port. (1981 (Reg. Sess., 1982), c. 1176, s. 1; 1985, c. 517, s. 1.)

§ 76A-32. Membership.

The Commission shall consist of three voting members, all appointed by the Governor. The president of the Morehead City Pilots' Association shall serve as an ex officio nonvoting member. All of the three members appointed by the Governor, shall be from Carteret County. One additional nonvoting ex officio member shall represent the maritime interests and shall be designated by the Governor. The Governor shall designate a voting member to serve at his pleasure as chairman. With the exception of the ex officio members, licensed pilots and members of their immediate families shall not be allowed to serve on the Commission. (1981 (Reg. Sess., 1982), c. 1176, s. 1.)

§ 76A-33. Term.

It shall be the duty of the Governor to make initial appointments to the Commission on July 1, 1982. One of the initial appointees shall serve an initial three-year term. One shall serve an initial two-year term and one for an initial one-year term. Thereafter, all appointments shall be for a three-year term. The representatives of the maritime interest shall be appointed for a one-year initial term and three-year terms thereafter. Any vacancy in the membership appointed by the Governor shall be filled by the Governor. (1981 (Reg. Sess., 1982), c. 1176, s. 1.)

§ 76A-34. Quorum.

A simple majority of voting members of the Commission shall constitute a quorum and may act in all cases. (1981 (Reg. Sess., 1982), c. 1176, s. 1.)

§ 76A-35. Duties and authority.

(a)   Rules and Regulations, Pilotage. - The Commission shall make and establish such rules and regulations as necessary and desirable respecting the qualifications, arrangements and station of pilots and for the control of navigation within the regulated area. In the development of such rules and regulations, the Commission should request the advice of the United States Coast Guard, the U.S. Corps of Engineers, the Pilots' Association, other maritime interests and any other party that the Commission might deem beneficial. However, the Commission may not establish rules and regulations concerning the Morehead City to Aurora water route except as they may apply to foreign vessels displacing over 60 gross tons.

(b)   Examination and Licensing. - The Commission may examine such persons who hold a federal pilot's license and who have complied with an apprentice course approved by the Commission as may offer themselves to be a pilot on the regulated area. The examination shall consist of, but not be limited to: a personal interview before the Commission; contact by the Commission with personal references; and a physical examination by a licensed physician based on a standard established by the Commission. Licenses shall be granted for a one-year period.

(c)   License Renewal. - Each license shall be renewed annually provided during the preceding year the holder thereof shall have complied with the provisions of this Subchapter and the reasonable rules and regulations as prescribed by the Commission under authority hereof. The Commission may for special considerations validate a license for less than a one-year period. Each license renewal submittal shall be accompanied with a physical examination comparable to the standards set in G.S. 76A-35(b).

(d)   Fine, License Suspension and Cancellation. - The Commission shall have the power to fine or call in and suspend or cancel the license of any pilot found to be derelict of duty, in violation of the reasonable rules and regulations as set out by the Commission or for other just cause. Grounds for suspension or cancellation shall include but not be limited to: citation by the United States Coast Guard and/or Commission for careless or neglectful duty resulting in damage to property or personal harm; absence, neglect of duty, absence from duty for a period longer than four weeks without written submission to and written approval from the Commission Chairman; other violations of regulations or in actions found by the Commission to be unduly disruptive of the pilotage and service and/or harmful to person or property.

The clear proceeds of fines levied pursuant to this subsection shall be remitted to the Civil Penalty and Forfeiture Fund in accordance with G.S. 115C-457.2.

(e) Pilots to Give Bond. - The Commission shall require of each pilot prior to granting his commission a bond with surety acceptable to the Commission in an amount not to exceed ten thousand dollars ($10,000). Every bond taken of a pilot shall be filed with and preserved by the Commission in trust for every person, firm or corporation, who shall be injured by the neglect or misconduct of such pilots, and any person, firm or corporation so injured may severally bring suit for the damage by each one sustained.

(f) Jurisdiction over Disputes as to Pilotage or Navigation. - Disputes between pilots or over matters related to navigation in the regulated area may be voluntarily appealed by one of the pilots to the Commission for resolution or so presented to the Commission by any interested party for resolution. If a resolution is not reached or the Commission decision is unacceptable to either party, normal legal recourse is available to resolve the dispute. (1981 (Reg. Sess., 1982), c. 1176, s. 1; 1985, c. 517, s. 2; 1998-215, s. 137(b); 2011-183, s. 127(b).)

§ 76A-36. Classes of licenses.

The Commission shall have general authority to issue three classes of licenses:

(1) Limited. - A license to pilot vessels whose draft does not exceed 25 feet combined with a maximum length to be fixed by Commission rules. Limited licenses may be issued to those who pass requirements established by statute and by the Commission to entitle such person to a limited license.

(2) Full. - A license to pilot any vessel. Full license shall be issued to all holders of a limited license who have in the opinion of the Commission

satisfactorily served at least one year under a limited license. Additionally, the Commission may issue a full license to anyone who in the Commission's judgments has sufficient credentials as established under G.S. 76A-35(b) to perform the pilotage task associated with a full license.

(3)   Apprentice. - A license to engage in a program, approved by the Commission, as apprentice pilot under the terms of G.S. 76A-42. (1981 (Reg. Sess., 1982), c. 1176, s. 1.)

§§ 76A-37 through 76A-41. Reserved for future codification purposes.

Article 5.

Pilots.

§ 76A-42. Apprentices.

The Commission when it deems necessary for the best interest of the State is hereby authorized to appoint in its discretion apprentices, none of whom shall be less than 21 nor more than 35 years of age, and to make and enforce reasonable rules and regulations relating thereto. Apprentices shall serve for a minimum of one year but no longer than three years in order to be eligible for a limited license. The Commission shall adopt rules and regulations to monitor the progress of apprentices on a regular basis to assure the progressive development of knowledge and skill necessary to obtain a limited license. That upon application of any person already partially qualified by prior experience, the Commission may waive the 35 maximum age limit and may vary the time requirements for the time period of such apprenticeship. (1981 (Reg. Sess., 1982), c. 1176, s. 1.)

§ 76A-43. Pilotage association.

In consideration that a mutual association for pilots has been formed, is operational and is expedient for effective management, the Commission shall recognize such a proper pilot association formed for the smooth business transactions in the provision of services. However, the Commission may prescribe such reasonable rules and regulations for the governance of such associations in its direct relationship with the Commission as it deems necessary. Any licensed pilot refusing to become a member of such association shall be subject to suspension or have his license revoked, at the discretion of the Commission. (1981 (Reg. Sess., 1982), c. 1176, s. 1.)

§ 76A-44. Number of pilots.

The Commission shall govern the number of pilots necessary to maintain an efficient pilotage service. Present active pilots shall continue to serve with the Commission's power of reduction to be effective only in the case of natural attrition except as provided in G.S. 76A-45. Docking masters shall not be deemed pilots for this section or any other section in this Subchapter. (1981 (Reg. Sess., 1982), c. 1176, s. 1.)

§ 76A-45. Pilot retirement.

The Commission shall have and is hereby given authority in its discretion and under such reasonable rules and regulations as it may prescribe to retire from active service any pilot who shall become physically or mentally unfit to perform a pilot's duties. Provided, however, that no pilot shall be retired, except with his consent for physical or mental disability unless and until such pilots shall have first been examined by the public health officer or county physician of his respective county of residence and such public health officer or physician shall have certified to the board the fact of such physical or mental disability. (1981 (Reg. Sess., 1982), c. 1176, s. 1.)

§ 76A-46. Compulsory use of pilots.

Every foreign vessel and every United States vessel sailing under register, including such vessels towing or being towed when underway or docking in the waters of the Morehead City Harbor and Beaufort Bar, either incoming or outgoing, and over 60 gross tons, shall employ and utilize a State licensed pilot. Every foreign vessel sailing including such vessels towing or being towed when underway or docking in the Morehead City to Aurora water route, and over 60 gross tons, shall employ and utilize a State licensed pilot. Any master of a vessel violating this section by failing to use a State licensed pilot shall be guilty of a Class 1 misdemeanor except as provided for in G.S. 76A-54. (1981 (Reg. Sess., 1982), c. 1176, s. 1; 1985, c. 517, s. 3; 1993, c. 539, s. 578; 1994, Ex. Sess., c. 14, s. 45, c. 24, s. 14(c).)

§ 76A-47. Pilotage rates.

The Commission shall set charges for pilotage services on a published tariff basis to be reviewed and revised annually as necessary. The initial publication of rates shall be those now in effect and subsequent revisions shall be preceded by public notice at least 30 days prior to publication. The rates may be based on the method chosen by the Commission and may be varied on a geographic or other basis which the Commission deems appropriate. In establishing pilotages' rates, the Commission shall consider, but not be limited to, factors such as vessels' lengths, tonnage, vessels' drafts, general design of vessels, distances for which pilotage services are to be provided, nature of waters to be traversed and the rates for comparable pilotage services in other ports. (1981 (Reg. Sess., 1982), c. 1176, s. 1.)

§ 76A-48. Vessels not liable for pilotage.

Any vessel, for reasons of safety, coming in from sea for harborage without assistance of a pilot, the wind and weather being such that such pilot assistance or service could not have been reasonably and safely given, shall not be liable for pilotage inward from sea. (1981 (Reg. Sess., 1982), c. 1176, s. 1.)

§§ 76A-49 through 76A-53. Reserved for future codification purposes.

Article 6.

Commission Funds.

§ 76A-54. Expenses of the Commission.

The pilots' association shall pay to the Commission, according to rules prescribed by the Commission, a percentage of all pilotage fees not to exceed two percent (2%) per annum for the purpose of providing funds to defray the necessary expense of the Commission. The appropriate percentage shall be set on an annual basis by the Commission. The fees paid shall be deposited to a special account with the State Treasurer in the name of the Commission and shall be administered by the Secretary of Commerce. Surpluses in the account in excess of three thousand dollars ($3,000) at the end of the fiscal year shall be returned to the pilots' association on a prorated basis determined and distributed by the Commission. That the Commission in carrying out its duties may incur necessary legal and auditing expenses and expenses for its travel and investigations which in addition to the one hundred dollar ($100.00) per meeting fee and other allowances allowed by law shall be paid from the foregoing funds. (1981 (Reg. Sess., 1982), c. 1176, s. 1.)

Chapter 77.

Rivers, Creeks, and Coastal Waters.

Article 1.

Commissioners for Opening and Clearing Streams.

§ 77-1. County commissioners to appoint commissioners.

Where any inland river or stream runs through the county, or is a line of their county, the boards of commissioners of the several counties may appoint commissioners to view such river or stream, and make out a scale of the expense of labor with which the opening and clearing thereof will be attended; and if the same is deemed within the ability of the county, and to be expedient, they may appoint and authorize the commissioners to proceed in the most expeditious manner in opening and clearing the same. (Code, s. 3706; 1887, c. 370; Rev., s. 5297; C.S., s. 7363.)

§ 77-2. Flats and appurtenances procured.

The board of county commissioners appointing the commissioners may direct them to purchase or hire a flat with a windlass and the appurtenances necessary to remove loose rock and other things, which may by such means be more easily removed, and allow the same to be paid for out of the county funds. (1785, c. 242, s. 2; R.C., c. 100, s. 3; Code, s. 3708; Rev., s. 5299; C. S., s. 7365.)

§ 77-3. Laid off in districts; passage for fish.

The board of county commissioners may appoint commissioners to examine and lay off the rivers and creeks in their county; and where the stream is a boundary between two counties, may lay off the same on their side; in doing so they shall allow three fourths for the owners of the streams for erecting slopes, dams and stands; and one-fourth part, including the deepest part, they shall leave open for the passage of fish, marking and designating the same in the best manner they can; and if mills are built across such stream, and slopes may be necessary, the commissioners shall lay off such slopes, and determine the length of time they shall be kept open; and such commissioners shall return to their respective boards of county commissioners a plan of such slopes, dams, and other parts of streams viewed and surveyed. (1787, c. 272, s. 1; R.C., c. 100, s. 5; Code, s. 3710; Rev., s. 5301; C.S., s. 7367.)

§ 77-4. Gates and slopes on milldams.

The commissioners appointed by the board of county commissioners to examine and lay off the rivers and creeks within the county, or where the stream is a boundary between counties, shall have power to lay off gates, with slopes attached thereto, upon any milldam built across such stream, of such dimensions and construction as shall be sufficient for the convenient passage of floating logs and other timber, in cases where it may be deemed necessary by the said board of county commissioners; and they shall return to the board of county commissioners appointing them a plan of such gates, slopes, and dams in writing. (1858-9, c. 26, s. 1; Code, s. 3712; Rev., s. 5302; C.S., s. 7368.)

§ 77-5. Owner to maintain gate and slope.

Upon the confirmation of the report made by the commissioners, and notice thereof given to the owner or keeper of said mill, it shall be his duty forthwith to construct, and thereafter to keep and maintain, at his expense, such gate and slope, for the use of persons floating logs and other timber as aforesaid, so long as said dam shall be kept up, or until otherwise ordered by the board of county commissioners. (1858-9, c. 26, s. 2; Code, s. 3713; Rev., s. 5303; C.S., s. 7369.)

§ 77-6. Gates and slopes discontinued.

The commissioners appointed as aforesaid, at any time that they may deem such gate and slope no longer necessary, may report the fact to their respective boards of county commissioners, and said boards of county commissioners may order the same to be discontinued. (1858-9, c. 26, s. 3; Code, s. 3714; Rev., s. 5304; C.S., s. 7370.)

§ 77-7. Failure of owner of dam to keep gates, etc.

If any owner or keeper of a mill, whose dam is across any stream, shall fail to build a gate and slope therein, or thereafter to keep and maintain the same as required by commissioners to lay off rivers and creeks, he shall be guilty of a Class 1 misdemeanor. (1858-9, c. 26, s. 4; Code, s. 3715; Rev., s. 3383; C.S., s. 7371; 1993, c. 539, s. 579; 1994, Ex. Sess., c. 24, s. 14(c).)

§ 77-8. Repairing breaks.

Wherever any stream of water which is used to propel machinery shall be by freshet or otherwise diverted from its usual channel so as to impair its power as used by any person, such person shall have power to repair the banks of such stream at the place where the break occurs, so as to cause the stream to return to its former channel. (1879, c. 53, s. 1; Code, s. 3716; Rev., s. 5305; C.S., s. 7372.)

§ 77-9. Entry upon lands of another to make repairs.

In case the break occurs on the lands of a different person from the one utilizing the stream, the person utilizing the stream shall have power to enter upon the lands of such other person to repair the same, and in case such person objects, the clerk of the superior court of the county in which the break occurs shall, upon application of the party utilizing the stream, appoint three disinterested freeholders, neither of whom shall be related to either party, who after being duly sworn shall lay off a road, if necessary, by which said person may pass over the lands of such other person to the break and repair said break from time to time as often as may be necessary, so as to cause the stream to return to its original channel, and assess any damage which may thereby be occasioned: Provided, the party upon whose land the work is proposed to be done shall have five days' notice in writing served on him or left at his place of residence: Provided further, that it shall be the duty of said commissioners to assess the damage of anyone on whose land the road shall be laid off to be paid by the applicant for said road: Provided, also, that either party shall have the right of appeal to the superior court. (1879, c. 53, s. 2; Code, s. 3717; Rev., s. 5306; C.S., s. 7373.)

§ 77-10. Draws in bridges.

Whenever the navigation of any river or creek which, in the strict construction of law, might not be considered a navigable stream, shall be obstructed by any bridge across said stream, except those under the supervision and control of the Board of Transportation, it shall be lawful for any person owning any boat plying on said stream to make a draw in such bridge sufficient for the passage of such boat; and the party owning such boat shall construct and maintain such draw at his own expense, and shall use the same in such manner as to delay travel as little as possible. (1879, c. 279, ss. 1, 2; Code, s. 3719; Rev., s. 5307; C.S., s. 7374; 1965, c. 493; 1973, c. 507, s. 5.)

§ 77-11. Public landings.

The board of county commissioners may establish public landings on any navigable stream or watercourse in the county upon petition in writing. Unless it shall appear to the board that the person owning the lands sought to be used for a public landing shall have had 20 days' notice of the intention to file such petition, the same shall be filed in the office of the clerk of the board until the succeeding meeting of the board, and notice thereof shall be posted during the same period at the courthouse door. At said meeting of the board, the allegations of the petition shall be heard, and if sufficient reason be shown, the board shall order the establishment of the public landing. The board shall at that time initiate proceedings under the Chapter entitled Eminent Domain. (1784, c. 206, s. 4; 1789, c. 303; 1790, c. 331, s. 3; 1793, c. 386; 1813, c. 862, s. 1; 1822, c. 1139, s. 2; R.C., c. 60, s. 1; c. 101, ss. 2, 4; 1869, c. 20, s. 8, subsec. 29; 1872-3, c. 189, s. 3; 1879, c. 82, s. 9; Code, ss. 2038, 2040, 2982; Rev., ss. 2684, 2685, 5308; 1917, c. 284, s. 33; 1919, c. 68; C.S., ss. 3667, 3762, 3763, 7375; 1981, c. 919, s. 10.)

Article 2.

Obstructions in Streams.

§ 77-12. Obstructing passage of boats.

If any person shall obstruct the free passage of boats along any river or creek, by felling trees, or by any other means whatever, he shall be guilty of a Class 1 misdemeanor. (1796, c. 460, s. 2; R.C., c. 100, s. 6; Code, s. 3711; Rev., s. 3561; C.S., s. 7376; 1993, c. 539, s. 580; 1994, Ex. Sess., c. 24, s. 14(c).)

§ 77-13. Obstructing streams a misdemeanor.

If any person, firm, or corporation shall fell any tree, or put any obstruction, except for the purposes of utilizing water as a motive power, in any branch, creek, stream, or other natural passage for water, whereby the natural flow of water through such passage is lessened or retarded, or whereby the navigation of such stream may be impeded, delayed, or prevented, the person, firm, or corporation so offending shall be guilty of a Class 2 misdemeanor. In addition to any fine or imprisonment imposed, the court may, in its discretion, order the person, firm, or corporation so offending to remove the obstruction and restore the affected waterway to an undisturbed condition, or allow authorized employees of the enforcing agency to enter upon the property and accomplish the removal of the obstruction and the restoration of the waterway to an undisturbed condition, in which case the costs of the removal and restoration shall be paid to the enforcing agency by the offending party. Nothing in this section shall prevent the erection of fish dams or hedges across any stream which do not extend across more than two thirds of its width at the point of obstruction. If the fish dams or hedges extend more than two thirds of the width of any stream, the said penalties shall attach. This section may be enforced by marine fisheries inspectors and wildlife protectors. Within the bounds of any county or municipality, this section may also be enforced by any law enforcement officer having territorial jurisdiction, or by the county engineer. This section may also be enforced by specially commissioned forest law-enforcement officers of the Department of Agriculture and Consumer Services for offenses occurring in woodlands. For purposes of this section, the term "woodlands" means all forested areas, including swamp and timber lands, cutover lands, and second-growth stands in previously cultivated sites. (1872-3, c. 107, ss. 1, 2; Code, s. 1123; Rev., s. 3559; C.S., s. 7377; 1975, c. 509; 1977, c. 771, s. 4; 1979, c. 493, s. 1; 1987, c. 641, s. 12; 1989, c. 727, s. 218(19); 1991, c. 152, s. 1; 1993, c. 539, s. 581; 1994, Ex. Sess., c. 24, s. 14(c); 1997-443, s. 11A.119(a); 2013-155, s. 3.)

§ 77-14. Obstructions in streams and drainage ditches.

If any person, firm or corporation shall fell any tree or put any slabs, stumpage, sawdust, shavings, lime, refuse or any other substances in any creek, stream, river or natural or artificial drainage ravine or ditch, or in any other outlet which serves to remove water from any land whatsoever whereby the drainage of said land is impeded, delayed or prevented, the person, firm or corporation so offending shall be guilty of a Class 2 misdemeanor: Provided, however, nothing herein shall prevent the construction of any dam or weir not otherwise prohibited by any valid local or State statute or regulation. In addition to any fine or imprisonment imposed, the court may, in its discretion, order the person, firm, or corporation so offending to remove the obstruction and restore the affected waterway to an undisturbed condition, or allow authorized employees of the enforcing agency to enter upon the property and accomplish the removal of the obstruction and the restoration of the waterway to an undisturbed condition, in which case the costs of the removal and restoration shall be paid to the enforcing agency by the offending party. This section may be enforced by marine fisheries inspectors and wildlife protectors. Within the boundaries of any county or municipality this section may also be enforced by any law enforcement officer having territorial jurisdiction, or by the county engineer. This section may also be enforced by specially commissioned forest law-enforcement officers of the Department of Agriculture and Consumer Services for offenses occurring in woodlands. For purposes of this section, the term "woodlands" means all forested areas, including swamp and timber lands, cutover lands and second-growth stands on previously cultivated sites. (1953, c. 1242; 1957, c. 524; 1959, cc. 160, 1125; 1961, c. 507; 1969, c. 790, s. 1; 1975, c. 509; 1977, c. 771, s. 4; 1979, c. 493, s. 1; 1987, c. 641, s. 13; 1989, c. 727, s. 218(20); 1991, c. 152, s. 2; 1993, c. 539, s. 582; 1994, Ex. Sess., c. 24, s. 14(c); 1997-443, s. 11A.119(a); 2013-155, s. 4.)

§§ 77-15 through 77-19. Reserved for future codification purposes.

Article 3.

Lands Adjoining Coastal Waters.

§ 77-20. Seaward boundary of coastal lands.

(a)   The seaward boundary of all property within the State of North Carolina, not owned by the State, which adjoins the ocean, is the mean high water mark. Provided, that this section shall not apply where title below the mean high water mark is or has been specifically granted by the State.

(b)   Notwithstanding any other provision of law, no agency shall issue any rule or regulation which adopts as the seaward boundary of privately owned property any line other than the mean high water mark. The mean high water mark also shall be used as the seaward boundary for determining the area of any property when such determination is necessary to the application of any rule or regulation issued by any agency.

(c)   For purposes of this Article, "agency" means any part, branch, division, or instrumentality of the State; any county, municipality, or special district; or any commission, committee, council, or board established by the State, or by any county or municipality.

(d)   The public having made frequent, uninterrupted, and unobstructed use of the full width and breadth of the ocean beaches of this State from time immemorial, this section shall not be construed to impair the right of the people to the customary free use and enjoyment of the ocean beaches, which rights remain reserved to the people of this State under the common law and are a part of the common heritage of the State recognized by Article XIV, Section 5 of the Constitution of North Carolina. These public trust rights in the ocean beaches are established in the common law as interpreted and applied by the courts of this State.

(e)   As used in this section, "ocean beaches" means the area adjacent to the ocean and ocean inlets that is subject to public trust rights. This area is in constant flux due to the action of wind, waves, tides, and storms and includes the wet sand area of the beach that is subject to regular flooding by tides and the dry sand area of the beach that is subject to occasional flooding by tides, including wind tides other than those resulting from a hurricane or tropical storm. The landward extent of the ocean beaches is established by the common law as interpreted and applied by the courts of this State. Natural indicators of the landward extent of the ocean beaches include, but are not limited to, the first line of stable, natural vegetation; the toe of the frontal dune; and the storm trash line. (1979, c. 618, s. 2; 1998-225, s. 5.1.)

§§ 77-21 through 77-29. Reserved for future codification purposes.

Article 4.

Lake Wylie Marine Commission.

§ 77-30. Definitions.

For purposes of this article:

(1)   "Board" means the board of commissioners of Mecklenburg and Gaston Counties, North Carolina and the county council of York County, South Carolina.

(2)   "Commission" means the Lake Wylie Marine Commission or its governing board as the case may be.

(3)   "Commissioner" means a member of the governing board of the Lake Wylie Marine Commission.

(4) "Three counties" means Mecklenburg and Gaston Counties, North Carolina, and York County, South Carolina.

(5) "Joint ordinance" means an ordinance substantially identical in content adopted separately by the board in each of the three counties.

(6) "Lake Wylie" means the impounded body of water along the Catawba River in the three counties extending from the base of Mountain Island Dam downstream to the Catawba Dam.

(7) "Shoreline area" means, except as restricted by a joint ordinance, the area within the three counties lying within 1000 feet of the mean high-water line (570 feet) on Lake Wylie. In addition, the shoreline area includes all islands within Lake Wylie and all peninsulas extending into the waters of Lake Wylie.

(8) "Wildlife Commission" means the North Carolina Wildlife Resources Commission and the South Carolina Department of Wildlife and Marine Resources. (1987, c. 683, s. 2; 1987 (Reg. Sess., 1988), c. 897, s. 1.)

§ 77-31. Authority to create and dissolve commission.

The three counties may by joint ordinance create the Lake Wylie Marine Commission. Upon its creation, the Commission has the powers, duties and responsibilities conferred upon it by joint ordinance subject to the laws of each applicable state. The provisions of any joint ordinance may be modified, amended, or rescinded by a subsequent joint ordinance. A county may unilaterally withdraw from participation as required by any joint ordinance or the provisions of this article, once the commission has been created. Any county may, by ordinance, unilaterally withdraw from the commission at the end of any budget period upon ninety days prior written notice. Upon the effectuation of the withdrawal, the Commission is dissolved and all property of the Commission must be distributed to or divided among the three counties and any other public agency or agencies serving the Lake Wylie area in a manner considered equitable by the Commission by resolution adopted prior to dissolution. (1987, c. 683, s. 2; 1987 (Reg. Sess., 1988), c. 897, s. 2.)

§ 77-32. Governing body.

Upon its creation, the commission shall have a governing board of seven. Except as otherwise provided for the first four-year period, each commissioner shall serve either a three or a four-year term, with commissioners to serve overlapping terms so that two commissioner appointments are made each year. Upon creation of the Commission, the Board of Commissioners of Gaston County shall appoint three commissioners and the boards of the other two counties shall appoint two each. These initial appointees shall serve until September thirtieth following their appointment. Thereafter, appointments must be made for terms beginning each October first by the respective boards of the three counties as follows:

(1) First Year: Three commissioners from Gaston, one appointed for a one-year term, one appointed for a three-year term and one appointed for a four-year term; two commissioners from Mecklenburg, one appointed for a one-year term and one appointed for a two-year term; two commissioners from York, one appointed for a two-year term and one appointed for a three-year term.

(2) Second Year: Two commissioners from Mecklenburg, one appointed for a three-year term and one appointed for a four-year term.

(3) Third Year: Two commissioners from York, one appointed for a three-year term and one appointed for a four-year term.

(4) Fourth Year: Two commissioners from Gaston, one appointed for a three-year term and one appointed for a four-year term.

(5) Fifth and Succeeding Years: Appointments for one three-year and one four-year term in rotation by county in the order set out above.

On the death of a commissioner, resignation, incapacity or inability to serve, as determined by the board appointing the commissioner, or removal of the commissioner for cause, as determined by the board appointing the commissioner, the board affected may appoint another commissioner to fill the unexpired term. (1987, c. 683, s. 3; 1987 (Reg. Sess., 1988), c. 897, s. 3.)

§ 77-33. Compensation and expenses of commissioners, consultants and staff.

The joint ordinance shall state the terms relating to compensation to commissioners, if any, compensation of consultants and staff members employed by the Commission, and reimbursement of expenses incurred by commissioners, consultants, and employees. The Commission is governed by these budgetary and accounting procedures as may be specified by joint ordinance. (1987, c. 683, s. 4; 1987 (Reg. Sess., 1988), c. 897, s. 4.)

§ 77-34. Meetings and election of officers; rules and regulations.

Upon creation of the Commission, its governing board shall meet at a time and place agreed upon by the boards of the three counties concerned. The commissioners shall elect a chairman and such officers as they may choose. All officers shall serve one-year terms. The governing board shall adopt such rules and regulations as it may consider necessary, not inconsistent with the provisions of this act or of any joint ordinance or the laws of the appropriate state, for the proper discharge of its duties and for the governance of the commission. In order to conduct business, a quorum must be present. The chairman may adopt those committees as may be authorized by such rules and regulations. The commission shall meet regularly at those times and places as may be specified in its rules and regulations or in any joint ordinance. However, meetings of the commission must be held in all three counties on a rotating basis so that an equal number of meetings is held in each county. Special meetings may be called as specified in the rules and regulations. As to meetings held within South Carolina, the provisions of Chapter 4 of Title 30, Code of Laws of South Carolina, 1976, (Freedom of Information Act) apply. As to meetings held within North Carolina, the provisions of that State's Open Meetings Law, Article 33C of Chapter 143 of the North Carolina General Statutes apply. (1987, c. 683, s. 5; 1987 (Reg. Sess., 1988), c. 897, s. 5.)

§ 77-35. Powers and duties.

(a) Within the limits of funds available to it and subject to the provisions of this act and of any joint ordinance the Commission may:

(1) Hire and fix the compensation of permanent and temporary employees and staff as it may consider necessary in carrying out its duties;

(2) Contract with consultants for such services as it may require;

(3) Contract with the States of North Carolina, South Carolina, or the federal government, or any agency, department, or subdivision of them for property or services as may be provided to or by these agencies and carry out the provisions of these contracts;

(4) Contract with persons, firms, and corporations generally as to all matters over which it has a proper concern and carry out the provisions of contracts;

(5) Lease, rent, purchase, or otherwise obtain suitable quarters and office space for its employees and staff, and lease, rent, purchase, or otherwise obtain furniture, fixtures, vessels, vehicles, firearms, uniforms, and other supplies and equipment necessary or desirable for carrying out the duties imposed in or under the authority of this article;

(6) Lease, rent, purchase, construct, otherwise obtain, maintain, operate, repair, and replace, either on its own or in cooperation with other public or private agencies or individuals, any of the following: boat docks, navigation aids, waterway markers, public information signs and notices, and other items of real and personal property designed to enhance public safety in Lake Wylie and its shoreline area, or protection of property in the shoreline area subject however to the provisions of Title 50 Code of Laws of South Carolina, 1976, or regulations promulgated under that title as to property within South Carolina, and Chapter 113 of the General Statutes of North Carolina and rules promulgated under that Chapter as to property within North Carolina.

(b) The Commission may accept, receive, and disburse in furtherance of its functions any funds, grants, services, or property made available by the federal government or its agencies or subdivisions, by the States of North Carolina or South Carolina or their agencies or subdivisions, or by private and civic sources.

(c) The governing bodies of the three counties may appropriate funds to the Commission out of surplus funds or funds derived from nontax sources. They may appropriate funds out of tax revenues and may also levy annually taxes for the payments of such appropriation as a special purpose, in addition to any allowed by the Constitution or in North Carolina as provided by G.S. 153A-149.

(d) The Commission is subject to those audit requirements as may be specified in any joint ordinance.

(e) In carrying out its duties and either in addition to or in lieu of exercising various provisions of the above authorization, the Commission may, with the agreement of the governing board of the county concerned, utilize personnel and property of or assign responsibilities to any officer or employee of any of the three counties. Such contribution in kind, if substantial, may with the agreement of the other two counties be considered to substitute in whole or in part for the financial contribution required of that county in support of the Commission.

(f) Unless otherwise specified by joint ordinance, each of the three counties shall annually contribute an equal financial contribution to the Commission in an amount appropriate to support the activities of the Commission in carrying out its duties. (1987, c. 683, s. 6; 1987 (Reg. Sess., 1988), c. 897, s. 6.)

§ 77-36. Filing and distribution of certified single ordinance text; effective date of ordinance and admissibility of evidence.

(a) A copy of the joint ordinance creating the Commission and of any joint ordinance amending or repealing the joint ordinance creating the Commission must be filed with the Executive Director of the North Carolina Wildlife Resources Commission and the Executive Director of the South Carolina Department of Wildlife and Marine Resources. When the Executive Directors receive ordinances that are in substance identical from all three counties concerned, they, in accordance with procedures agreed upon, shall, within 10 days, certify this fact and distribute a certified single ordinance text to the following:

(1) The Secretary of State of North Carolina and the Secretary of State of South Carolina;

(2) The clerk to the governing board of each of the three counties;

(3) The clerk of superior court of Mecklenburg and Gaston Counties and the clerk of court of York County. Upon request, the Executive Directors also shall send a certified single copy of any and all applicable joint ordinances to the chairman of the Commission;

(4) A newspaper of general circulation in the three counties.

(b)   Unless a joint ordinance specifies a later date, it shall take effect when the Executive Directors' certified text has been submitted to the Secretaries of State for filing. Certifications of the Executive Directors under the seal of the Commission as to the text or amended text of any joint ordinance and of the date or dates of submission to the Secretaries of State is admissible in evidence in any court. Certifications by any clerk of superior court or county clerk of court of the text of any certified ordinance filed with him by the Executive Directors is admissible in evidence and the Executive Directors' submission of the ordinance for filing to the clerk shall constitute prima facie evidence that the ordinance was on the date of submission also submitted for filing with the Secretary of State. Except for the certificate of a clerk as to receipt and date of submission, no evidence may be admitted in court concerning the submission of the certified text of any ordinance by the Executive Directors to any person other than the Secretary of State. (1987, c. 683, s. 7; 1987 (Reg. Sess., 1988), c. 897, s. 7.)

§ 77-37. Regulations for Lake Wylie and shoreline area.

(a)   Except as limited in subsection (b) of this section, by restrictions in any joint ordinance and by other supervening provisions of law, the Commission may make regulations applicable to Lake Wylie and its shoreline area concerning all matters relating to or affecting the use of Lake Wylie. These regulations may not conflict with or supersede provisions of general or special acts or of regulations of state agencies promulgated under the authority of general law. No regulations adopted under the provisions of this section may be adopted by the Commission except after public hearing, with publication of notice of the hearing in a newspaper of general circulation in the three counties at least 10 days before the hearing. In lieu of or in addition to passing regulations supplementary to state law and regulations concerning the operation of vessels on Lake Wylie, the Commission may, after public notice, request that the North Carolina Wildlife Resources Commission and the South Carolina Department of Wildlife and Marine Resources pass local regulations on this subject in accordance with the procedure established by appropriate state law.

(b)   Violation of any regulation of the Commission commanding or prohibiting an act is a Class 3 misdemeanor.

(c)   The regulations promulgated under this section take effect upon passage or upon such dates as may be stipulated in the regulations except that no regulation may be enforced unless adequate notice of the regulation has been posted in or on Lake Wylie or its shoreline area. Adequate notice as to a regulation affecting only a particular location may be by a sign, uniform waterway marker, posted notice, or other effective method of communicating the essential provisions of the regulation in the immediate vicinity of the location in question. Where a regulation applies generally as to Lake Wylie or its shoreline area, or both, there must be a posting of notices, signs, or markers communicating the essential provisions in at least three different places throughout the area and it must be printed in a newspaper of general circulation in the three counties.

(d)   A copy of each regulation promulgated under this section must be filed by the Commission with the following persons:

(1)   The Secretaries of State of North and South Carolina;

(2)   The clerk of superior court of Mecklenburg and Gaston Counties and the clerk of court of York County;

(3)   The Executive Directors of the Wildlife Resources Commission of North Carolina and South Carolina Wildlife and Marine Resources Department.

(e)   Any official designated in subsection (d) above may issue certified copies of regulations filed with him under the seal of his office. These certified copies may be received in evidence in any proceeding.

(f)   Publication and filing of regulations promulgated under this section as required above is for informational purposes and is not a prerequisite to their validity if they in fact have been duly promulgated, the public has been notified as to the substance of regulations, a copy of the text of all regulations is in fact available to any person who may be affected and no party to any proceeding has been prejudiced by any defect that may exist with respect to publication and filing. Rules and regulations promulgated by the Commission under the provisions of other sections of this article relating to internal governance of the Commission need not be filed or published. Where posting of any sign, notice, or marker or the making of other communication is essential to the validity of a regulation duly promulgated, it is presumed in any proceeding that prior notice was given and maintained and the burden lies upon the party asserting to the contrary to prove lack of adequate notice of any regulation. (1987, c. 683, s. 8; 1987 (Reg. Sess., 1988), c. 897, s. 8; 1993, c. 539, s. 583; 1994, Ex. Sess., c. 24, s. 14(c).)

§ 77-38. Authority of law enforcement officers and special officers.

(a)   Where a joint ordinance so provides, all law enforcement officers, or those officers as may be designated in the joint ordinance, with territorial jurisdiction as to any part of Lake Wylie or its shoreline area, within the limitations of their subject matter jurisdiction, have the authority of peace officers in enforcing the laws over all of Lake Wylie and its shoreline area.

(b)   Where a joint ordinance provides it, the Commission may hire special officers to patrol and enforce the laws on Lake Wylie and its shoreline area. These special officers have and may exercise all the powers of peace officers generally within the area in question and shall take the oaths and are subject to all provisions of law relating to law enforcement officers.

(c)   Every criminal violation must be tried in the county where it occurred. However, a certificate of training by the South Carolina Criminal Justice Academy, or a similar certificate issued by the North Carolina Criminal Justice Education and Training Standards Commission or the North Carolina Sheriffs' Education and Training Standards Commission will suffice for certification in both states for the purposes of this article.

(d)   Where a law enforcement officer with jurisdiction over any part of Lake Wylie or its shoreline area is performing duties relating to the enforcement of the laws on Lake Wylie or in its shoreline area, he has such extraterritorial jurisdiction as may be necessary to perform his duties. These duties include investigation of crimes an officer reasonably believes have been, or are about to be, committed within the area in question. This includes traversing by reasonable routes from one portion of this area to another although across territory not within the boundaries of Lake Wylie and its shoreline area; conducting prisoners in custody to a court or detention facilities as may be authorized by law, although this may involve going outside the area in question; execution of process connected with any criminal offense alleged to have been committed within the boundaries in question, except that this process may not be executed by virtue of this provision beyond the boundaries of the three counties. This also includes continuing pursuit of and arresting any violator or suspected violator as to which grounds for arrest arose within the area in question.

(e)   Where law enforcement officers are given additional territorial jurisdiction under the provisions of this section, this is considered an extension of the duties of the office held and no officer shall take any additional oath or title of office. (1987, c. 683, s. 9; 1987 (Reg. Sess., 1988), c. 897, s. 9.)

§§ 77-39 through 77-49. Reserved for future codification purposes.

Article 5.

High Rock Lake Marine Commission.

§ 77-50. Definitions.

For purposes of this Article:

(1) "Boards" means the Boards of Commissioners of Davidson and Rowan Counties.

(2) "Commission" means the High Rock Lake Marine Commission or its governing board, as the case may be.

(3) "Commissioner" means a member of the governing board of the High Rock Lake Marine Commission.

(4) High Rock Reservoir, known for purposes of this Article as "High Rock Lake", means the impounded body of water along the Yadkin River in the two counties extending from High Rock Dam, located at mile 253 on the Yadkin River, upstream approximately 19 miles.

(5) "Joint ordinance" means an ordinance substantially identical in content adopted separately by the board in each of the two counties.

(6) "Shoreline area" means, except as restricted by a joint ordinance, the area within the two counties lying within 500 feet of the normal full pool elevation of 655 (Yadkin, Inc. datum) on High Rock Lake. In addition, the shoreline area shall include all islands within High Rock Lake and all peninsulas extending into the waters of High Rock Lake.

(7) "Two counties" means Davidson and Rowan Counties.

(8) "Wildlife Commission" means the North Carolina Wildlife Resources Commission. (1993, c. 355, s. 1.)

§ 77-51. Creation of Commission authorized.

The two counties may by joint ordinance create the High Rock Lake Marine Commission. The Boards shall hold a public hearing on the joint ordinance to create the Commission. The location of the public hearing shall be determined by the Boards and established by resolution. The Boards shall cause notice of the hearing to be published once a week for two successive calendar weeks in a newspaper of general circulation in each county. The notice shall be published the first time not less than 10 days nor more than 25 days before the date fixed for the hearing. Upon its creation the Commission shall enjoy the powers and have the duties and responsibilities conferred upon it by joint ordinance, subject to the provisions of this Article and the laws of the State of North Carolina. The provisions of any joint ordinance may be modified, amended, or rescinded by a subsequent joint ordinance. A county may unilaterally withdraw from participation as required by any joint ordinance or the provisions of this Article, once the Commission has been created. Any county may unilaterally withdraw from the Commission at the end of its fiscal year, by written notification to the other county and the Commission of its intent to withdraw, with notification 90 days prior to the end of the fiscal year. Upon the effectuation of the withdrawal, the Commission is dissolved, and all property of the Commission shall be distributed to or divided among the two counties and any other public agency or agencies serving the High Rock Lake area in a manner considered equitable by the Commission by resolution adopted prior to dissolution. (1993, c. 355, s. 2.)

§ 77-52. Terms of members.

Upon its creation, the Commission shall have a governing board of nine commissioners. Except as otherwise provided for the first three-year period, each commissioner shall serve a three-year term, with commissioners to serve overlapping terms. Upon creation of the Commission, the Boards shall appoint four commissioners each. Another alternating commissioner shall serve two-year terms. This alternating commissioner shall initially be appointed by the Davidson County Board of Commissioners, then by the Rowan County Board of Commissioners, and thereafter shall alternate between the two Boards.

These appointees shall serve until December 31 following their appointment. Thereafter, appointments shall be made for terms beginning each January 1 by the respective Boards of the two counties as follows:

Initial appointments: Four commissioners from Davidson County, one appointed for a one-year term, one appointed for a two-year term, and two appointed for three-year terms; four commissioners from Rowan County, one appointed for a one-year term, two appointed for two-year terms, and one appointed for a three-year term. Subsequent appointees shall serve three-year terms. The alternating commissioner, to be initially appointed by Davidson County, shall initially serve a one-year term and thereafter serve a two-year term. (1993, c. 355, s. 3.)

§ 77-53. Compensation; budgetary and accounting procedures.

The joint ordinance shall state the terms relating to compensation to commissioners, if any, compensation of consultants and staff members employed by the Commission, and reimbursement of expenses incurred by commissioners, consultants, and employees. The Commission shall be governed by these budgetary and accounting procedures as may be specified by joint ordinance and the applicable laws of North Carolina. (1993, c. 355, s. 4.)

§ 77-54. Organization and meetings.

Upon creation of the Commission, its governing board shall meet at a time and place agreed upon by the Boards. The commissioners shall elect a chairman and such other officers as they may choose. All officers shall serve one-year terms. The governing board shall adopt such rules and regulations as it may consider necessary, not inconsistent with the provisions of this Article or of any joint ordinance or the laws of the State of North Carolina, for the proper discharge of its duties and for the governance of the Commission. In order to conduct business, a quorum must be present. The chairman may appoint those committees as may be authorized by such rules and regulations. The Commission shall meet regularly at those times and places as may be specified in its rules and regulations or in any joint ordinance. However, meetings of the Commission shall be held in the two counties on a rotating basis so that an equal number of meetings is held in each county. Special meetings may be called as specified in the rules and regulations. The provisions of the Open Meetings Law, Article 33C of Chapter 143 of the General Statutes apply. (1993, c. 355, s. 5.)

§ 77-55. Powers of Commission; administrative provision.

(a)   Within the limits of funds available to it and subject to the provisions of this Article and of any joint ordinance the Commission may:

(1)   Hire and fix the compensation of permanent and temporary employees and staff as it may consider necessary in carrying out its duties;

(2)   Contract with consultants for such services as it may require;

(3)   Contract with the State of North Carolina or the federal government, or any agency or department or subdivision of them, for property or services as may be provided to or by these agencies, and carry out the provisions of such contracts;

(4)   Contract with persons, firms, and corporations generally as to all matters over which it has a proper concern, and carry out the provisions of such contracts;

(5)   Lease, rent, purchase, or otherwise obtain suitable quarters and office space for its employees and staff, and lease, rent, purchase, or otherwise obtain furniture, fixtures, vehicles, uniforms, and other supplies and equipment necessary or desirable for carrying out the duties imposed in or under the authority of this Article; and

(6)   Lease, rent, purchase, construct, otherwise obtain, maintain, operate, repair, and replace, either on its own or in cooperation with other public or private agencies or individuals, any of the following: boat docks, navigation aids, waterway markers, public information signs and notices, and other items of real and personal property designed to enhance public recreation, public safety in High Rock Lake and its shoreline area, or protection of property in the shoreline area, subject, however, to the provisions of Chapter 113 of the General Statutes and rules promulgated under that Chapter as to property within North Carolina.

(b) The Commission may accept, receive, and disburse in furtherance of its functions any funds, grants, services, or property made available by the federal government or its agencies or subdivisions, or by private and civic sources.

(c) The Boards may appropriate funds to the Commission out of surplus funds or funds derived from nontax sources. They may appropriate funds out of tax revenues and may also levy annually taxes for the payment of such appropriation as a special purpose, in addition to any allowed by the North Carolina Constitution or as provided by G.S. 153A-149.

(d) The Commission shall be subject to such audit requirements as may be specified in any joint ordinance.

(e) In carrying out its duties, and either in addition to or in lieu of exercising various provisions of the above authorizations, the Commission may, with the agreement of the Board of Commissioners of the county concerned, utilize personnel and property of or assign responsibilities to any officer or employee of any of the two counties. Such contribution in kind, if substantial, may with the agreement of the other county be considered to substitute in whole or in part for the financial contribution required of such county in support of the Commission.

(f) Unless otherwise specified by joint ordinance, each of the two counties shall annually contribute an equal financial contribution to the Commission in an amount appropriate to support the activities of the Commission in carrying out its duties. (1993, c. 355, s. 6.)

§ 77-56. Filing and publication of joint ordinances.

(a) A copy of the joint ordinance creating the Commission and of any joint ordinance amending or repealing the joint resolution creating the Commission shall be filed with the Executive Director of the Wildlife Commission. When the Executive Director receives ordinances that are in substance identical from the two counties concerned, the Executive Director shall, within 10 days, certify this fact and distribute a certified single ordinance text to the following:

(1) The Secretary of State.

(2) The clerk to the governing board of each of the two counties.

(3)   The clerk of superior court of Davidson and Rowan Counties. Upon request, the Executive Director shall also send a certified single copy of any and all applicable joint ordinances to the chairman of the Commission.

(4)   A newspaper of general circulation in the two counties.

(b)   Unless a joint ordinance specifies a later date, it shall take effect when the Executive Director's certified text has been submitted to the Secretary of State for filing. Certifications of the Executive Director under the seal of the Commission as to the text or amended text of any joint ordinance and of the date or dates of submission to the Secretary of State shall be admissible in evidence in any court. Certifications by any clerk of superior court of the text of any certified ordinance filed with him by the Executive Director is admissible in evidence and the Executive Director's submission of the resolution for filing to the clerk shall constitute prima facie evidence that such resolution was on the date of submission also submitted for filing with the Secretary of State. Except for the certificate of a clerk as to receipt and date of submission, no evidence may be admitted in court concerning the submission of the certified text of any ordinance by the Executive Director to any person other than the Secretary of State. (1993, c. 355, s. 7.)

§ 77-57. Regulatory authority.

(a)   Except as limited in subsection (b) below, by restrictions in any joint ordinance, and by other supervening provisions of law, the Commission may make regulations applicable to High Rock Lake and its shoreline area concerning all matters relating to or affecting the use of High Rock Lake. These regulations may not conflict with or supersede provisions of general or special acts or of regulations of State agencies promulgated under the authority of general law. No regulations adopted under the provisions of this section may be adopted by the Commission except after public hearing, with publication of notice of the hearing in a newspaper of general circulation in the two counties at least 10 days before the hearing. In lieu of or in addition to passing regulations supplementary to State law and regulations concerning the operation of vessels on High Rock Lake, the Commission may, after public notice, request that the Wildlife Resources Commission pass local regulations on this subject in accordance with the procedure established by appropriate State law.

(b) Violation of any regulation of the Commission commanding or prohibiting an act shall be a Class 3 misdemeanor.

(c) The regulations promulgated under this section take effect upon passage or upon such dates as may be stipulated in the regulations except that no regulation may be enforced unless adequate notice of the regulation has been posted in or on High Rock Lake or its shoreline area. Ordinances providing regulations for specific areas shall clearly establish the boundaries of the affected area by including a map of the regulated area, with the boundaries clearly drawn, or by setting out the boundaries in a written description, or by a combination of these techniques. Adequate notice as to a regulation affecting only a particular location shall be given in the following manner. When an ordinance providing regulations for a specific area is proposed, owners of the parcel of land involved as shown on the county tax listing, and the owners of land within 500 feet of the proposed area to be regulated, as shown on the county tax listing, shall be mailed a notice of the proposed classification by first-class mail at the last addresses listed for such owners on the county tax abstracts. This mailing requirement does not apply in regulations affecting the entire lake. Notice shall also be given by a sign, uniform waterway marker, posted notice, or other effective method of communicating the essential provisions of the regulation in the immediate vicinity of the location in question. Where a regulation applies generally as to High Rock Lake or its shoreline area, or both, there must be a posting of notices, signs, or markers communicating the essential provisions in at least three different places throughout the area, and it shall be printed in a newspaper of general circulation in the two counties.

(d) A copy of each regulation promulgated under this section must be filed by the Commission with the following persons:

(1) The Secretary of State;

(2) The clerks of superior court of Davidson and Rowan Counties;

(3) The Executive Director of the Wildlife Resources Commission; and

(4) The federal Energy Regulatory Commission licensee for High Rock Lake.

(e) Any official designated in subsection (d) above may issue certified copies of regulations filed with the official under the seal of the official's office. Such certified copies may be received in evidence in any proceeding.

(f) Publication and filing of regulations promulgated under this section as required above are for informational purposes and is not a prerequisite to their validity if they in fact have been duly promulgated, the public has been notified as to the substance of the regulations, a copy of the text of all regulations is in fact available to any person who may be affected, and no party to any proceeding has been prejudiced by any defect that may exist with respect to publication and filing. Rules and regulations promulgated by the Commission under the provisions of other sections of this Article relating to internal governance of the Commission need not be filed or published. Where posting of any sign, notice, or marker, or the making of other communication is essential to the validity of a regulation duly promulgated, it is presumed in any proceeding that prior notice was given and maintained and the burden lies upon the party asserting to the contrary to prove lack of adequate notice of any regulation. (1993, c. 355, s. 8; 1993 (Reg. Sess., 1994), c. 767, s. 27.)

§ 77-58. Enforcement.

(a) Where a joint ordinance so provides, all law enforcement officers, or those officers as may be designated in the joint ordinance, with territorial jurisdiction as to any part of High Rock Lake or its shoreline area within the limitations of their subject matter jurisdiction, have the authority of peace officers in enforcing the laws over all of High Rock Lake and its shoreline area. A certificate of training issued by the North Carolina Criminal Justice Education and Training Standards Commission or the North Carolina Sheriffs' Education and Training Standards Commission will suffice for certification for the purposes of this Article.

(b) Every criminal violation shall be tried in the county where it occurred.

(c) Where a law enforcement officer with jurisdiction over any part of High Rock Lake or its shoreline area is performing duties relating to the enforcement of the laws on High Rock Lake or in its shoreline area, the officer shall have such extraterritorial jurisdiction as may be necessary to perform the officer's duties. These duties include investigations of crimes an officer reasonably believes have been, or are about to be, committed within the area in question. This includes traversing by reasonable routes from one portion of this area to another although across territory not within the boundaries of High Rock Lake and its shoreline area; conducting prisoners in custody to a court or to detention facilities as may be authorized by law, although this may involve going outside the area in question; execution of process connected with any criminal offense alleged to have been committed within the boundaries in question, except that this process may not be executed by virtue of this provision beyond the boundaries of the two counties. This also includes continuing pursuit of and arresting any violator or suspected violator as to which grounds for arrest arose within the area in question.

(d)   Where law enforcement officers are given additional territorial jurisdiction under the provisions of this section, this shall be considered an extension of the duties of the office held and no officer shall take any additional oath or title of office. (1993, c. 355, s. 9.)

§§ 77-59 through 77-69. Reserved for future codification purposes.

Article 6.

Mountain Island Lake Marine Commission.

§ 77-70. Definitions.

For purposes of this Article:

(1)   "Board" means the board of commissioners of one of the three counties.

(2)   "Commission" means the Mountain Island Lake Marine Commission or its governing board, as the case may be.

(3)   "Commissioner" means a member of the governing board of the Mountain Island Lake Marine Commission.

(4)   "Joint resolution" means a resolution or ordinance substantially identical in content adopted separately by the governing boards in each of the three counties.

(5)   "Mountain Island Lake" means the impounded body of water along the Catawba River in the three counties extending from the Cowans Ford Dam downstream to the Mountain Island Dam.

(6) "Shoreline area" means, except as modified by a joint resolution, the area within the three counties lying within 1,000 feet of the full pond elevation contour on Mountain Island Lake. In addition, the shoreline area includes all islands within Mountain Island Lake and all peninsulas extending into the waters of Mountain Island Lake.

(7) "Three counties" means Gaston, Lincoln, and Mecklenburg Counties.

(8) "Wildlife Commission" means the North Carolina Wildlife Resources Commission. (1997-257, s. 1.)

§ 77-71. Authority to create Commission; withdrawal from and dissolution of Commission.

The three counties may by joint resolution create the Mountain Island Lake Marine Commission. Upon its creation the Commission has the powers, duties, and responsibilities conferred upon it by joint resolution, subject to the provisions of this Article. The provisions of any joint resolution may be modified, amended, or rescinded by a subsequent joint resolution. A county may unilaterally withdraw from participation as provided by any joint resolution or the provisions of this Article, once the Commission has been created, and any county may unilaterally withdraw from the Commission at the end of any budget period upon 90 days prior written notice. Upon the effectuation of the withdrawal, the Commission is dissolved, and all property of the Commission must be distributed to or divided among the three counties and any other public agency or agencies serving the Mountain Island Lake area in a manner considered equitable by the Commission by resolution adopted by it prior to dissolution. (1997-257, s. 1.)

§ 77-72. Membership; terms.

Upon its creation, the Commission shall have a governing board of seven. Except as otherwise provided for the initial appointees, each commissioner shall serve a three-year term. Upon creation of the Commission, the Boards of Commissioners of Gaston County and Mecklenburg County shall appoint three commissioners each, and the Board of Commissioners of Lincoln County shall appoint one commissioner. Of the initial appointees:

(1) One commissioner appointed by Gaston County and one member appointed by Mecklenburg County shall serve one-year terms;

(2) One commissioner appointed by Gaston County and one member appointed by Mecklenburg County shall serve two-year terms; and

(3) One member appointed by Gaston County, one member appointed by Mecklenburg County, and the member appointed by Lincoln County shall serve three-year terms.

Any commissioner who has served two consecutive terms, including any initial term of less than three years, may not be reappointed to a third consecutive term. Such a member may, however, be appointed to serve again after the expiration of the term of the member's successor.

On the death of a commissioner, resignation, incapacity, or inability to serve, as determined by the board appointing that commissioner, or removal of the commissioner for cause, as determined by the board appointing that commissioner, the board affected may appoint another commissioner to fill the unexpired term. (1997-257, s. 3.)

§ 77-73. Compensation; budget.

The joint resolution of the three counties shall state the terms relating to compensation to commissioners, if any, compensation of consultants and staff members employed by the Commission, and reimbursement of expenses incurred by commissioners, consultants, and employees. The Commission shall be governed by those budgetary and accounting procedures specified by joint resolution. (1997-257, s. 4.)

§ 77-74. Organization and meetings.

Upon creation of the Commission, its governing board shall meet at a time and place agreed upon by the boards of the three counties concerned. The commissioners shall elect a chairman and officers as they choose. All officers shall serve one-year terms. The governing board shall adopt rules and regulations as it deems necessary, not inconsistent with the provisions of this Article or of any joint resolution, for the proper discharge of its duties and for the governance of the Commission. In order to conduct business, a quorum must be present. The chairman may adopt those committees as authorized by those rules and regulations. The Commission shall meet regularly at times and places as specified in its rules and regulations or in any joint resolution. However, meetings of the Commission must be held in all three counties on a rotating basis so that an equal number of meetings is held in each county. Special meetings may be called as specified in the rules and regulations. The provisions of the Open Meetings Law, Article 33C of Chapter 143 of the General Statutes, shall apply. (1997-257, s. 5.)

§ 77-75. Powers of the Commission; administration and funding.

(a) Within the limits of funds available to it and subject to the provisions of this Article and of any joint resolution, the Commission may:

(1) Hire and fix the compensation of permanent and temporary employees and staff as it may deem necessary in carrying out its duties;

(2) Contract with consultants for services it requires;

(3) Contract with the State of North Carolina or the federal government, or any agency or department, or subdivision of them, for property or services as may be provided to or by these agencies and carry out the provisions of these contracts;

(4) Contract with persons, firms, and corporations generally as to all matters over which it has a proper concern, and carry out the provisions of contracts;

(5) Lease, rent, purchase, or otherwise obtain suitable quarters and office space for its employees and staff, and lease, rent, purchase, or otherwise obtain furniture, fixtures, vessels, vehicles, firearms, uniforms, and other supplies and equipment necessary or desirable for carrying out the duties imposed in or under the authority of this Article; and

(6) Lease, rent, purchase, construct, otherwise obtain, maintain, operate, repair, and replace, either on its own or in cooperation with other public or private agencies or individuals, any of the following: boat docks, navigation aids, waterway markers, public information signs and notices, and other items of real and personal property designed to enhance public safety in Mountain Island Lake and its shoreline area, or protection of property in the shoreline area subject however to Chapter 113 of the General Statutes and rules promulgated under that Chapter.

(b) The Commission may accept, receive, and disburse in furtherance of its functions any funds, grants, services, or property made available by the federal government or its agencies or subdivisions, by the State of North Carolina or its agencies or subdivisions, or by private and civic sources.

(c) The governing boards of the three counties may appropriate funds to the Commission out of surplus funds or funds derived from nontax sources. They may appropriate funds out of tax revenues and may also levy annually property taxes for the payments of such appropriation as a special purpose, in addition to any allowed by the Constitution, or as provided by G.S. 153A-149.

(d) The Commission shall be subject to those audit requirements as may be specified in any joint resolution.

(e) In carrying out its duties and either in addition to or in lieu of exercising various provisions of the above authorization, the Commission may, with the agreement of the governing board of the county concerned, utilize personnel and property of or assign responsibilities to any officer or employee of any of the three counties. Such contribution in kind, if substantial, may with the agreement of the other two counties be deemed to substitute in whole or in part for the financial contribution required of that county in support of the Commission.

(f) Unless otherwise specified by joint resolution, each of the three counties shall annually contribute an equal financial contribution to the Commission in an amount appropriate to support the activities of the Commission in carrying out its duties. (1997-257, s. 6.)

§ 77-76. Filing and publication of joint ordinances.

(a) A copy of the joint resolution creating the Commission and of any joint resolution amending or repealing the joint resolution creating the Commission shall be filed with the Executive Director of the Wildlife Commission. When the Executive Director receives resolutions that are in substance identical from all three counties concerned, the Executive Director shall within 10 days so certify and distribute a certified single resolution text to the following:

(1) The Secretary of State;

(2) The clerk to the governing board of each of the three counties;

(3) The clerks of Superior Court of Lincoln, Mecklenburg, and Gaston Counties. Upon request, the Executive Director also shall send a certified single copy of any and all applicable joint resolutions to the chairman of the Commission; and

(4) A newspaper of general circulation in the three counties.

(b) Unless a joint resolution specifies a later date, it shall take effect when the Executive Director's certified text has been submitted to the Secretary of State for filing. Certifications of the Executive Director under the seal of the Commission as to the text or amended text of any joint resolution and of the date or dates of submission to the Secretary of State shall be admissible in evidence in any court. Certifications by any clerk of superior court of the text of any certified resolution filed with him by the Executive Director is admissible in evidence and the Executive Director's submission of the resolution for filing to the clerk shall constitute prima facie evidence that that resolution was on the date of submission also submitted for filing with the Secretary of State. Except for the certificate of a clerk as to receipt and date of submission, no evidence may be admitted in court concerning the submission of the certified text of any resolution by the Executive Director to any person other than the Secretary of State. (1997-257, s. 7.)

§ 77-77. Regulatory authority.

(a) Except as limited in subsection (b) of this section, by restrictions in any joint resolution, and by other supervening provisions of law, the Commission may make regulations applicable to Mountain Island Lake and its shoreline area concerning all matters relating to or affecting the use of Mountain Island

Lake. These regulations may not conflict with or supersede provisions of general or special acts or of regulations of State agencies promulgated under the authority of general law. No regulations adopted under this section may be adopted by the Commission except after public hearing, with publication of notice of the hearing being given in a newspaper of general circulation in the three counties at least 10 days before the hearing. In lieu of or in addition to passing regulations supplementary to State law and regulations concerning the operation of vessels on Mountain Island Lake, the Commission may, after public notice, request that the Wildlife Commission pass local regulations on this subject in accordance with the procedure established by appropriate State law.

(b)   Violation of any regulation of the Commission commanding or prohibiting an act shall be a Class 3 misdemeanor.

(c)   The regulations promulgated under this section take effect upon passage or upon dates as stipulated in the regulations, except that no regulation may be enforced unless adequate notice of the regulation has been posted in or on Mountain Island Lake or its shoreline area. Adequate notice as to a regulation affecting only a particular location may be by a sign, uniform waterway marker, posted notice, or other effective method of communicating the essential provisions of the regulation in the immediate vicinity of the location in question. Where a regulation applies generally as to Mountain Island Lake or its shoreline area, or both, there must be a posting of notices, signs, or markers communicating the essential provisions in at least three different places throughout the area, and it must be printed in a newspaper of general circulation in the three counties.

(d)   A copy of each regulation promulgated under this section must be filed by the Commission with the following persons:

(1)   The Secretary of State;

(2)   The clerks of Superior Court of Gaston, Lincoln, and Mecklenburg Counties; and

(3)   The Executive Director of the Wildlife Commission.

(e)   Any official designated in subsection (d) above may issue certified copies of regulations filed with him under the seal of his office. Those certified copies may be received in evidence in any proceeding.

(f) Publication and filing of regulations promulgated under this section as required above is for informational purposes and shall not be a prerequisite to their validity if they in fact have been duly promulgated, the public has been notified as to the substance of regulations, a copy of the text of all regulations is in fact available to any person who may be affected, and no party to any proceeding has been prejudiced by any defect that may exist with respect to publication and filing. Rules and regulations promulgated by the Commission under the provisions of other sections of this Article relating to internal governance of the Commission need not be filed or published. Where posting of any sign, notice, or marker or the making of other communication is essential to the validity of a regulation duly promulgated, it shall be presumed in any proceeding that prior notice was given and maintained and the burden lies upon the party asserting to the contrary to prove lack of adequate notice of any regulation. (1997-257, s. 8.)

§ 77-78. Enforcement.

(a) Where a joint resolution so provides, all law enforcement officers, or those officers as may be designated in the joint resolution, with territorial jurisdiction as to any part of Mountain Island Lake or its shoreline area shall, within the limitations of their subject matter jurisdiction, have the authority of peace officers in enforcing the laws over all of Mountain Island Lake and its shoreline area.

(b) Where a joint resolution provides it, the Commission may hire special officers to patrol and enforce the laws on Mountain Island Lake and its shoreline area. These special officers have and exercise all the powers of peace officers generally within the area in question and shall take the oaths and be subject to all provisions of law relating to law enforcement officers.

(c) Unless a joint resolution provides otherwise, all courts in the three counties within the limits of their subject matter jurisdiction shall have concurrent jurisdiction as to all criminal offenses arising within the boundaries of Mountain Island Lake and its shoreline area.

(d) Where a law enforcement officer with jurisdiction over any part of Mountain Island Lake or its shoreline area is performing duties relating to the enforcement of the laws on Mountain Island Lake or in its shoreline area, the officer has the extraterritorial jurisdiction necessary to perform his duties. These duties include investigation of crimes an officer reasonably believes have been, or are about to be, committed within the area in question. This includes traversing by reasonable routes from one portion of that area to another although across territory not within the boundaries of Mountain Island Lake and its shoreline area; conducting prisoners in custody to court or detention facilities as authorized by law, although this may involve going outside the area in question; execution of process connected with any criminal offense alleged to have been committed within the boundaries in question, except that such process may not be executed by virtue of this provision beyond the boundaries of the three counties. This also includes continuing pursuit of and arresting any violator or suspected violator as to which grounds for arrest arose within the area in question.

(e) Where law enforcement officers are given additional territorial jurisdiction under the provisions of this section, this shall be deemed an extension of the duties of the office held, and no officer shall take any additional oath or title of office. (1997-257, s. 9.)

§ 77-79: Reserved for future codification purposes.

Article 6A.

Lake Lure Marine Commission.

§ 77-80. Definitions.

For purposes of this Article:

(1) "Board" means the Board of Commissioners of the Town of Lake Lure.

(2) "Commission" means the Lake Lure Marine Commission or its governing board, as the case may be.

(3) "Commissioner" means a member of the governing board of the Lake Lure Marine Commission.

(4) Lake Lure Reservoir, known for purposes of this Article as "Lake Lure" or "the waters of Lake Lure", means the body of water along the Broad River in Rutherford County, impounded by the dam at Tumbling Shoals, and lying below the 995-foot contour line above sea level.

(5) "Shoreline area" means the area submerged by the dam at Tumbling Shoals, lying below 955 feet above mean sea level of the normal full pond elevation of 992 feet above mean sea level, on Lake Lure.

(6) "Wildlife Commission" means the North Carolina Wildlife Resources Commission. (2003-332, s. 1.)

§ 77-81. Creation of Commission authorized.

The Board of Commissioners of the Town of Lake Lure may by ordinance create the Lake Lure Marine Commission. The Board shall hold a public hearing on the ordinance to create the Commission. The location of the public hearing shall be determined by the Boards and established by resolution. The Board shall cause notice of the hearing to be published once a week for two successive calendar weeks in a newspaper of general circulation in Rutherford County. The notice shall be published the first time not less than 10 days nor more than 25 days before the date fixed for the hearing. Upon its creation the Commission shall enjoy the powers and have the duties and responsibilities conferred upon it by the Lake Lure municipal ordinance, subject to the provisions of this Article and the laws of the State of North Carolina. The provisions of any ordinance may be modified, amended, or rescinded by a subsequent ordinance. (2003-332, s. 1.)

§ 77-82. Governing board.

Upon its creation, the Commission shall have a governing board. The governing board shall, unless otherwise stated by ordinance, be the Board of Commissioners of the Town of Lake Lure. (2003-332, s. 1.)

§ 77-83. Compensation; budgetary and accounting procedures.

The municipal ordinance shall state the terms relating to compensation to commissioners, if any, compensation of consultants and staff members employed by the Commission, and reimbursement of expenses incurred by commissioners, consultants, and employees. The Commission shall be governed by these budgetary and accounting procedures as may be specified by the municipal ordinance and the applicable laws of North Carolina. (2003-332, s. 1.)

§ 77-84. Organization and meetings.

Upon creation of the Commission, its governing board shall meet at a time and place set by the Town of Lake Lure ordinance. Unless otherwise stated in the ordinance, the mayor of the Town of Lake Lure shall act as the presiding officer. The governing board shall adopt such rules and regulations as it may consider necessary, not inconsistent with the provisions of this Article or of any ordinance of the Town of Lake Lure or the laws of the State of North Carolina, for the proper discharge of its duties and for the governance of the Commission. In order to conduct business, a quorum must be present. The presiding officer may appoint those committees as may be authorized by such rules and regulations. The Commission shall meet regularly at those times and places as may be specified in its rules and regulations or in the Town of Lake Lure municipal ordinance. Special meetings may be called as specified in the rules and regulations. The provisions of the Open Meetings Law, Article 33C of Chapter 143 of the General Statutes, apply. (2003-332, s. 1.)

§ 77-85. Powers of Commission; administrative provision.

(a)   Within the limits of funds available to it, and subject to the provisions of this Article and of the Town of Lake Lure municipal ordinance, the Commission may:

(1)   Hire and fix the compensation of permanent and temporary employees and staff as it may consider necessary in carrying out its duties;

(2)   Contract with consultants for such services as it may require;

(3) Contract with the State of North Carolina or the federal government, or any agency or department or subdivision of them, for property or services as may be provided to or by these agencies, and carry out the provisions of such contracts;

(4) Contract with persons, firms, and corporations generally as to all matters over which it has a proper concern, and carry out the provisions of such contracts;

(5) Lease, rent, purchase, or otherwise obtain suitable quarters and office space for its employees and staff, and lease, rent, purchase, or otherwise obtain furniture, fixtures, vehicles, uniforms, and other supplies and equipment necessary or desirable for carrying out the duties imposed in or under the authority of this Article; and

(6) Lease, rent, purchase, construct, otherwise obtain, maintain, operate, repair, and replace, either on its own or in cooperation with other public or private agencies or individuals, any of the following: boat docks, navigation aids, waterway markers, public information signs and notices, and other items of real and personal property designed to enhance public recreation, public safety on the waters of Lake Lure and its shoreline area, or protection of property in the shoreline area, subject, however, to the provisions of Chapter 113 of the General Statutes and rules promulgated under that Chapter as to property within North Carolina.

(b) The Commission may accept, receive, and disburse in furtherance of its functions any funds, grants, services, or property made available by the federal government or its agencies or subdivisions, or by private and civic sources.

(c) The Board of Commissioners of the Town of Lake Lure may appropriate funds to the Commission out of surplus funds or funds derived from nontax sources. It may appropriate funds out of tax revenues and may also levy annually taxes for the payment of such appropriation as a special purpose, in addition to any allowed by the North Carolina Constitution or as provided by G.S. 160A-209.

(d) The Commission shall be subject to such audit requirements as may be specified in the municipal ordinance.

(e) In carrying out its duties, and either in addition to or in lieu of exercising various provisions of the above authorizations, the Commission may, with the agreement of the Board of Commissioners of the Town of Lake Lure, utilize personnel and property of or assign responsibilities to any officer or employee of the Town of Lake Lure. Such contribution in kind, if substantial, may with agreement between the Board and the Commission be considered to substitute in whole or in part for the financial contribution required of the Town in support of the Commission. (2003-332, s. 1.)

§ 77-86. Filing and publication of applicable municipal ordinances.

(a)   A copy of the initial municipal ordinance creating the Commission and of any ordinance amending or repealing the resolution creating the Commission shall be filed with:

(1)   The Executive Director of the Wildlife Commission.

(2)   The Secretary of State.

(3)   The clerk to the Town of Lake Lure.

(4)   The clerk of superior court of Rutherford County. Upon request, the Executive Director shall also send a certified single copy of any and all applicable ordinances to the chairman of the Commission.

(5)   A newspaper of general circulation in Rutherford County.

(b)   Unless the municipal ordinance specifies a later date, it shall take effect when the text has been submitted to the Secretary of State for filing. Certifications of the Board under the seal of the Commission as to the text or amended text of any municipal ordinance and of the date or dates of submission to the Secretary of State shall be admissible in evidence in any court. Certifications by the clerk of superior court of Rutherford County of the text of any certified ordinance filed with the clerk by the Board is admissible in evidence and the Board's submission of the resolution for filing to the clerk shall constitute prima facie evidence that such resolution was on the date of submission also submitted for filing with the Secretary of State. Except for the certificate of a clerk as to receipt and date of submission, no evidence may be admitted in court concerning the submission of the certified text of any ordinance by the Board to any person other than the Secretary of State. (2003-332, s. 1.)

§ 77-87. Regulatory authority.

(a)   Except as limited in subsection (b) of this section, by restrictions in any municipal ordinance, and by other supervening provisions of law, the Commission may make regulations applicable to Lake Lure and its shoreline area concerning all matters relating to or affecting the use of Lake Lure. These regulations may not conflict with provisions of general or special acts or of regulations of State agencies promulgated under the authority of general law. No regulations adopted under the provisions of this section may be adopted by the Commission except after public hearing, with publication of notice of the hearing in a newspaper of general circulation in Rutherford County at least 10 days before the hearing. In lieu of or in addition to passing regulations supplementary to State law and regulations concerning the operation of vessels on Lake Lure, the Commission may, after public notice, request that the Wildlife Resources Commission pass local regulations on this subject in accordance with the procedure established by appropriate State law.

(b)   Violation of any regulation of the Commission commanding or prohibiting an act shall be a Class 3 misdemeanor.

(c)   The regulations promulgated under this section take effect upon passage or upon such dates as may be stipulated in the regulations except that no regulation may be enforced unless adequate notice of the regulation has been posted in or on Lake Lure or its shoreline area. Ordinances providing regulations for specific areas shall clearly establish the boundaries of the affected area by including a map of the regulated area, with the boundaries clearly drawn, by setting out the boundaries in a written description, or by a combination of these techniques. Adequate notice as to a regulation affecting only a particular location shall be given in the following manner. When an ordinance providing regulations for a specific area is proposed, owners of the parcel of land involved as shown on the county tax listing, and the owners of land within 500 feet of the proposed area to be regulated, as shown on the county tax listing, shall be mailed a notice of the proposed classification by first-class mail at the last addresses listed for such owners on the county tax abstracts. This mailing requirement does not apply in regulations affecting the entire lake. Notice shall also be given by a sign, uniform waterway marker, posted notice, or other effective method of communicating the essential provisions of the regulation in the immediate vicinity of the location in question. Where a regulation applies generally as to the waters of Lake Lure or its shoreline area, or both, there must be a posting of notices, signs, or markers communicating the essential provisions in at least three different places throughout the area, and it shall be printed in a newspaper of general circulation in Rutherford County.

(d)   A copy of each regulation promulgated under this section must be filed by the Commission with the following persons:

(1)   The Secretary of State;

(2)   The clerk of superior court of Rutherford County;

(3)   The Executive Director of the Wildlife Resources Commission; and

(4)   The federal Energy Regulatory Commission licensee for Lake Lure, if other than the Town of Lake Lure.

(e)   Any official designated in subsection (d) of this section may issue certified copies of regulations filed with the official under the seal of the official's office. Such certified copies may be received in evidence in any proceeding.

(f)   Publication and filing of regulations promulgated under this section as required above are for informational purposes and are a prerequisite to their validity if they in fact have been duly promulgated, the public has been notified as to the substance of the regulations, a copy of the text of all regulations is in fact available to any person who may be affected, and no party to any proceeding has been prejudiced by any defect that may exist with respect to publication and filing. Rules and regulations promulgated by the Commission under the provisions of other sections of this Article relating to internal governance of the Commission need not be filed or published. Where posting of any sign, notice, or marker, or the making of other communication is essential to the validity of a regulation duly promulgated, it is presumed in any proceeding that prior notice was given and maintained, and the burden lies upon the party asserting to the contrary to prove lack of adequate notice of any regulation. (2003-332, s. 1.)

§ 77-88. Enforcement.

(a)   Where a municipal ordinance so provides, all law enforcement officers, or those officers as may be designated in the municipal ordinance, with territorial jurisdiction as to any part of the waters of Lake Lure or its shoreline area within the limitations of their subject matter jurisdiction, have the authority of peace officers in enforcing the laws over all of the waters of Lake Lure and its shoreline area. A certificate of training issued by the North Carolina Criminal Justice Education and Training Standards Commission or the North Carolina Sheriffs' Education and Training Standards Commission will suffice for certification for the purposes of this Article.

(b)　　Where a law enforcement officer with jurisdiction over any part of the waters of Lake Lure or its shoreline area is performing duties relating to the enforcement of the laws on the waters of Lake Lure or in its shoreline area, the officer shall have such extraterritorial jurisdiction as may be necessary to perform the officer's duties. These duties include investigations of crimes an officer reasonably believes have been, or are about to be, committed within the area in question. This includes traversing by reasonable routes from one portion of this area to another although across territory not within the boundaries of the waters of Lake Lure and its shoreline area; conducting prisoners in custody to a court or to detention facilities as may be authorized by law, although this may involve going outside the area in question; execution of process connected with any criminal offense alleged to have been committed within the boundaries in question, except that this process may not be executed by virtue of this provision beyond the boundaries of Rutherford County. This also includes continuing pursuit of and arresting any violator or suspected violator as to which grounds for arrest arose within the area in question.

(c)　　Reserved for future codification purposes.

(d)　　Where law enforcement officers are given additional territorial jurisdiction under the provisions of this section, this shall be considered an extension of the duties of the office held, and no officer shall take any additional oath or title of office. (2003-332, s. 1.)

§ 77-89: Reserved for future codification purposes.

Article 7.

Roanoke River Basin Bi-State Commission.

Part 1. Roanoke River Basin Bi-State Commission.

§ 77-90. Definitions.

The following definitions apply in this Article:

(1)   "Commission" means the Roanoke River Basin Bi-State Commission.

(2)   "Roanoke River Basin" or "Basin" means that land area designated as the Roanoke River Basin by the North Carolina Department of Environment and Natural Resources pursuant to G.S. 143-215.8B and the Virginia State Water Control Board pursuant to Code of Virginia § 62.1-44.38. (2002-177, s. 1.)

§ 77-91. Commission established; purposes.

There is established the Roanoke River Basin Bi-State Commission. The Commission shall be composed of members from the State of North Carolina and the Commonwealth of Virginia. The purposes of the Commission shall be to:

(1)   Provide guidance and make recommendations to local, state, and federal legislative and administrative bodies, and to others as it deems necessary and appropriate, for the use, stewardship, and enhancement of the water, and other natural resources, for all citizens within the Basin.

(2)   Provide a forum for discussion of issues affecting the Basin's water quantity and water quality and issues affecting other natural resources.

(3)   Promote communication, coordination, and education among stakeholders within the Basin.

(4)   Identify problems and recommend appropriate solutions.

(5)   Undertake studies and prepare, publish, and disseminate information through reports, and in other forms, related to water quantity, water quality, and other natural resources of the Basin. (2002-177, s. 1.)

§ 77-92. Membership; terms of office; eligibility for appointment.

(a)   The Roanoke River Basin Bi-State Commission shall consist of 18 members with each state appointing nine members. The North Carolina delegation to the Commission shall consist of the six members of the General Assembly of North Carolina appointed to the North Carolina Roanoke River Basin Advisory Committee and three nonlegislative members who represent different geographical areas of the North Carolina portion of the Basin and who reside within the Basin's watershed, to be appointed by the Governor of North Carolina. The Virginia delegation to the Commission shall be appointed as determined by the Commonwealth of Virginia.

(b)   Members of the North Carolina House of Representatives, the North Carolina Senate, the Virginia House of Delegates, the Virginia Senate, and federal legislators, who have not been appointed to the Commission and whose districts include any portion of the Basin, may serve as nonvoting ex officio members of the Commission.

(c)   Except as provided in this subsection, members of the North Carolina delegation to the Commission shall serve at the pleasure of the Governor of North Carolina. The Governor of North Carolina may not remove a legislative member of the North Carolina delegation to the Commission during the legislator's term of office, except that the Governor may remove any member of the North Carolina delegation to the Commission for misfeasance, malfeasance, or nonfeasance as provided in G.S. 143B-13. A legislative member of the North Carolina delegation to the Commission who ceases to be a member of the General Assembly of North Carolina shall cease to be a member of the Commission. The terms of members of the Virginia delegation to the Commission shall be determined by the Commonwealth of Virginia.

(d)   Each state's delegation to the Commission may meet separately to discuss Basin-related issues affecting their state and may report their findings independently of the Commission. (2002-177, s. 1; 2005-37, ss. 2, 3; 2012-200, s. 28(a).)

§ 77-93. Powers and duties.

(a)   The Commission shall have no regulatory authority.

(b) To perform its duties and objectives, the Commission shall have the following powers:

(1) To develop rules and procedures for the conduct of its business or as may be necessary to perform its duties and carry out its objectives, including, but not limited to, selecting a chairman and vice-chairman, rotating chairmanships, calling meetings, and establishing voting procedures. Rules and procedures developed pursuant to this subdivision shall be effective upon an affirmative vote by a majority of the Commission members.

(2) To establish standing and ad hoc advisory committees pursuant to G.S. 77-94 and the Virginia Roanoke River Basin Advisory Committee established pursuant to Chapter 5.4 of Title 62.1 of the Code of Virginia, which shall be constituted in a manner to ensure a balance between recognized interests. The Commission shall determine the purpose of each advisory committee.

(3) To seek, apply for, accept, and expend gifts, grants and donations, services, and other aid from public or private sources. With the exception of funds provided by the planning district commissions, councils of governments, and commissions and funds appropriated by the General Assemblies of Virginia and North Carolina, the Commission may accept funds only after an affirmative vote by a majority of the members of the Commission or by following any other procedures that are established by the Commission for the conduct of its business.

(4) To establish a nonprofit corporation to assist in the details of administering its affairs and in raising funds.

(5) To enter into contracts and execute all instruments necessary or appropriate.

(6) To perform any lawful acts necessary or appropriate for the furtherance of its work. (2002-177, s. 1; 2012-200, s. 28(b).)

§ 77-94. Standing and ad hoc committees.

To facilitate communication among stakeholders in the Basin, and to maximize participation by all interested parties, the Commission shall establish both standing and ad hoc committees. The Commission shall appoint the members of the standing and ad hoc committees in accordance with guidelines adopted by the Commission. The standing committees shall include all of the following:

(1)   Permit holders. - The Commission shall identify those entities that hold permits issued by a federal, state, or local regulatory agency pertaining to the water of the Basin. The entities may recommend representatives to be appointed to the committees by the Commission.

(2)   Roanoke River Basin interest groups. - The Commission shall identify interest groups that may recommend representatives to be appointed to the committees by the Commission.

(3)   Public officials and governmental entities. - The committees shall be composed of representatives of each county, city, and town located completely or partially within the Basin. Also, other governmental entities that the Commission deems appropriate may recommend one member to be appointed to the committees by the Commission. The committees may also include the United States Senators from North Carolina and Virginia or their designees, and any member of the United States House of Representatives or the Representative's designee, whose district includes any portion of the Basin, if the members elect to serve on the committees.

(4)   Agriculture, forestry, and soil and water conservation districts. - The Commission shall identify persons who represent agricultural and forestry interests throughout the Basin and representatives from the soil and water conservation districts within the Basin and shall appoint representatives from these groups to the committees. (2002-177, s. 1.)

§ 77-95. Staffing and support.

(a)   The North Carolina Department of Environment and Natural Resources and the Virginia Department of Environmental Quality shall provide staff support to the Commission. Additional staff may be hired or contracted by the Commission through funds raised by or provided to it. The duties and compensation of any additional staff shall be determined and fixed by the Commission, within available resources.

(b)   All agencies of the State of North Carolina and the Commonwealth of Virginia shall cooperate with the Commission and, upon request, shall assist the

Commission in fulfilling its responsibilities. The North Carolina Secretary of Environment and Natural Resources and the Virginia Secretary of Natural Resources or their designees shall each serve as the liaison between their respective state agencies and the Commission. (2002-177, s. 1.)

§ 77-96. Funding.

(a)   The Commission shall annually adopt a budget that shall include the Commission's estimated expenses. Funding for the Commission shall be shared and apportioned between the State of North Carolina and the Commonwealth of Virginia. The appropriation of public funds to the Commission shall be provided through each state's regular process for appropriating public funds. The North Carolina councils of governments and commissions named in G.S. 77-103(b)(5) shall bear a proportion of North Carolina's share of the expenses, which may be in the form of in-kind contributions.

(b)   The Commission shall designate a fiscal agent.

(c)   The accounts and records of the Commission showing the receipt and disbursement of funds from whatever source derived shall be in the form that the North Carolina Auditor and the Virginia Auditor of Public Accounts prescribe, provided that the accounts shall correspond as nearly as possible to the accounts and records for such matters maintained by similar enterprises. The accounts and records of the Commission shall be subject to an annual audit by the North Carolina Auditor and the Virginia Auditor of Public Accounts or their legal representatives, and the costs of the audit services shall be borne by the Commission. The results of the audits shall be delivered to the Joint Legislative Commission on Governmental Operations of the General Assembly of North Carolina and as provided by the Commonwealth of Virginia. (2002-177, s. 1.)

§ 77-97. Compensation and expenses of Commission members.

(a)   The appointed members of the North Carolina delegation to the Commission shall receive per diem, subsistence, and travel expenses as follows:

(1) Commission members who are members of the General Assembly at the rate established in G.S. 120-3.1.

(2) Commission members who are officials or employees of the State or of local government agencies at the rate established in G.S. 138-6.

(3) All other Commission members at the rate established in G.S. 138-5.

(b) The members of the Virginia delegation to the Commission shall receive compensation as provided by the Commonwealth of Virginia.

(c) All expenses shall be paid from funds appropriated or otherwise available to the Commission. (2002-177, s. 1.)

§ 77-98. Annual report.

The Commission shall submit an annual report, including any recommendations, on or before 1 October of each year to the Governor of North Carolina, the Environmental Review Commission of the General Assembly of North Carolina, the Governor of Virginia, and the General Assembly of Virginia. (2002-177, s. 1; 2007-495, s. 22.)

§ 77-99. Termination.

The General Assembly of North Carolina may terminate the Commission by repealing this Part. The Commission shall terminate if the General Assembly of Virginia repeals the provisions of the Code of Virginia that are comparable to this Part. (2002-177, s. 1.)

§§ 77-100 through 77-102: Reserved for future codification purposes.

Part 2. Roanoke River Basin Advisory Committee.

§ 77-103: Repealed by Session Laws 2011-266, s. 1.25(a), effective July 1, 2011.

§ 77-104: Repealed by Session Laws 2011-266, s. 1.25(a), effective July 1, 2011.

§ 77-105: Repealed by Session Laws 2011-266, s. 1.25(a), effective July 1, 2011.

§ 77-106: Repealed by Session Laws 2011-266, s. 1.25(a), effective July 1, 2011.

§ 77-107: Reserved for future codification purposes.

§ 77-108: Reserved for future codification purposes.

§ 77-109: Reserved for future codification purposes.

Article 8.

River Basins Advisory Commissions.

§ 77-110. Definitions.

The following definitions apply in this Article:

(1) "Commission" or "commissions" means (i) the Catawba/Wateree River Basin Advisory Commission, (ii) the Yadkin/Pee Dee River Basin Advisory Commission, or (iii) both commissions, as required by the context.

(2) "River basin" or "river basins" means (i) that land area designated as the Catawba River Basin pursuant to G.S. 143-215.22G and that land area designated as the Catawba/Wateree River Basin by the South Carolina Department of Health and Environmental Control, (ii) that land area designated as the Yadkin (Yadkin-Pee Dee) River Basin pursuant to G.S. 143-215.22G and that land area designated as the Yadkin/Pee Dee River Basin by the South Carolina Department of Health and Environmental Control, or (iii) both river basins, as required by the context. (2004-83, s. 1.)

§ 77-111. Commissions established; purposes.

There is established the Catawba/Wateree River Basin Advisory Commission and the Yadkin/Pee Dee River Basin Advisory Commission. The commissions shall be constituted as described in this Article and there shall be a separate commission for each river basin. The commissions shall be permanent bodies composed of members from the State of North Carolina and the State of South Carolina. The purpose of each commission shall be to:

(1) Provide guidance and make recommendations to local, state, and federal legislative and administrative bodies, and to others as it considers necessary and appropriate, for the use, stewardship, and enhancement of the water, and other natural resources, for all citizens within the river basins.

(2) Provide a forum for discussion of issues affecting the river basin's water quantity and water quality, and issues affecting other natural resources.

(3) Promote communication, coordination, and education among stakeholders within the river basins.

(4) Identify problems and recommend appropriate solutions.

(5) Undertake studies related to water quantity, water quality, and other natural resources in the river basin based on existing data available from agencies located in either state.

(6) Determine the optimum approach to comprehensively and collaboratively provide recommendations for integrated river management including, but not limited to, the total assimilative capacity of the river basin. (2004-83, s. 1.)

§ 77-112. Powers and duties.

(a) The authority granted to each commission shall be advisory in nature and in no way shall either commission be construed to have any regulatory authority.

(b) Neither commission shall have any authority to obligate or otherwise bind the State of North Carolina, the State of South Carolina, or any agency or subdivision of either state.

(c) To achieve its purposes, each commission shall have all of the following powers and duties:

(1) To develop rules and procedures for the conduct of its business or as may be necessary to perform its duties and carry out its objectives including, but not limited to, calling meetings and establishing voting procedures. Rules and procedures developed pursuant to this item shall be effective upon an affirmative vote by a majority of the commission members.

(2) To establish standing and ad hoc committees, which shall be constituted in a manner to ensure a balance between recognized interests and states. The commissions shall determine the purpose of each standing or ad hoc committee.

(3) To seek, apply for, accept, and expend gifts, grants, donations, services, and other aid from public or private sources. The commissions may accept or expend funds only after an affirmative vote by a majority of the members of the commissions.

(4) To exercise the powers of a body corporate, including the power to sue and be sued, and adopt and use a common seal and alter the same.

(5) To enter into contracts and execute all instruments necessary or appropriate to achieve the purposes of the commissions.

(6)   To designate a fiscal agent.

(7)   To perform any lawful acts necessary or appropriate to achieve the purposes of the commissions. (2004-83, s. 1.)

§ 77-113. Membership; terms of office; eligibility for appointment; meetings.

(a)   The Catawba/Wateree River Basin Advisory Commission shall be composed of 15 members as follows:

(1)   Two members of the North Carolina House of Representatives whose districts include a part of the North Carolina portion of the river basin, to be appointed by the Speaker of the North Carolina House of Representatives.

(2)   Two members of the North Carolina Senate whose districts include a part of the North Carolina portion of the river basin, to be appointed by the President Pro Tempore of the North Carolina Senate.

(3)   Two members of the South Carolina House of Representatives, to be appointed by the Speaker of the South Carolina House of Representatives.

(4)   Two members of the South Carolina Senate, to be appointed by the President Pro Tempore of the South Carolina Senate.

(5)   One person from South Carolina representing a water or sewer municipal utility to be appointed by the South Carolina legislative members of the Commission.

(6)   One person from a nonprofit land conservation trust operating within the North Carolina portion of the river basin, appointed by the Governor of North Carolina.

(7)   The President of Duke Power or the President's designee.

(8)   The Chair of the Bi-State Catawba River Task Force or the Chair's designee.

(9)   The Chief Executive Officer of Carolina's Partnership, Inc., or the Chief Executive Officer's designee.

(10) One person to represent the following commissions, appointed jointly by the three chief executive officers of the commissions: the Lake Wylie Marine Commission established pursuant to Article 4 of Chapter 77 of the General Statutes, the Mountain Island Lake Marine Commission established pursuant to Article 6 of Chapter 77 of the General Statutes, and the Lake Norman Marine Commission established pursuant to Chapter 1089 of the 1969 Session Laws.

(11) One member of a lake homeowner's association located on the Catawba/Wateree River whose members reside in South Carolina, to be appointed by the President Pro Tempore of the South Carolina Senate.

(b) The Yadkin/Pee Dee River Basin Advisory Commission shall be composed of 15 members as follows:

(1) Two members of the North Carolina House of Representatives whose districts include a part of the North Carolina portion of the river basin, to be appointed by the Speaker of the North Carolina House of Representatives.

(2) Two members of the North Carolina Senate whose districts include a part of the North Carolina portion of the river basin, to be appointed by the President Pro Tempore of the North Carolina Senate.

(3) Two members of the South Carolina House of Representatives, to be appointed by the Speaker of the South Carolina House of Representatives.

(4) Two members of the South Carolina Senate, to be appointed by the President Pro Tempore of the South Carolina Senate.

(5) One person from South Carolina representing a water or sewer municipal utility to be appointed by the South Carolina legislative members of the Commission.

(6) One person from South Carolina representing the agricultural community to be appointed by the South Carolina legislative members of the Commission.

(7) One person from a water or sewer municipal utility, appointed by the Governor of North Carolina.

(8) The President of Progress Energy or the President's designee.

(9) The President of Alcoa Power Generating, Inc., (APGI) or the President's designee.

(10) The President of Weyerhaeuser or the President's designee.

(11) A representative of the land development industry, whose organization does business within the Yadkin/Pee Dee River Basin and who shall be appointed by the Chair of the Commission.

(c) Each member appointed to the commissions pursuant to subdivisions (1) and (2) of subsections (a) and (b) of this section shall serve at the pleasure of the appointing authority so long as the member remains a Representative or Senator. Each member appointed to the commissions pursuant to subdivisions (3) and (4) of subsections (a) and (b) of this section shall serve as provided by the General Assembly of South Carolina. Each member appointed to the commissions pursuant to subdivisions (7) through (9) of subsection (a) and subdivisions (8) through (10) of subsection (b) of this section shall serve for so long as the member continues in the qualifying position or, if the member is a designee, at the pleasure of the designating authority. Each member appointed to the commissions pursuant to subdivisions (6) and (10) of subsection (a) and subdivisions (7) and (11) of subsection (b) of this section shall serve a term of two years and may be reappointed to serve no more than three consecutive full terms or 84 consecutive months, whichever is greater. The term of a person appointed to the commission pursuant to subdivision (10) of subsection (a) of this section shall expire on 1 January of even-numbered years. The term of a person appointed to the commission pursuant to subdivision (6) of subsection (a) of this section shall expire on 1 January of odd-numbered years. The term of a member who is appointed to the commissions pursuant to subdivisions (5) and (11) of subsection (a) and subdivisions (5) and (6) of subsection (b) of this section shall serve as provided by the General Assembly of South Carolina. An appointment to fill a vacancy on the commissions shall be for the unexpired portion of the term. A vacancy on the commissions shall be filled in the same manner as the original appointment. Members of the commissions who are appointed from or reside in North Carolina may be removed by the Governor of North Carolina for misfeasance, malfeasance, or nonfeasance, as provided in G.S. 143B-13.

(d) The legislative members of each commission may appoint additional members to the commission to serve as advisory members as the legislative members consider necessary.

(e) The members of each commission shall elect a Chair, Vice-Chair, and any other officers they consider necessary and shall determine the length of the term of office, not to exceed two years, of each officer. The Chair and the Vice-Chair shall not be from the same state and the Chair shall be rotated between the State of North Carolina and the State of South Carolina.

(f) Each commission shall meet upon the call of the Chair. A majority of each commission shall constitute a quorum for the transaction of business.

(g) The legislative members of the commissions from each state may meet separately to discuss river basin-related issues affecting their state and may report their findings independently of the commissions. (2004-83, s. 1; 2005-37, s. 1.)

§ 77-114. Staffing; meeting facilities; assistance by agencies.

(a) The North Carolina Department of Environment and Natural Resources and the South Carolina Department of Health and Environmental Control shall provide staff support and facilities to each commission within the existing programs of the respective agencies. Additional staff may be hired or contracted by each commission through funds raised by or provided to it. The duties and compensation of any additional staff shall be determined and fixed by each commission, within available resources.

(b) All agencies of the State of North Carolina and the State of South Carolina shall cooperate with the commissions and, upon request, shall assist each commission in fulfilling its responsibilities. The North Carolina Secretary of Environment and Natural Resources and the Commissioner of the South Carolina Department of Health and Environmental Control or their designees shall each serve as the liaison between their respective state agencies and each commission.

(c) The commissions may obtain information and data upon request from all state officers, agents, agencies, and departments of the State of North Carolina and the State of South Carolina while in discharge of their duties. (2004-83, s. 1.)

§ 77-115. Funding.

(a) Each commission shall annually adopt a budget that shall include the estimated income and expenses of each commission. Funding for the commissions shall be shared and apportioned between the State of North Carolina and the State of South Carolina as each state may provide through its regular appropriations process.

(b) The accounts and records of each commission showing the receipt and disbursement of funds from whatever source derived shall be in the form that the Auditor of North Carolina and the State Auditor of South Carolina prescribe. The accounts and records of each commission shall be subject to an annual audit by the Auditor of North Carolina and the State Auditor of South Carolina or their legal representatives. The cost of the annual audits shall be borne by each commission. The results of the audits shall be delivered to the Joint Legislative Commission on Governmental Operations of the General Assembly of North Carolina and to the General Assembly of South Carolina as the General Assembly of South Carolina shall provide. (2004-83, s. 1.)

§ 77-116. Compensation and expenses of members of the commissions.

(a) Members of the commissions who are appointed from or reside in North Carolina shall receive no salary for their service on the commissions but may be paid, within available resources, per diem, subsistence, and travel expenses as follows:

(1) Members of the commissions who are members of the General Assembly at the rate established in G.S. 120-3.1.

(2) Members of the commissions who are officials or employees of the State or of local government agencies at the rate established in G.S. 138-6.

(3) All other members of the commissions at the rate established in G.S. 138-5.

(b) Members of the commissions who are appointed from or reside in South Carolina shall be compensated as provided by the General Assembly of South Carolina.

(c)   All expenses shall be paid from funds appropriated or otherwise available to the commissions. (2004-83, s. 1.)

§ 77-117. Annual report.

The commissions shall submit annual reports, including any recommendations, on or before 1 October of each year to the Governor of North Carolina, the Environmental Review Commission of the General Assembly of North Carolina, the Governor of South Carolina, and the General Assembly of South Carolina, as the Governor, the General Assembly of South Carolina, or the Commissioner of the South Carolina Department of Health and Environmental Control shall provide. (2004-83, s. 1.)

§ 77-118. Termination.

The General Assembly of North Carolina may terminate the commissions by repealing this Article. The commissions shall terminate if the General Assembly of South Carolina repeals the provisions of the South Carolina Code of Laws that are comparable to this Article. (2004-83, s. 1.)

§ 77-119. Reserved for future codification purposes.

§ 77-120. Reserved for future codification purposes.

§ 77-121. Reserved for future codification purposes.

§ 77-122. Reserved for future codification purposes.

§ 77-123. Reserved for future codification purposes.

§ 77-124. Reserved for future codification purposes.

Article 9.

Clean Coastal Water and Vessel Act.

§ 77-125. Definitions.

The following definitions apply in this Article:

(1) Department. - Department of Environment and Natural Resources.

(2) Large vessel marina. - A marina that has docking facilities and has more than 10 wet slips for vessels of 26 feet or more that have marine sanitation devices. The term includes privately and publicly owned marinas and anchorages.

(3) Marine sanitation device. - As defined in 33 U.S.C. § 1322. The term does not include "portable toilets" as defined in this act.

(4) Portable toilet. - A self-contained mobile toilet facility and holding tank for sewage.

(5) Pumpout facility. - The term includes stations affixed permanently to a dock, mobile stations mounted to a golf cart or hand truck, direct slipside connections, pumpout vessels, and tanker trucks.

(6) Sewage. - Treated or untreated human waste. As used in this act, the term includes effluent produced or held by any type of marine sanitation device.

(7) Vessel. - As defined in G.S. 75A-2. (2009-345, s. 1; 2010-180, s. 21(b).)

§ 77-126. Marina pumpout facilities and services required in certain areas; marinas and local government may apply for grant funds.

(a) The owner or operator, as appropriate, of any large vessel marina that is located on coastal waters designated as a no discharge zone by the Environmental Protection Agency or that is located in a county or municipality that has adopted a resolution to petition the Environmental Protection Agency for a no discharge zone designation shall either (i) install and maintain an operational pumpout facility at the marina that is available to customers patronizing the marina or (ii) contract with an outside service provider to provide pumpout services on a regular basis to the marina.

(b) The owner or operator, as appropriate, of a large vessel marina may apply for any private, State, or federal grant funds that are available for the purpose of assisting with the cost of installing and maintaining a pumpout facility. A county or municipality may also apply for any private, State, or federal grant funds that are available for the purpose of assisting with the cost of installing and maintaining a pumpout facility. (2009-345, s. 1; 2010-180, s. 21(b).)

§ 77-127. Department of Environment and Natural Resources establish pumpout facility criteria; inspection of pumpout facilities and vessels docked or moored at a marina.

(a) The Department of Environment and Natural Resources shall establish appropriate criteria for pumpout facilities and pumpout services provided at large vessel marinas that offer docking services to the general public. The criteria shall include requirements that the facility or services be available to the public, the pumpout facility be open during normal hours, and the pumpout facility be used for its intended purpose. The criteria also shall include a requirement that these marinas maintain records regarding the pumpout facility or services. The Department also shall develop guidelines for inspections of pumpout facilities at such marinas and of vessels that are docked or moored at these marinas.

(b) The Department also shall establish appropriate criteria for pumpout facilities and pumpout services provided at privately owned large vessel marinas that do not offer docking services to the general public. The criteria shall include requirements that the facility or services be made reasonably available to members of the private marina and the pumpout facility be used for its intended purpose. The criteria also shall include a requirement that these marinas maintain records regarding the pumpout facility or services. The Department also shall develop guidelines for inspections of pumpout facilities at such marinas and of vessels that are docked or moored at these marinas. (2009-345, s. 1; 2010-180, s. 21(b).)

§ 77-128. Vessel owner and operator required to keep log of pumpout dates.

(a)   Any owner or operator of a vessel that has a marine sanitation device shall maintain a record of the date of each pumpout of the marine sanitation device and the location of the pumpout facility. Each record shall be maintained for a period of one year from the date of the pumpout.

(b)   A violation of this section is punishable as a Class 3 misdemeanor. No civil penalty shall be assessed under G.S. 77-130 for a violation of this section. (2009-345, s. 1; 2010-180, s. 21(b).)

§ 77-129. No discharge of treated or untreated sewage in coastal waters; duty of marina owner or operator to report unlawful discharge.

(a)   No person shall discharge treated or untreated sewage into coastal waters, including effluent produced or held by any type of marine sanitation device into coastal waters. The owner or operator of a vessel with a marine sanitation device shall keep the overboard waste discharge valves of the device secure by acceptable methods set forth under 33 C.F.R. § 159.7(b) so as to prevent the discharge of treated or untreated sewage, except when lawfully discharging sewage at a pumpout facility. A violation of this section is punishable as a Class 1 misdemeanor and also may be assessed a civil penalty pursuant to G.S. 77-130.

(b)   If the owner or operator of a large vessel marina knows that the owner or operator of any vessel docked or moored at the marina knowingly and unlawfully discharged sewage, including effluent produced or held by a marine sanitation device, in coastal waters in violation of this section, then the marina owner or operator shall report the unlawful discharge to the appropriate law enforcement agency. A marina owner or operator who fails to report an unlawful discharge pursuant to this subsection may be assessed a civil penalty pursuant to G.S. 77-130. (2009-345, s. 1; 2010-180, s. 21(b).)

§ 77-130. Enforcement.

(a)   The following officers have authority to enforce this Article and to inspect a large vessel marina or vessel subject to this Article:

(1)   Wildlife protectors.

(2)   Marine fisheries inspectors.

(3)   Any sworn local law enforcement officer with jurisdiction to enforce the laws in the county or municipality in which the marina or vessel is located.

(4)   United States Coast Guard personnel.

(b)   Officers enforcing the provisions of this Article shall report violations to the Department.

(c)   Unless provided otherwise by this Article, a civil penalty of not more than ten thousand dollars ($10,000) may be assessed by the Secretary of Environment and Natural Resources against any person who violates this Article. If any action or failure for which a penalty may be assessed under this section is continuous, the Secretary of Environment and Natural Resources may assess a penalty not to exceed ten thousand dollars ($10,000) per day for so long as the violation continues. (2009-345, s. 1; 2010-180, s. 21(b).)

§ 77-131. Application of Article.

The provisions of this Article apply only to the following:

(1)   A large vessel marina that is located on coastal waters designated by the Environmental Protection Agency as a no discharge zone or that is located in a county or municipality that has adopted a resolution to petition the Environmental Protection Agency for a no discharge zone designation.

(2) A vessel in coastal waters that is designated as a no discharge zone by the Environmental Protection Agency. (2009-345, s. 1; 2010-180, s. 21(a), (b).)

§ 77-132. Rule-making authority.

The Department shall adopt rules to implement this Article. (2009-345, s. 1; 2010-180, s. 21(b).)

§ 77-133: Reserved for future codification purposes.

§ 77-134: Reserved for future codification purposes.

§ 77-135: Reserved for future codification purposes.

§ 77-136: Reserved for future codification purposes.

§ 77-137: Reserved for future codification purposes.

§ 77-138: Reserved for future codification purposes.

§ 77-139: Reserved for future codification purposes.

Article 10.

Falls Lake Watershed Association.

§ 77-140. Definitions.

The following definitions apply in this Article:

(1)   "Board of directors" has the same meaning as in G.S. 55A-1-40.

(2)   "Falls Lake watershed" means those natural areas of drainage including all tributaries contributing to the supply of Falls Lake, the specific limits of which are designated by the Environmental Management Commission pursuant to G.S. 143-213.

(3)   "Local government" means a county, city, town, or incorporated village that is located in whole or in part within the Falls Lake watershed. Local government also includes any water or sewer authority that is created pursuant to Article 1 of Chapter 162A of the General Statutes that provides service within the Falls Lake watershed.

(4)   "Nonprofit corporation" has the same meaning as in G.S. 55A-1-40. (2010-155, s. 1.)

§ 77-141. Falls Lake Watershed Association criteria for creation; board of directors; purpose; meetings; and records.

(a)   Local governments may elect to incorporate the Falls Lake Watershed Association nonprofit corporation or establish the Association using an existing nonprofit corporation. The Association shall only be comprised of local governments that choose to participate in the Association.

(b)   Each local government that elects to participate in the Association shall appoint a representative and an alternate representative to serve on the board of directors of the Association. The first board of directors that is appointed to the Association shall adopt bylaws that govern the operation of the Association.

(c)   The purposes of the Association may include, but are not limited to:

(1)   Providing a forum for sharing information in order to assist local governments in complying with State and federal laws that pertain to the water quality in the Falls Lake watershed.

(2)   Providing a mechanism for participating local governments to coordinate and fund common technical resources.

(3)   Planning for and conducting water quality monitoring in the Falls Lake watershed in coordination with the Department of Environment and Natural Resources.

(4)   Coordinating with the Department of Environment and Natural Resources in the development of a transparent and accessible system for recording and maintaining nutrient offsets and credits that complies with any rules adopted to protect and restore water quality in the Falls Lake watershed.

(5)   Providing a public forum to review and discuss innovative approaches to restore, protect, and maintain water quality in the Falls Lake watershed.

(6)   Conducting and evaluating scientific research that describes or predicts conditions related to or affecting water quality in the Falls Lake watershed, including the reservoir.

(d)   The Association shall be subject to the requirements for meetings of public bodies pursuant to Article 33C of Chapter 143 of the General Statutes.

(e)   The Association shall be subject to the requirements for public records pursuant to Chapter 132 of the General Statutes. (2010-155, s. 1.)

§ 77-142. Memoranda of understanding.

To the extent allowed by law, the Department of Environment and Natural Resources may enter into memoranda of understanding with the Association to implement the purposes in G.S. 77-141(c). (2010-155, s. 1.)

§ 77-143. Authority.

The authority granted pursuant to this Article is in addition to and not in derogation of any other authority granted to local governments under any other provision of law. (2010-155, s. 1.)

Chapter 78.

Securities Law.

§§ 78-1 through 78-25. Repealed by Session Laws 1973, c. 1380.

Chapter 78A.

North Carolina Securities Act.

Article 1.

Title and Definitions.

§ 78A-1. Title.

This Chapter shall be known and may be cited as the North Carolina Securities Act. (1925, c. 190, s. 1; 1927, c. 149, s. 1; 1943, c. 104, s. 1; 1973, c. 1380.)

§ 78A-2. Definitions.

When used in this Chapter, unless the context otherwise requires:

(1) "Administrator" means the Secretary of State.

(2) "Dealer" means any person engaged in the business of effecting transactions in securities for the account of others or for his own account. "Dealer" does not include:

a. A salesman,

b. A bank, savings institution, or trust company,

c. A person who has no place of business in this State if

1. He effects transactions in this State exclusively with or through (i) the issuers of the securities involved in the transactions, (ii) other dealers, or (iii) banks, savings institutions, trust companies, insurance companies, investment companies as defined in the Investment Company Act of 1940, pension or profit-sharing trusts, or other financial institutions or institutional buyers, whether acting for themselves or as trustees, or

2. In the case of a person registered as a dealer with the Securities and Exchange Commission under the Securities Exchange Act of 1934 and in one or more states, during any period of 12 consecutive months he does not effect more than 15 purchases or sales in this State in any manner with persons other than those specified in clause 1, whether or not the dealer or any of the purchasers or sellers is then present in this State, or

d. An issuer if

1. The security is exempted under subdivisions (1), (2), (3), (4), (5), (7), (9), (10), (11), (13), or (14) of G.S. 78A-16, or the security is a security covered under federal law, or the transaction is exempted under G.S. 78A-17, except for G.S. 78A-17(19) if the security is a viatical settlement contract, or the transaction is in a security covered under federal law, and such exemption has not been denied or revoked under G.S. 78A-18, or

2. The security is registered under this Chapter and it is offered and sold through a registered dealer, or

3. All of the following conditions are met: (i) No commission or other remuneration is paid or given directly or indirectly for soliciting any prospective purchaser in this State; (ii) the total amount of the offering, both within and without this State, does not exceed two million five hundred thousand dollars ($2,500,000); and (iii) the total number of purchasers, both within and without this State, does not exceed 100. Provided, however, the Administrator may by rule or order waive the condition imposed by subdivision (iii) hereof; or

4. The security is issued by an open-end management company that is registered under the Investment Company Act of 1940 and so long as no sales load is paid or given, directly or indirectly.

e. A person who acts as a business broker with respect to a transaction involving the offer or sale of all of the stock or other equity interests in any closely held corporation provided that such stock or other equity interest is sold to no more than one person, as that term is defined herein.

f. An individual who represents an issuer in effecting transactions in a security described in sub-subdivision (2)d. of this section or a security covered under federal law, provided no commission or other special remuneration is paid or given directly or indirectly for soliciting any prospective purchaser in this State.

(2a) "Entity" includes a corporation, joint-stock company, limited liability company, business trust, limited partnership or other partnership in which the interests of the partners are evidenced by a security, trust in which the interests of the beneficiaries are evidenced by a security, any other unincorporated organization in which two or more persons have a joint or common economic interest evidenced by a security, and government or political subdivision of a government.

(3) "Fraud," "deceit," and "defraud" are not limited to common-law deceit.

(4) "Guaranteed" means guaranteed as to payment of principal, interest, dividends, or other distributions.

(5) "Issuer" means any person who issues or proposes to issue any security, except that

a. With respect to certificates of deposit, voting-trust certificates, or collateral-trust certificates, or with respect to certificates of interest or shares in an unincorporated investment trust not having a board of directors or persons performing similar functions or of the fixed, restricted-management, or unit type, the term "issuer" means the person or persons performing the acts and assuming the duties of depositor or manager pursuant to the provisions of the trust or other agreement or instrument under which the security is issued; and

b. With respect to certificates of interest or participation in oil, gas, or mining titles or leases or in payments out of production under such titles or leases, there is not considered to be any "issuer."

c. With respect to a viatical settlement contract, "issuer" means a person involved in creating, offering, transferring, or selling to an investor any interest in a viatical settlement contract, including, but not limited to, fractional or pooled interests.

(6) "Nonissuer" means not directly or indirectly for the benefit of the issuer.

(7) "Person" means an individual, an entity, a partnership in which the interests of the partners are not evidenced by a security, a trust in which the interests of the beneficiaries are not evidenced by a security, or an unincorporated organization.

(8) a. "Sale" or "sell" includes every contract of sale of, contract to sell, or disposition of, a security or interest in a security for value.

b. "Offer" or "offer to sell" includes every attempt or offer to dispose of, or solicitation of an offer to buy, a security or interest in a security for value.

c. Any security given or delivered with, or as a bonus on account of, any purchase of securities or any other thing is considered to constitute part of the subject of the purchase and to have been offered and sold for value.

d. A purported gift of assessable stock or other ownership interest obligating the owner to make future payments is considered to involve an offer and sale.

e. Every sale or offer of a warrant or right to purchase or subscribe to another security of the same or another issuer, as well as every sale or offer of a security which gives the holder a present or future right or privilege to convert into another security of the same or another issuer, is considered to include an offer of the other security.

f. The terms defined in this subdivision and the term "purchase" as used in this Chapter do not include any of the following:

1. Any bona fide loan, pledge, or other transaction creating a bona fide security interest.

2. Any stock split and any security dividend or distribution, whether the entity distributing the dividend or distribution is the issuer of the security or not, if nothing of value is given by security holders for the dividend or distribution other than the surrender of a right to a cash or property dividend or distribution when

each security holder may elect to take the dividend or distribution in cash or property or in securities.

3. 4. Repealed by Session Laws 2001-201, s. 6, effective October 1, 2001.

(9) "Salesman" means any individual other than a dealer who represents a dealer in effecting or attempting to effect purchases or sales of securities. "Salesman" does not include an individual who represents a dealer in effecting transactions in this State limited to those transactions described in section 15(h)(2) of the Securities Exchange Act of 1934 (15 U.S.C. § 78o(h)(2)). A partner, executive officer, or director of a dealer, or a person occupying a similar status or performing similar functions, is a salesman only if that person otherwise comes within this definition.

(10) "Securities Act of 1933," "Securities Exchange Act of 1934," "Public Utility Holding Company Act of 1935," "Investment Company Act of 1940," and "Internal Revenue Code" mean the federal statutes of those names as amended before or after April 1, 1975.

(11) "Security" means any note; stock; treasury stock; bond; debenture; evidence of indebtedness; certificate of interest or participation in any profit-sharing agreement; collateral-trust certificate; preorganization certificate or subscription; transferable share; investment contract including without limitation any investment contract taking the form of a whiskey warehouse receipt or other investment of money in whiskey or malt beverages; voting-trust certificate; certificate of deposit for a security; certificate of interest or participation in an oil, gas, or mining title or lease or in payments out of production under a title or lease; viatical settlement contract or any fractional or pooled interest in a viatical settlement contract; or, in general, any interest or instrument commonly known as a "security," or any certificate of interest or participation in, temporary or interim certificate for, receipt for guarantee of, or warrant or right to subscribe to or purchase, any of the foregoing. "Security" does not include any insurance or endowment policy, funding agreement, as defined in G.S. 58-7-16, or annuity contract under which an insurance company promises to pay (i) a fixed sum of money either in a lump sum or periodically for life or for some other specified period, or (ii) benefits or payments or value that vary so as to reflect investment results of any segregated portfolio of investments or of a designated separate account or accounts in which amounts received or retained in connection with a contract have been placed if the delivering or issuing insurance company has currently satisfied the Commissioner of Insurance that it is in compliance with G.S. 58-7-95.

(11a) "Security covered under federal law" means any security that is a covered security under section 18(b) of the Securities Act of 1933 (15 U.S.C. § 77r(b)) or rules or regulations adopted under that section.

(12) "State" means any state, territory, or possession of the United States, the District of Columbia, and Puerto Rico.

(13) "Viatical settlement contract" means an agreement for the purchase, sale, assignment, transfer, or devise of all or any portion of the death benefit or ownership of a life insurance policy or contract for consideration which is less than the expected death benefit of the life insurance policy or contract. "Viatical settlement contract" does not include:

a. The assignment, transfer, sale, or devise of a death benefit of a life insurance policy or contract made by the viator to an insurance company or to a viatical settlement provider or broker licensed pursuant to the Viatical Settlements Act (Part 5 of Article 58 of Chapter 58 of the General Statutes);

b. The assignment of a life insurance policy or contract to a bank, savings bank, savings and loan association, credit union, or other licensed lending institution as collateral for a loan; or

c. The exercise of accelerated benefits pursuant to the terms of a life insurance policy or contract and consistent with applicable law. (1925, c. 190, s. 2; 1927, c. 149, s. 2; 1933, c. 432; 1943, c. 104, ss. 2, 3; 1955, c. 436, s. 1; 1973, c. 1380; 1983, c. 817, ss. 1-3; 1987, c. 849, s. 1; 1989, c. 12, s. 1; 1993 (Reg. Sess., 1994), c. 600, s. 3; 1995, c. 509, s. 35; 1997-419, ss. 1-4; 2001-201, ss. 2, 3, 4, 5, 6; 2001-436, s. 6; 2011-284, s. 61.)

§§ 78A-3 through 78A-7. Reserved for future codification purposes.

Article 2.

Fraudulent and Other Prohibited Practices.

§ 78A-8. Sales and purchases.

It is unlawful for any person, in connection with the offer, sale or purchase of any security, directly or indirectly:

(1)   To employ any device, scheme, or artifice to defraud,

(2)   To make any untrue statement of a material fact or to omit to state a material fact necessary in order to make the statements made, in the light of the circumstances under which they are made, not misleading or,

(3)   To engage in any act, practice, or course of business which operates or would operate as a fraud or deceit upon any person. (1973, c. 1380.)

§ 78A-9. Misleading filings.

It is unlawful for any person to make or cause to be made, in any document filed with the Administrator or in any proceeding under this Chapter, any statement which is, at the time and in the light of the circumstances under which it is made false or misleading in any material respect. (1973, c. 1380.)

§ 78A-10. Unlawful representations concerning registration or exemption.

(a)   Neither (i) the fact that an application for registration under Article 5 or a registration statement under Article 4 has been filed nor (ii) the fact that a person or security is effectively registered constitutes a finding by the Administrator that any document filed under this Chapter is true, complete, and not misleading. Neither any such fact nor the fact that an exemption or exception is available for a security or a transaction means that the Administrator has passed in any way upon the merits or qualifications of, or recommended or given approval to, any person, security, or transaction.

(b)   It is unlawful to make, or cause to be made, to any prospective purchaser, customer, or client any representation inconsistent with subsection (a). (1973, c. 1380.)

§ 78A-11. Unlawful telephone rooms.

It is unlawful for any person to willfully manage, supervise, control, or own, directly or indirectly, either alone or in association with others, any telephone room in this State. For purposes of this section, "telephone room" means an enterprise in which two or more persons engage in telephone communications with members of the public using two or more telephones at one location, or more than one location in a common scheme or enterprise, in violation of G.S. 78A-8 or G.S. 78A-12. It is an affirmative defense to a prosecution under this section that the person acted in good faith and did not directly or indirectly induce an act or acts constituting a violation of G.S. 78A-8 or G.S. 78A-12. (1991, c. 456, s. 1.)

§ 78A-12. Manipulation of market.

(a)   In addition to the prohibitions of G.S. 78A-8, it is unlawful for any person to do any of the following:

(1)   Willfully quote a fictitious price with respect to a security.

(2)   Effect a transaction in a security which involves no change in the beneficial ownership of the security, for the purpose of creating a false or misleading appearance of active trading in a security, or a false or misleading appearance of activity with respect to the market for the security.

(3)   Enter an order for the purchase of a security with the knowledge that, at substantially the same time, an order of substantially the same size, and at substantially the same price, for the sale of the security has been, or will be, entered by or for the same person, or an affiliated person, for the purpose of creating a false or misleading appearance of active trading in a security, or a false or misleading appearance of activity with respect to the market for the security.

(4)   Enter an order for the sale of a security with knowledge that, at substantially the same time, an order of substantially the same size, and at substantially the same price, for the purchase of the security has been, or will be, entered by or for the same person, or an affiliated person, for the purpose of creating a false or misleading appearance of active trading in a security, or a false or misleading appearance of activity with respect to the market for the security.

(5) Employ any other deceptive or fraudulent device, scheme, or artifice to manipulate the market in a security, including the issuance, with the intent to deceive or defraud, of analyses, reports, or financial statements that are false or misleading in any material respect.

(b) A transaction effected in compliance with the applicable provisions of the Securities Exchange Act of 1934 and the rules and regulations of the Securities and Exchange Commission thereunder is not manipulation of the market under subsection (a) of this section. (1991, c. 456, s. 1; 2003-413, s. 1.)

§ 78A -13. Disclosures required in offer and sale of viaticals.

(a) Disclosures Required Prior to Signing of Purchase Agreement or Transfer of Consideration. - The following disclosures shall be required in the offer and sale of viatical settlement contracts, whether such offer and sale is pursuant to an exemption from registration or pursuant to the registration of such securities, and shall be conspicuously displayed in each viatical settlement purchase agreement or in a separate document signed by the viatical settlement purchaser and by the issuer or its sales agent:

(1) Disclosures prior to payment of consideration. - On or before the date the viatical settlement purchaser remits consideration pursuant to the purchase agreement, the viatical settlement purchaser shall be provided the following written disclosures:

a. The name, principal business, and mailing addresses, and telephone number of the issuer;

b. The suitability standards for prospective purchasers as set forth by rule or order promulgated by the Administrator;

c. A description of the issuer's type of business organization and the state in which the issuer is organized or incorporated;

d. A brief description of the business of the issuer;

e. If the issuer retains ownership or becomes the beneficiary of the insurance policy, an audit report from an independent certified public accountant together with a balance sheet and related statements of income, retained earnings, and cash flows that reflect the issuer's financial position, the results of the issuer's operations, and the issuer's cash flows as of a date within six months before the date of the initial issuance of the securities described in this subdivision. The financial statements shall be prepared in conformity with generally accepted accounting principles. If the date of the audit report is more than 120 days before the date of the initial issuance of the securities described in this subdivision, the issuer shall provide unaudited interim financial statements;

f.   The names of all directors, officers, partners, members, or trustees of the issuer;

g.   A description of any order, judgment, or decree that is final as to the issuing entity of any state, federal, or foreign governmental agency or administrator, or of any state, federal, or foreign court of competent jurisdiction (i) revoking, suspending, denying, or censuring, for cause, any license, permit, or other authority of the issuer or of any director, officer, partner, member, trustee, or person owning or controlling, directly or indirectly ten percent (10%) or more of the outstanding interest or equity securities of the issuer, to engage in the securities, commodities, franchise, insurance, real estate, or lending business or in the offer or sale of securities, commodities, franchises, insurance, real estate, or loans, (ii) permanently restraining, enjoining, barring, suspending, or censuring any such person from engaging in or continuing any conduct, practice, or employment in connection with the offer or sale of securities, commodities, franchises, insurance, real estate, or loans, (iii) convicting any such person of, or pleading nolo contendere by any such person to, any felony or misdemeanor involving a security, commodity, franchise, insurance, real estate, or loan, or any aspect of the securities, commodities, franchise, insurance, real estate, or lending business, or involving dishonesty, fraud, deceit, embezzlement, fraudulent conversion, or misappropriation of property, or (iv) holding any such person liable in a civil action involving breach of a fiduciary duty, fraud, deceit, embezzlement, fraudulent conversion, or misappropriation of property. This subdivision does not apply to any order, judgment, or decree that has been vacated or overturned or is more than 10 years old;

h.   Notice of the purchaser's right to rescind or cancel the investment and receive a refund;

i.   A statement to the effect that any projected rate of return to the purchaser from the purchase of a viatical settlement contract or any fractionalized or pooled interest therein is based on an estimated life expectancy for the person insured under the life insurance policy; that the return on the purchase may vary substantially from the expected rate of return based upon the actual life expectancy of the insured that may be less than, may be equal to, or may greatly exceed the estimated life expectancy; and that the rate of return would be higher if the actual life expectancy were less than, and lower if the actual life expectancy were greater than, the estimated life expectancy of the insured at the time the viatical settlement contract was closed;

j. A statement that the purchaser should consult with his or her tax advisor regarding the tax consequences of the purchase of the viatical settlement contract or any fractionalized or pooled interest therein; and

k. Any other information as may be prescribed by rule or order of the Administrator.

(2) Disclosures prior to closing. - At least five business days prior to the date the purchase agreement is signed, the viatical settlement purchaser shall receive the following written disclosures:

a. The name, address, and telephone number of the issuing insurance company and the name, address, and telephone number of the state or foreign country regulator of the insurance company;

b. The total face value of the insurance policy and the percentage of the insurance policy the purchaser will own;

c. The insurance policy number, issue date, and type;

d. If a group insurance policy, the name, address, and telephone number of the group and, if applicable, the material terms and conditions of converting the policy to an individual policy, including the amount of increased premiums;

e. If a term insurance policy, the term and the name, address, and telephone number of the person who will be responsible for renewing the policy if necessary;

f. Whether the insurance policy is beyond the state statute for contestability and the reason therefor;

g. The insurance policy premiums and terms of premium payments;

h. The amount of the purchaser's money that will be set aside to pay premiums;

i. The name, address, and telephone number of the person who will be the insurance policy owner and the person who will be responsible for paying premiums;

j. The date on which the purchaser will be required to pay premiums and the amount of the premium, if known;

k. A statement of risk factors associated with investment in viatical settlement contracts, including, but not limited, to the following:

1. The purchaser will receive no returns (i.e., dividends and interest) until the insured dies.

2. The actual annual rate of return on a viatical settlement contract is dependent upon an accurate projection of the insured's life expectancy, and the actual date of the insured's death. An annual "guaranteed" rate of return is not determinable.

3. The viaticated life insurance contract should not be considered a liquid purchase since it is impossible to predict the exact timing of its maturity and the funds probably are not available until the death of the insured. There is no established secondary market for resale of these products by the purchaser.

4. The purchaser may lose all benefits or may receive substantially reduced benefits if the insurer goes out of business during the term of the viatical investment.

5. The purchaser is responsible for payment of the insurance premium or other costs related to the policy, if required by the terms of the viatical purchase agreement. These payments may reduce the purchaser's return. If a party other than the purchaser is responsible for the payment, the name and address of that party also shall be disclosed.

6. If the purchaser is responsible for payment of the insurance premiums or other costs related to the policy or if the insured returns to health, the amount of the premiums, if applicable.

7. The name and address of any person providing escrow services and the relationship to the issuer.

8. The amount of any trust fees or other expenses to be charged to the viatical settlement purchaser shall be disclosed.

9. Whether the purchaser is entitled to a refund of all or part of his or her investment under the settlement contract if the policy is later determined to be null and void.

10. A disclosure that group policies may contain limitations or caps in the conversion rights; that additional premiums may have to be paid if the policy is converted; the name of the party responsible for the payment of the additional premiums; and, if a group policy is terminated and replaced by another group policy, that there may be no right to convert the original coverage.

11. A disclosure of the risks associated with policy contestability including, but not limited to, the risk that the purchaser will have no claim or only a partial claim to death benefits should the insurer rescind the policy within the contestability period.

12. A disclosure of whether the purchaser will be the owner of the policy in addition to being the beneficiary, and if the purchaser is the beneficiary only and not also the owner, the special risks associated with that status, including, but not limited to, the risk that the beneficiary may be changed or the premium may not be paid.

13. The experience and qualifications of the person who determines the life expectancy of the insured, i.e., in-house staff, independent physicians, and specialty firms that weigh medical and actuarial data; the information this projection is based on; and the relationship of the projection maker to the viatical settlement provider, if any.

14. Disclosure to an investor shall include distribution of a brochure describing the process of investment in viatical settlements. The NAIC's form for the brochure shall be used unless the Administrator prescribes one by rule or order.

I. Any other information as may be prescribed by rule or order of the Administrator.

(b) Disclosures Required Upon Assignment or Sale of Underlying Insurance Policy. - The issuer shall provide the viatical settlement purchaser with at least the following disclosures no later than at the time of the assignment, transfer, or sale of all or a portion of an insurance policy underlying the viatical settlement contract, and the disclosure shall be contained in a document signed by the viatical settlement purchaser and by the issuer or its sales agent:

(1) Disclose all the life expectancy certifications obtained by the provider in the process of determining the price paid to the viator.

(2) State whether premium payments or other costs related to the policy have been escrowed. If escrowed, state the date upon which the escrowed funds will be depleted; whether the purchaser will be responsible for payment of premiums thereafter and, if so, the amount of the premiums; and the name and address of the escrow agent.

(3) State whether premium payments or other costs related to the policy have been waived. If waived, disclose whether the investor will be responsible for payment of the premiums if the insurer that wrote the policy terminates the waiver after purchase and the amount of those premiums.

(4) Disclose the type of policy offered or sold, i.e., whole life, term life, universal life, or a group policy certificate, any additional benefits contained in the policy, and the current status of the policy.

(5) If the policy is term insurance, disclose the special risks associated with term insurance including, but not limited to, the purchaser's responsibility for additional premiums if the viator continues the term policy at the end of the current term.

(6) State whether the policy is contestable.

(7) State whether the insurer that wrote the policy has any additional rights that could negatively affect or extinguish the purchaser's rights under the viatical settlement contract, what these rights are, and under what conditions these rights are activated.

(8) State the name and address of the person responsible for monitoring the insured's condition. Describe how often the monitoring of the insured's condition is done, how the date of death is determined, and how and when this information will be transmitted to the purchaser.(2001-436, s. 7.)

§ 78A-14. Advertising of Viatical Settlement Contracts.

(a) The purpose of this section is to provide prospective viatical settlement purchasers with clear and unambiguous statements in the advertisement of viatical settlement contracts and to assure the clear, truthful, and adequate disclosure of the benefits, risks, limitations, and exclusions of any contract or purchase agreement offered or sold. This purpose is intended to be accomplished by the establishment of guidelines and standards of permissible and impermissible conduct in the advertising of viatical settlement contracts to assure that product descriptions are presented in a manner that prevents unfair, deceptive, or misleading advertising and is conducive to accurate presentation and description of viatical settlement contracts through the advertising media and material used by issuers of viatical settlement contracts and their sales agents.

(b) This section shall apply to any advertising of viatical settlement contracts intended for dissemination in this State, including Internet advertising viewed by persons located in this State. Where disclosure requirements are established pursuant to federal regulation, this section shall be interpreted so as to minimize or eliminate conflict with federal regulation wherever possible.

(c) Every person offering or selling viatical settlement contracts shall establish and, at all times, maintain a system of control over the content, form, and method of dissemination of all advertisements of these securities. All advertisements, regardless of by whom written, created, designed, or presented, shall be the responsibility of the issuer. A system of control shall include regular routine notification, at least once a year, to agents and others authorized by the issuer who disseminate advertisements of the requirements and procedures for approval before the use of any advertisements not furnished by the issuer.

(d) Advertisements shall be truthful and not misleading in fact or by implication. The form and content of an advertisement of a contract or purchase agreement, product, or service shall be sufficiently complete and clear so as to avoid deception. It shall not have the capacity or tendency to mislead or deceive. Whether an advertisement has the capacity or tendency to mislead or deceive shall be determined by the Administrator from the overall impression that the advertisement may be reasonably expected to create upon a person of average education or intelligence within the segment of the public to which it is directed.

(e) Certain viatical settlement contract advertisements are deemed false and misleading on their face and are prohibited. False and misleading viatical settlement advertisements include, but are not limited to, the following representations:

(1) "Guaranteed", "fully secured", "100 percent secured", "fully insured", "secure", "safe", "backed by rated insurance companies", "backed by federal law", "backed by state law", or "state guaranty funds", or similar representations;

(2) "No risk", "minimal risk", "low risk", "no speculation", "no fluctuation", or similar representations;

(3) "Qualified or approved for individual retirement accounts (IRAs), Roth IRAs, 401(k) plans, simplified employee pensions (SEP), 403(b), Keogh plans, TSA, other retirement account rollovers", "tax deferred", or similar representations;

(4) Utilization of the word "guaranteed" to describe the fixed return, annual return, principal, earnings, profits, investment, or similar representations;

(5) "No sales charges or fees" or similar representations;

(6) "High yield", "superior return", "excellent return", "high return", "quick profit", or similar representations;

(7) Purported favorable representations or testimonials about the benefits of contracts or purchase agreements as an investment, taken out of context from newspapers, trade papers, journals, radio and television programs, and all other forms of print and electronic media.

(f) All information required to be disclosed under this section shall be set out conspicuously and in close conjunction with the statements to which such information relates or under appropriate captions of such prominence that it shall not be minimized, rendered obscure or presented in an ambiguous fashion, or intermingled with the context of the advertisement so as to be confusing or misleading.

(g) An advertisement shall not:

(1) Omit material information or use words, phrases, statements, references, or illustrations if the omission or use has the capacity, tendency, or

effect of misleading or deceiving purchasers or prospective purchasers as to the nature or extent of any benefit, loss covered, premium payable, or state or federal tax consequence. The fact that the contract or purchase agreement offered is made available for inspection before consummation of the sale, or an offer is made to refund the payment if the purchaser is not satisfied or that the contract or purchase agreement includes a "free look" period that satisfies or exceeds legal requirements, does not remedy misleading statements.

(2) Use the name or title of a life insurance company or a policy unless the insurer has approved the advertisement.

(3) Represent that premium payments will not be required to be paid on the policy that is the subject of a contract or purchase agreement in order to maintain that policy, unless that is the fact.

(4) State or imply that interest charged on an accelerated death benefit or a policy loan is unfair, inequitable, or in any manner an incorrect or improper practice.

(5) State or imply that a contract or purchase agreement, benefit, or service has been approved or endorsed by a group of individuals, society, association, or other organization unless that is the fact and unless any relationship between an organization and the seller or its agents is disclosed. If the entity making the endorsement or testimonial is owned, controlled, or managed by the seller or its agents, or receives any payment or other consideration from the seller or its agents for making an endorsement or testimonial, that fact shall be disclosed in the advertisement.

(6) Contain statistical information unless it accurately reflects recent and relevant facts. The source of all statistics used in an advertisement shall be identified.

(7) Disparage insurers, providers, brokers, dealers, salesmen, insurance producers, policies, services, or methods of marketing.

(8) Use a trade name, group designation, name of the parent company of an issuer, name of a particular division of the issuer, service mark, slogan, symbol, or other device or reference without disclosing the name of the issuer, if the advertisement would have the capacity or tendency to mislead or deceive as to the true identity of the issuer, or to create the impression that a company

other than the issuer would have any responsibility for the financial obligation under a contract or purchase agreement.

(9)   Use any combination of words, symbols, or physical materials that by their content, phraseology, shape, color, or other characteristics are so similar to a combination of words, symbols, or physical materials used by a government program or agency or otherwise appear to be of such a nature that they tend to mislead prospective purchasers into believing that the solicitation is in some manner connected with a government program or agency.

(10)   Create the impression that the issuer, its financial condition or status, the payment of its claims, or the merits, desirability, or advisability of its contracts or purchase agreement forms are recommended or endorsed by any government entity.

(h)   The words "free", "no cost", "without cost", "no additional cost", "at no extra cost", or words of similar import shall not be used with respect to any benefit or service unless true. An advertisement may specify the charge for a benefit or a service, may state that a charge is included in the payment, or use other appropriate language.

(i)   Testimonials, appraisals, or analysis used in advertisements must be genuine; represent the current opinion of the author; be applicable to the contract or purchase agreement, product, or service advertised, if any; and be accurately reproduced with sufficient completeness to avoid misleading or deceiving prospective purchasers as to the nature or scope of the testimonials, appraisals, analysis, or endorsement. In using testimonials, appraisals, or analysis, the issuer makes as its own all the statements contained therein, and the statements are subject to all the provisions of this section.

(j)   If the individual making a testimonial, appraisal, analysis, or an endorsement has a financial interest in the issuer or related entity as a stockholder, director, officer, employee, or otherwise, or receives any benefit directly or indirectly other than required union scale wages, that fact shall be prominently disclosed in the advertisement.

(k)   When an endorsement refers to benefits received under a contract or purchase agreement, all pertinent information shall be retained for a period of five years after its use.

(l)   The name of the issuer shall be clearly identified in all advertisements about the issuer or its contract or purchase agreements, products, or services, and if any specific contract or purchase agreement is advertised, the contract or purchase agreement shall be identified either by form number or some other appropriate description. If an application is part of the advertisement, the name of the issuer shall be shown on the application.

(m)   An advertisement may state that issuer is registered in the state where the advertisement appears, provided it does not exaggerate that fact or suggest or imply that a competing issuer may not be so licensed. The advertisement may ask the audience to consult the issuer's web site or contact the department of insurance and/or the state securities regulatory agency to find out if the state requires licensing or registration and, if so, whether the issuer or its sales agents are licensed.

(n)   The name of the actual issuer shall be stated in all of its advertisements. An advertisement shall not use a trade name, any group designation, name of any affiliate or controlling entity of the issuer, service mark, slogan, symbol, or other device in a manner that would have the capacity or tendency to mislead or deceive as to the true identity of the actual issuer or create the false impression that an affiliate or controlling entity would have any responsibility for the financial obligation of the issuer.

(o)   An advertisement shall not directly or indirectly create the impression that any state or federal governmental agency endorses, approves, or favors:

(1)   Any issuer or its business practices or methods of operation;

(2)   The merits, desirability, or advisability of any contract or purchase agreement;

(3)   Any contract or purchase agreement; or

(4)   Any policy or life insurance company.

(p)   If the advertiser emphasizes the speed with which the viatication will occur, the advertising must disclose the average time frame from completed application to the date of offer and from acceptance of the offer to receipt of the funds by the viator. (2001-436, s. 7.)

§ 78A-15. Reserved for future codification purposes.

Article 3.

Exemptions.

§ 78A-16. Exempt securities.

The following securities are exempted from G.S. 78A-24 and 78A-49(d):

(1) Any security (including a revenue obligation) issued or guaranteed by the United States, any state, any political subdivision of a state, or any agency or corporate or other instrumentality of one or more of the foregoing; or any certificate of deposit for any of the foregoing;

(2) Any security issued or guaranteed by Canada, any Canadian province, any political subdivision of any such province, any agency of one or more of the foregoing, or any other foreign government with which the United States currently maintains diplomatic relations, if the security is recognized as a valid obligation by the issuer or guarantor;

(3) Any security issued by and representing an interest in or a debt of, or guaranteed by, any bank organized under the laws of the United States, or any bank, savings institution, or trust company organized and supervised under the laws of any state;

(4) Any security issued by and representing an interest in or a debt of, or guaranteed by, any federal savings and loan association, or any building and loan or similar association organized under the laws of any state and authorized to do business in this State;

(5) Any security issued by and representing an interest in or a debt of, or guaranteed by, any insurance company organized under the laws of any state and authorized to do business in this State; but this exemption does not apply to an annuity contract, investment contract, or similar security under which the promised payments are not fixed in dollars but are substantially dependent upon the investment results of a segregated fund or account invested in securities unless the issuing or delivering company has satisfied the Commissioner of Insurance that it is in compliance with G.S. 58-7-95;

(6) Any security issued or guaranteed by any federal credit union or any credit union, industrial loan association, or similar association organized and supervised under the laws of this State;

(7) Any security issued or guaranteed by any railroad, other common carrier, public utility, or holding company of one of the foregoing which is (i) subject to the jurisdiction of the Interstate Commerce Commission; (ii) a registered holding company under the Public Utility Holding Company Act of 1935 or a subsidiary of such a company within the meaning of that act; (iii) regulated in respect of its rates and charges by a governmental authority of the United States or any state; or (iv) regulated in respect of the issuance or guarantee of the security by a governmental authority of the United States, any state, Canada, or any Canadian province;

(8) Repealed by Session Laws 2001, c. 149, s. 1.

(9) Any security issued by any person organized and operated not for private profit but exclusively for religious, educational, benevolent, charitable, fraternal, social, athletic, or reformatory purposes, or as a chamber of commerce or trade or professional association provided, however, that the Administrator may by rule or order impose conditions upon this exemption either generally or in relation to specific securities or transactions;

(10) Any commercial paper which arises out of a current transaction or the proceeds of which have been or are to be used for current transactions, and which evidences an obligation to pay cash within nine months of the date of issuance, exclusive of days of grace, or any renewal of such paper which is likewise limited, or any guarantee of such paper or of any such renewal;

(11) Any interest in an employees' stock or equity purchase, option, savings, pension, profit-sharing or other similar benefit plan;

(12) Any bond or note secured by lien on vessels shown by policies of marine insurance taken out in responsible companies to be of value, after deducting any and all other indebtedness secured by prior lien, of not less than one hundred twenty-five percent (125%) of the par amount of such bonds or notes;

(13) Any capital stock issued by a professional corporation organized pursuant to the provisions of the Professional Corporation Act, Chapter 55B;

(14) Any security issued by (i) any mutual association or agricultural marketing association organized or domesticated and existing under Subchapter IV or Subchapter V, respectively, of Chapter 54 of the General Statutes of North Carolina; or (ii) any electric or telephone membership corporation organized or domesticated and existing under Chapter 117 of the General Statutes of North Carolina.

(15) Any security listed or approved for listing upon notice of issuance on an exchange registered with the United States Securities and Exchange Commission or quoted or approved for quotation upon notice of issuance on an automated quotation system operated by a national securities association registered with the United States Securities and Exchange Commission, provided such security or class of securities, exchange or system is approved by rule of the Administrator; any other security of the same issuer which is of senior or substantially equal rank; any security called for by subscription rights or warrants so listed or approved; or any warrant or right to purchase or subscribe to any of the foregoing. (1925, c. 190, s. 3; 1927, c. 149, s. 3; 1931, c. 243, s. 5; 1955, c. 436, s. 2; 1967, c. 1233, s. 1; 1973, c. 1380; 1981, c. 624, s. 1; 1983, c. 817, ss. 4, 5; 1989 (Reg. Sess., 1990) c. 803, s. 1; 2001-149, s. 1; 2001-201, s. 7.)

§ 78A-17. Exempt transactions.

Except as otherwise provided in this Chapter, the following transactions are exempted from G.S. 78A-24 and G.S. 78A-49(d):

(1) Any isolated nonissuer transaction, whether effected through a dealer or not.

(2) Any nonissuer distribution other than by a controlling person of an outstanding security if

a. A recognized securities manual contains the names of the issuer's officers and directors, a balance sheet of the issuer as of a date within 18 months, and a profit and loss statement for either the fiscal year preceding that date or the most recent year of operations, or

b. A registered dealer files with the Administrator such information relating to the issuer as the Administrator may by rule or order require, or

c. The security has a fixed maturity or a fixed interest or dividend provision and there has been no default during the current fiscal year or within the three preceding fiscal years, or during the existence of the issuer and any predecessors if less than three years, in the payment of principal, interest, or dividends on the security.

(3) Any nonissuer transaction effected by or through a registered dealer pursuant to an unsolicited order or offer to buy; but the Administrator may by rule require that the customer acknowledge upon a specified form that the sale was unsolicited, and that a signed copy of each such form be preserved by the dealer for a specified period.

(4) Any transaction between the issuer or other person on whose behalf the offering is made and an underwriter, or among underwriters.

(5) Any transaction in a bond or other evidence of indebtedness secured by a lien or security interest in real or personal property, or by an agreement for the sale of real estate or chattels, if the entire security interest or agreement, together with all the bonds or other evidences of indebtedness secured thereby, is offered and sold as a unit.

(6) Any transaction by an executor, administrator, sheriff, marshal, receiver, trustee in bankruptcy, guardian, or conservator.

(7) Any transaction executed by a person holding a bona fide security interest without any purpose of evading this Chapter.

(8) Any offer or sale to an entity which has a net worth in excess of one million dollars ($1,000,000) as determined by generally accepted accounting principles, bank, savings institution, trust company, insurance company, investment company as defined in the Investment Company Act of 1940, pension or profit-sharing trust, or other financial institution or institutional buyer, or to a dealer, whether the purchaser is acting for itself or in some fiduciary capacity.

(9) Any transaction pursuant to an offer directed by the offeror to not more than 25 persons, other than those persons designated in subdivision (8), in this State during any period of 12 consecutive months, whether or not the offeror or any of the offerees is then present in this State, if the seller reasonably believes that all the buyers in this State are purchasing for investment. The Administrator may by rule or order withdraw, amend, or further condition this exemption for

any security or security transaction. There is established a fee of one hundred fifty dollars ($150.00) to recover costs for any filing required.

(10)   Any offer or sale of a preorganizational certificate or subscription if: (i) no commission or other remuneration is paid or given directly or indirectly for soliciting any prospective subscriber; (ii) no public advertising or solicitation is used in connection with the offer or sale; (iii) the number of subscribers does not exceed 10 and the number of offerees does not exceed 25; and (iv) no payment is made by any subscriber.

(11)   Any transaction pursuant to an offer to existing security holders of the issuer, including persons who at the time of the transaction are holders of convertible securities, nontransferable warrants, or transferable warrants exercisable within not more than 90 days of their issuance, if (i) no commission or other remuneration (other than a standby commission) is paid or given directly or indirectly for soliciting any security holder in this State, or (ii) the issuer first files a notice specifying the terms of the offer and the Administrator does not by order disallow the exemption within the next 10 full business days.

(12)   Any offer (but not a sale) of a security for which registration statements have been filed under both this Chapter and the Securities Act of 1933 if no stop order or refusal order is in effect and no public proceeding or examination looking toward such an order is pending under either act.

(13)   Any offer or sale by a domestic entity of its own securities if (i) the entity was organized for the purpose of promoting community, agricultural or industrial development of the area in which the principal office is located, (ii) the offer or sale has been approved by resolution of the county commissioners of the county in which its principal office is located, and, if located in a municipality or within two miles of the boundaries thereof, by resolution of the governing body of such municipality, (iii) no commission or other remuneration is paid or given directly or indirectly for soliciting any prospective buyer in this State, and (iv) the entity is both organized and operated principally to promote some community, industrial, or agricultural development that confers a public benefit rather than organized and operated principally to generate a pecuniary profit.

(14)   Any offer, sale or issuance of securities pursuant to an employees' stock or equity purchase, option, savings, pension, profit-sharing, or other similar benefit plan that is exempt under the provisions of G.S. 78A-16(11).

(15) Any offer or sale of limited partnership interests in a partnership organized under the North Carolina Uniform Limited Partnership Act for the sole purpose of constructing, owning and operating a low and moderate income rental housing project located in North Carolina if the total amount of the offering and the total number of limited partners, both within and without this State for each such partnership, does not exceed five hundred thousand dollars ($500,000) and 100 respectively. This exemption shall be allowed without limitation as to (i) the number, either in total or within any time period, of separate partnerships which may be formed by the same general partner or partners, sponsors or individuals in which partnership interests are offered; (ii) the period over which such offerings can be made; (iii) the amount of each limited partner's investment; or (iv) the period over which such investment is payable to the partnership. For purposes of this subdivision (15), the term "low and moderate rental housing project" means:

a. Any housing project with respect to which a mortgage is insured or guaranteed under section 221(d)(3) or 221(d)(4) or 236 of the National Housing Act, or any housing project financed or assisted by direct loan, mortgage insurance or guaranty, or tax abatement under similar provisions of federal, State or local laws, whether now existing or hereafter enacted; or

b. Any housing project, some or all of the units of which are available for occupancy by families or individuals eligible to receive subsidies under section 8 of the United States Housing Act of 1937, as amended, or under the provisions of other federal, State or local law authorizing similar levels of subsidy for lower income families, whether now existing or hereafter enacted; or

c. Any housing project with respect to which a loan is made, insured or guaranteed under Title V, section 515, of the Housing Act of 1949, or under similar provisions of other federal, State or local laws, whether now existing or hereafter enacted.

(16) Any offer to purchase or to sell or any sale or issuance of a security, other than a security covered under federal law, pursuant to a plan approved by the Administrator after a hearing conducted pursuant to the provisions of G.S. 78A-30 or any transaction incident to any other judicially or governmentally approved reorganization in which a security is issued in exchange for one or more outstanding securities, claims or property interests, or partly in such exchange and partly cash.

(17) Any transaction that is exempt pursuant to rules established by the Administrator creating limited offering transactional exemptions that are consistent with the objectives of compatibility with federal limited offering exemptions and uniformity among the states. There is established a fee of one hundred fifty dollars ($150.00) to recover costs for any filing required by such rules.

(18) Any transaction incident to a class vote by security holders, pursuant to the articles of incorporation or similar organizational document or the applicable statute governing the internal affairs of the entity, on a merger, conversion, consolidation, share exchange, reclassification of securities, or sale of an entity's assets in consideration of the issuance of securities of another entity.

(19) Any offer or sale of any viatical settlement contract or any fractionalized or pooled interest therein by the issuer in a transaction that meets all of the following criteria:

a. The underlying viatical settlement transaction with the viator was not in violation of any applicable state or federal law; and

b. The offer and sale of such contract or interest therein is conducted in accordance with such conditions as the Administrator requires by rule or order, including conditions governing advertising, suitability standards, financial statements, the investor's right of rescission, and the disclosure of information to offerees and purchasers.

The Administrator may establish a fee to recover costs for any filing required by such rules, not to exceed five hundred dollars ($500.00). (1925, c. 190, s. 4; 1927, c. 149, s. 4; 1935, cc. 90, 154; 1955, c. 436, s. 3; 1959, c. 1185; 1967, c. 1233, ss. 2, 3; 1971, c. 572, s. 1; 1973, c. 1380; 1977, c. 162; c. 610, s. 1; 1979, c. 647, s. 1; 1981, c. 624, s. 2; 1981 (Reg. Sess., 1982), c. 1263, ss. 1, 2; 1983, c. 509, ss. 1, 2; c. 817, ss. 6, 7; 1997-419, s. 5; 2001-197, s. 1; 2001-201, ss. 8, 9, 10, 11, 12; 2001-436, s. 8; 2002-126, ss. 29A.22, 29A.23; 2004-203, s. 6.)

§ 78A-18. Denial and revocation of exemptions.

(a) The Administrator may by order deny or revoke any exemption specified in subdivision (9), (11), or (15) of G.S. 78A-16 or in 78A-17 with respect to a specific security or transaction. No such order may be entered without appropriate prior notice to all interested parties, opportunity for hearing, and written findings of fact and conclusions of law, except that the Administrator may by order summarily deny or revoke any of the specified exemptions pending final determination of any proceeding under this section. Upon the entry of a summary order, the Administrator shall promptly notify all interested parties that it has been entered and of the reasons therefor and that within 20 days of the receipt of a written request the matter will be scheduled for hearing in accordance with Chapter 150B of the General Statutes. If no hearing is requested and none is ordered by the Administrator, the order will remain in effect until it is modified or vacated by the Administrator. If a hearing is requested or ordered, the Administrator, after notice of an opportunity for hearing to all interested persons, may not modify or vacate the order or extend it until final determination. No order under this subsection may operate retroactively. No person may be considered to have violated G.S. 78A-24 or 78A-49(d) by reason of any offer or sale effected after the entry of an order under this subsection if he sustains the burden of proof that he did not know, and in the exercise of reasonable care could not have known, of the order.

(b) In a civil or administrative proceeding brought under this Chapter, the burden of proving an exemption or an exception from a definition is upon the person claiming it. In a criminal proceeding brought under this Chapter, the State has no initial burden of producing evidence to show that the defendant's actions do not fall within the exemption or exception; however, once the defendant introduces evidence to show that his conduct is within the exemption or exception, the burden of persuading the trier of fact that the exemption or exception does not apply falls upon the State. (1925, c. 190, ss. 5, 11; 1927, c. 149, ss. 5, 11; 1973, c. 1380; 1975, c. 19, s. 20; 1987, c. 849, s. 2; 1989 (Reg. Sess., 1990), c. 803, s. 2; 2001-126, s. 1; 2001-149, s. 2.)

§§ 78A-19 through 78A-23. Reserved for future codification purposes.

Article 4.

Registration and Notice Filing Procedures of Securities.

§ 78A-24. Registration requirement.

It is unlawful for any person to offer or sell any security in this State unless (i) it is registered under this Chapter, (ii) the security or transaction is exempted under G.S. 78A-16 or 78A-17 and such exemption has not been denied or revoked under G.S. 78A-18, or (iii) it is a security covered under federal law. (1925, c. 190, s. 6; 1927, c. 149, s. 6; 1955, c. 436, s. 4; 1973, c. 1380; 1997-419, ss. 6, 7.)

§ 78A-25. Registration by notification.

(a) The following securities may be registered by notification whether or not they are also eligible for registration by coordination under G.S. 78A-26:

(1) Any security whose issuer and any predecessors have been in continuous operation for at least five years if

a. There has been no default during the current fiscal year or within the three preceding fiscal years in the payment of principal, interest, dividends, or distributions on any security of the issuer (or any predecessor) with a fixed maturity or a fixed interest or dividend or distribution provision, and

b. The issuer and any predecessors during the past three fiscal years have had average net earnings, determined in accordance with generally accepted accounting principles, (i) which are applicable to all securities without a fixed maturity or a fixed interest or dividend or distribution provision outstanding at the date the registration statement is filed and equal at least five percent (5%) of the amount of such outstanding securities (as measured by the maximum offering price or the market price on a day, selected by the registrant, within 30 days before the date of filing the registration statement, whichever is higher, or book value on a day, selected by the registrant, within 90 days of the date of filing the registration statement to the extent that there is neither a readily determinable market price nor a cash offering price), or (ii) which, if the issuer and any predecessors have not had any security of the type specified in clause (i) outstanding for three full fiscal years, equal at least five percent (5%) of the amount (as measured in clause (i)) of all securities which will be outstanding if all the securities being offered or proposed to be offered (whether or not they are proposed to be registered or offered in this State) are issued;

(2) Any security (other than a certificate of interest or participation in an oil, gas, or mining title or lease or in payments out of production under such a title

or lease) registered for nonissuer distribution if (i) any security of the same class has been registered under this Chapter or a predecessor law within five years of the date of filing the registration statement, or (ii) the security being registered was originally issued within five years of the date of filing the registration statement pursuant to an exemption under this Chapter or a predecessor law;

(3) Any bonds or notes secured by a first mortgage upon agricultural lands used and valuable for agricultural purposes (not including oil, gas or mining property or leases) and the principal value of the bonds or notes does not exceed sixty percent (60%) of the then fair market value of the lands and improvements thereon;

(4) Any bonds or notes secured by a first mortgage on city, town, or village real estate situated in any state or in Canada if the principal value of the bonds and notes does not exceed sixty percent (60%) of the fair market value of the land and improvements thereon and the real estate is used principally to produce through rental a net annual income or has a fair net rental value at least equal to the annual interest on the bonds and notes, plus not less than three percent (3%) of the principal of said mortgage indebtedness;

(5) Any bond or note secured by a first lien on collateral pledged as security with a bank or trust company as trustee, which bank or trust company is incorporated under the laws of and subject to examination and supervision by the United States or by a state of the United States, and which collateral shall consist of (i) a principal amount of first mortgage bonds or notes meeting the requirements of G.S. 78A-25(a)(3) or 78A-25(a)(4) or (ii) a principal amount of obligations of the United States or (iii) cash equal to not less than one hundred percent (100%) of the principal secured, or (iv) a principal amount of obligations meeting the requirements of (i), (ii) or (iii) of this subdivision in any combination.

(b) A registration statement under this section shall contain the following information and be accompanied by the following documents in addition to the information specified in G.S. 78A-28(c) and the consent to service of process required by G.S. 78A-63(f):

(1) A statement demonstrating eligibility for registration by notification;

(2) With respect to the issuer and any significant subsidiary: its name, address, and form of organization; the state (or foreign jurisdiction) and the date of its organization; and the general character and location of its business;

(3)   With respect to any person on whose behalf any part of the offering is to be made in a nonissuer distribution: his name and address; the amount of securities of the issuer held by him as of the date of the filing of the registration statement; and a statement of his reasons for making the offering;

(4)   A description of the security being registered;

(5)   The information and documents specified in subdivisions (8), (10) and (12) of G.S. 78A-27(b); and

(6)   In the case of any registration under G.S. 78A-25(a)(2) which does not also satisfy the conditions of G.S. 78A-25(a)(1), a balance sheet of the issuer as of a date within four months prior to the filing of the registration statement, and a summary of earnings for each of the two fiscal years preceding the date of the balance sheet and for any period between the close of the last fiscal year and the date of the balance sheet, or for the period of the issuer's and any predecessors' existence if less than two years.

(c)   If no stop order is in effect and no proceeding is pending under G.S. 78A-29, a registration statement under this section automatically becomes effective at three o'clock Raleigh, North Carolina time in the afternoon of the tenth full business day after the filing of the registration statement or the last amendment, or at such earlier time as the Administrator determines. (1927, c. 149, s. 8; 1955, c. 436, s. 6; 1973, c. 1380; 1975, c. 144, s. 1; 2001-201, s. 13; 2003-413, s. 2.)

§ 78A-26. Registration by coordination.

(a)   Any security for which a registration statement has been filed under the Securities Act of 1933 in connection with the same offering may be registered by coordination.

(b)   A registration statement under this section shall contain the following information and be accompanied by the following documents in addition to the information specified in G.S. 78A-28(c) and the consent to service of process required by G.S. 78A-63(f):

(1)   One copy of the latest form of prospectus filed under the Securities Act of 1933;

(2) A copy of the articles of incorporation and bylaws or their substantial equivalents currently in effect, a copy of any agreements with or among underwriters, a copy of any indenture or other instrument governing the issuance of the security to be registered, and a specimen or copy of the security;

(3) If the Administrator requests, any other information or copies of any other documents filed under the Securities Act of 1933; and

(4) An undertaking to forward all future amendments to the federal prospectus, other than an amendment which merely delays the effective date of the registration statement, promptly and in any event not later than the first business day after they are forwarded to or filed with the Securities and Exchange Commission, whichever first occurs.

(c) A registration statement under this section automatically becomes effective at the moment the federal registration statement becomes effective if all the following conditions are satisfied: (i) no stop order is in effect and no proceeding is pending under G.S. 78A-29; (ii) the registration statement has been on file with the Administrator for at least 10 days; and (iii) a statement of the maximum proposed offering price and the maximum underwriting discounts and commissions expressed as a percentage of the final offering price has been on file for two full business days or such shorter period as the Administrator permits by rule or otherwise and the offering is made within those limitations. The registrant shall promptly notify the Administrator by telephone or telegram of the date and time when the federal registration statement became effective and the content of the price amendment, if any, and shall promptly file a post-effective amendment containing the information and documents in the price amendment. "Price amendment" means the final federal amendment which includes a statement of the offering price, underwriting and selling discounts or commissions, amount of proceeds, conversion rates, call prices, and other matters dependent upon the offering price. Upon failure to receive the required notification and post-effective amendment with respect to the price amendment, the Administrator may enter a stop order without notice or hearing, retroactively denying effectiveness to the registration statement or suspending its effectiveness until compliance with this subsection, if he promptly notifies the registrant by telephone or telegram (and promptly confirms by letter or telegram when he notifies by telephone) of the issuance of the order. If the registrant proves compliance with the requirements of this subsection as to notice and post-effective amendment, the stop order is void as of the time of its entry. The Administrator may by rule or otherwise waive either or both of the conditions specified in clauses (ii) and (iii). If the federal registration statement becomes effective before all the conditions in this subsection are satisfied and they are not waived, the registration statement automatically becomes effective as soon as all the conditions are satisfied. If the registrant advises the Administrator of the date when the federal registration statement is expected to become effective, the Administrator shall promptly advise the registrant by telephone or telegraph, at the registrant's expense, whether all the conditions are satisfied and whether he then contemplates the institution of a proceeding under G.S. 78A-29; but this advice by the Administrator does not preclude the institution of such a proceeding at any time. (1925, c. 190, s. 6; 1927, c. 149, s. 6; 1955, c. 436, s. 4; 1973, c. 1380; 1981, c. 624, s. 6.)

§ 78A-27. Registration by qualification.

(a) Any security may be registered by qualification upon the following conditions.

(b) A registration statement under this section shall contain the following information and be accompanied by the following documents in addition to the information specified in G.S. 78A-28(c) and the consent to service of process required by G.S. 78A-63(f):

(1) With respect to the issuer and any significant subsidiary: its name, address, and form of organization; the state or foreign jurisdiction and date of its organization; the general character and location of its business; a description of its physical properties and equipment; and a statement of the general competitive conditions in the industry or business in which it is or will be engaged;

(2) With respect to every director and officer of the issuer or person occupying a similar status or performing similar functions: his name, address, and principal occupation for the past five years; the amount of securities of the issuer held by him as of a specified date within 30 days of the filing of the registration statement; the amount of the securities covered by the registration statement to which he has indicated his intention to subscribe; and a description of any material interest in any material transaction with the issuer or any significant subsidiary effected within the past three years or proposed to be effected;

(3) With respect to persons covered by subdivision (2): the remuneration paid during the past 12 months or fiscal year and estimated to be paid during the next fiscal year, directly or indirectly, by the issuer (together with all predecessors, parents, subsidiaries, and affiliates) to all those persons in the aggregate;

(4) With respect to any person owning of record or beneficially if known, ten percent (10%) or more of the outstanding shares of any class of equity security of the issuer: the information specified in subdivision (2) other than his occupation;

(5) With respect to every promoter if the issuer was organized within the past three years: the information specified in subdivision (2), any amount paid to him within that period or intended to be paid to him, and the consideration for any such payment;

(6) With respect to any person on whose behalf any part of the offering is to be made in a nonissuer distribution: his name and address; the amount of securities of the issuer held by him as of the date of the filing of the registration statement; a description of any material interest in any material transaction with the issuer or any significant subsidiary effected within the past three years or proposed to be effected; and a statement of his reasons for making the offering;

(7) The capitalization and long-term debt (on both current and a pro forma basis) of the issuer and any significant subsidiary including a description of each security outstanding or being registered or otherwise offered, and a statement of the amount and kind of consideration (whether in the form of cash, physical assets, services, patents, goodwill, or anything else) for which the issuer or any subsidiary has issued any of its securities within the past three years or is obligated to issue any of its securities;

(8) The kind and amount of securities to be offered; the proposed offering price or the method by which it is to be computed; any variation therefrom at which any proportion of the offering is to be made to any person or class of persons other than the underwriters, with a specification of any such person or class; the basis upon which the offering is to be made if otherwise than for cash; the estimated aggregate underwriting and selling discounts or commissions and finders' fees (including separately, cash, securities, contracts, or anything else of value to accrue to the underwriters or finders in connection with the offering) or, if the selling discounts or commissions are variable, the basis of determining them and their maximum and minimum amounts; the estimated amounts of

other selling expenses, including legal, engineering, and accounting charges; the name and address of every underwriter and every recipient of a finder's fee; a copy of any underwriting or selling-group agreement pursuant to which the distribution is to be made, or the proposed form of any such agreement whose terms have not yet been determined; and a description of the plan of distribution of any securities which are to be offered otherwise than through an underwriter;

(9) The estimated cash proceeds to be received by the issuer from the offering; the purposes for which the proceeds are to be used by the issuer; the amount to be used for each purpose; the order or priority in which the proceeds will be used for the purposes stated; the amount of any funds to be raised from other sources to achieve the purposes stated; the sources of any such funds; and, if any part of the proceeds is to be used to acquire any property (including goodwill) otherwise than in the ordinary course of business, the names and addresses of the vendors, the purchase price, the names of any persons who have received commissions in connection with the acquisition, and the amounts of any such commissions and any other expense in connection with the acquisition (including the cost of borrowing money to finance the acquisition);

(10) A description of any stock options or other security options outstanding, or to be created in connection with the offering, together with the amount of any such options held or to be held by every person required to be named in subdivisions (2), (4), (5), (6), or (8) and by any person who holds or will hold ten percent (10%) or more in the aggregate of any such options;

(11) The dates of, parties to, and general effect concisely stated of, every management or other material contract made or to be made otherwise than in the ordinary course of business if it is to be performed in whole or in part at or after the filing of the registration statement or was made within the past two years, together with a copy of every such contract; and a description of any pending litigation or proceeding to which the issuer is a party and which materially affects its business or assets (including any such litigation or proceeding known to be contemplated by governmental authorities);

(12) A copy of any prospectus, pamphlet, circular, form letter, advertisement, or other sales literature intended as of the effective date to be used in connection with the offering; if the security is a viatical settlement contract, the prospectus and advertising shall comply with G.S. 78A-13 and G.S. 78A-14 relating to the offering of viatical settlement contracts;

(13) A specimen or copy of the security being registered; a copy of the issuer's articles of incorporation and bylaws, or their substantial equivalents, as currently in effect; and a copy of any indenture or other instrument covering the security to be registered;

(14) A signed or conformed copy of an opinion of counsel as to the legality of the security being registered (with an English translation if it is in a foreign language), which shall state whether the security when sold will be legally issued, fully paid, and nonassessable, and, if a debt security, a binding obligation of the issuer;

(15) The written consent of any accountant, engineer, appraiser, or other person whose profession gives authority to a statement made by him, if any such person is named as having prepared or certified a report or valuation (other than a public and official document or statement) which is used in connection with the registration statement;

(16) A balance sheet of the issuer as of a date within four months prior to the filing of the registration statement; a profit and loss statement and analysis of surplus for each of the three fiscal years preceding the date of the balance sheet and for any period between the close of the last fiscal year and the date of the balance sheet, or for the period of the issuer's and any predecessors' existence if less than three years; and, if any part of the proceeds of the offering is to be applied to the purchase of any business, the same financial statements which would be required if that business were the registrant; and

(17) Such additional information as the Administrator requires by rule or order.

(c) A registration statement under this section becomes effective when the Administrator so orders.

(d) The Administrator may by rule or order require as a condition of registration under this section that a prospectus containing any designated part of the information specified in subsection (b) be sent or given to each person to whom an offer is made before or concurrently with (i) the first written offer made to him (otherwise than by means of a public advertisement) by or for the account of the issuer or any other person on whose behalf the offering is being made, or by any underwriter or dealer who is offering part of an unsold allotment or subscription taken by him as a participant in the distribution, (ii) the confirmation of any sale made by or for the account of any such person, (iii) payment pursuant to any such sale, or (iv) delivery of the security pursuant to any such sale, whichever first occurs. (1927, c. 149, s. 9; 1955, c. 436, s. 7; 1973, c. 1380; 1975, c. 19, s. 21; 2001-436, s. 9.)

§ 78A-28. Provisions applicable to registration generally.

(a) A registration statement may be filed by the issuer, any other person on whose behalf the offering is to be made, or a registered dealer.

(b) Every person filing a registration statement shall pay a filing fee of two thousand dollars ($2,000). When a registration statement is withdrawn before the effective date or a pre-effective stop order is entered under G.S. 78A-29, the Administrator shall retain the filing fee. A registration statement relating to redeemable securities to be offered for a period in excess of one year, other than securities covered under federal law, must be renewed annually by payment of a renewal fee of one hundred dollars ($100.00) and by filing any documents or reports that the Administrator may by rule or order require.

(c) Every registration statement shall specify (i) the amount of securities to be offered in this State; (ii) the states in which a registration statement or similar document in connection with the offering has been or is expected to be filed; and (iii) any adverse order, judgment, or decree entered in connection with the offering by the regulatory authorities in each state or by any court or the Securities and Exchange Commission.

(d) Any document filed under this Chapter or a predecessor law within five years preceding the filing of a registration statement may be incorporated by reference in the registration statement to the extent that the document is currently accurate.

(e) The Administrator may by rule or otherwise permit the omission of any item of information or document from any registration statement.

(f) In the case of a nonissuer distribution, information may not be required under G.S. 78A-27 or 78A-28(i) unless it is known to the person filing the registration statement or to the persons on whose behalf the distribution is to be made, or can be furnished by them without unreasonable effort or expense.

(g) The Administrator may by rule or order require as a condition of registration by qualification or coordination (i) that any security issued within the past three years or to be issued to a promoter for a consideration substantially different from the public offering price, or to any person for a consideration other than cash, be deposited in escrow; and (ii) that the proceeds from the sale of the registered security in this State be impounded until the issuer receives a specified amount from the sale of the securities either in this State or elsewhere. The Administrator may by rule or order determine the conditions of any escrow or impounding required hereunder, but he may not reject a depository solely because of location in another state.

(h) Except during the time a stop order is in effect under G.S. 78A-29, a registration statement relating to redeemable securities to be offered for a period in excess of one year, other than securities covered under federal law, expires on December 31 of each year or some other date not more than one year from its effective date as the Administrator may by rule or order provide. Every other registration statement is effective for one year from its effective date, or any longer period during which the security is being offered or distributed in a nonexempted transaction by or for the account of the issuer or other person on whose behalf the offering is being made or by any underwriter or dealer who is still offering part of an unsold allotment or subscription taken by him as a participant in the distribution, except during the time a stop order is in effect under G.S. 78A-29. All outstanding securities of the same class as a registered security are considered to be registered for the purpose of any nonissuer transaction (i) so long as the registration statement is effective and (ii) between the thirtieth day after the entry of any stop order suspending or revoking the effectiveness of the registration statement under G.S. 78A-29 (if the registration statement did not relate in whole or in part to a nonissuer distribution) and one year from the effective date of the registration statement. A registration statement may not be withdrawn for one year from its effective date if any securities of the same class are outstanding. A registration statement may be withdrawn otherwise only in the discretion of the Administrator.

(i) So long as a registration statement is effective, the Administrator may by rule or order require the person who filed the registration statement to file reports, not more often than quarterly, to keep reasonably current the information contained in the registration statement and to disclose progress of the offering.

(j) A registration statement filed in accordance with subsection (b) of this section may be amended after its effective date to increase the securities specified as proposed to be offered. Such an amendment becomes effective when the Administrator so orders. Every person filing such an amendment shall pay a filing fee of fifty dollars ($50.00) with respect to the additional securities proposed to be offered. (1973, c. 1380; 1979, 2nd Sess., c. 1148, s. 1; 1981, c. 452; c. 624, s. 3; c. 682, s. 14; 1983, c. 713, ss. 45-47; 1998-212, s. 29A.9(b).)

§ 78A-29. Denial, suspension, and revocation of registration.

(a) The Administrator may issue a stop order denying effectiveness to, or suspending or revoking the effectiveness of, any registration statement if he finds

(1) That the order is in the public interest and

(2) That:

a. The registration statement as of its effective date or as of any earlier date in the case of an order denying effectiveness, or any amendment under G.S. 78A-28(j) as of its effective date, or any report under G.S. 78A-28(i) is incomplete in any material respect or contains any statement which was, in the light of the circumstances under which it was made, false or misleading with respect to any material fact; or

b. Any provision of this Chapter or any rule, order, or condition lawfully imposed under this Chapter has been willfully violated, in connection with the offering, by (i) the person filing the registration statement, (ii) the issuer, any partner, officer, or director of the issuer, any person occupying a similar status or performing similar functions, or any person directly or indirectly controlling or controlled by the issuer, but only if the person filing the registration statement is directly or indirectly controlled by or acting for the issuer, or (iii) any underwriter; or

c. The security registered or sought to be registered is the subject of an administrative stop order or similar order or a permanent or temporary injunction of any court of competent jurisdiction entered under any other federal or state act applicable to the offering; but (i) the Administrator may not institute a proceeding against an effective registration statement under paragraph c more than one year from the date of the order or injunction relied on, and (ii) he may not enter an order under paragraph c on the basis of an order or injunction entered under any other state act unless that order or injunction was based on facts which would currently constitute a ground for a stop order under this section; or

d. The issuer's enterprise or method of business includes or would include activities which are illegal where performed; or

e. The offering has worked or tended to work a fraud upon purchasers or would so operate; or

f. The offering has been or would be made with unreasonable amounts of underwriters' and sellers' discounts, commissions, or other compensation, or promoters' profits or participation, or unreasonable amounts or kinds of options; or

g. When a security is sought to be registered by notification, it is not eligible for such registration; or

h. When a security is sought to be registered by coordination, there has been a failure to comply with the undertaking required by G.S. 78A-26(b)(4); or

i. The applicant or registrant has failed to pay the proper fees; but the Administrator may enter only a denial order under this paragraph and he shall vacate any such order when the deficiency has been corrected.

The Administrator may not institute a stop-order proceeding against an effective registration statement on the basis of a fact or transaction known to him when the registration statement became effective unless the proceeding is instituted within the next 30 days.

(b) The following provisions govern the application of G.S. 78A-29(a)(2)f:

(1) The Administrator may not enter a stop order against a registration statement based on one or more of the grounds set forth in paragraph f of G.S. 78A-29(a)(2) if the offering, or the dealer, or any dealers, making or participating in the offering, is subject to rules, promulgated by any national securities association registered with the Securities and Exchange Commission pursuant to section 15A of the Securities Exchange Act of 1934, providing safeguards against unreasonable profits or unreasonable rates or commissions or other charges, and such rules are complied with.

(2) The Administrator may by rule or order require such evidence of compliance with such rules as he may deem advisable.

(c) The Administrator may by order summarily postpone or suspend the effectiveness of the registration statement pending final determination of any proceeding under this section. Upon the entry of the order, the Administrator shall promptly notify each person specified in subsection (d) that it has been entered and of the reasons therefor and that within 20 days after the receipt of a written request the matter will be scheduled for hearing in accordance with chapter 150B of the General Statutes. If no hearing is requested and none is ordered by the Administrator, the order will remain in effect until it is modified or vacated by the Administrator. If a hearing is requested or ordered, the Administrator, after notice of an opportunity for hearing to each person specified in subsection (d), may modify or vacate the order or extend it until final determination.

(d) No stop order may be entered under any part of this section except the first sentence of subsection (c) without (i) appropriate prior notice to the applicant or registrant, the issuer, and the person on whose behalf the securities are to be or have been offered, (ii) opportunity for hearing, and (iii) written findings of fact and conclusions of law.

(e) The Administrator may vacate or modify a stop order if he finds that the conditions which prompted entry have changed or that it is otherwise in the public interest to do so. (1973, c. 1380; 2001-126, s. 2.)

§ 78A-30. Application to exchange securities.

(a) When application is made for approval to issue securities or to deliver other consideration (whether or not the security or transaction is exempt from registration or qualification other than by the provisions of G.S. 78A-17(16) or not required to be qualified) in exchange for one or more bona fide securities, claims, or property interests, or partly in such exchange and partly in cash, the Administrator is expressly authorized to approve the terms and conditions of such issuance and exchange or such delivery and exchange and the fairness of such terms and conditions, and is expressly authorized to hold a hearing upon the fairness of such terms and conditions, at which all persons to whom it is proposed to issue securities or to deliver such other consideration in such exchange have the right to appear. Notice of such hearing shall be mailed by

United States Mail, Postage Prepaid, to all persons to whom it is proposed to issue securities or to deliver such other consideration in such exchange, not less than 10 days prior to such hearing, and such notice shall be effective upon mailing. The application for approval to issue securities or to deliver other consideration shall be in such form, contain such information and be accompanied by such documents as shall be required by rule or order of the Administrator.

(b) The Administrator shall be required to hold a hearing on an application for approval within 30 days after the filing of the application and supporting documents required by rule of the Administrator. Provided, however, if the securities or the transaction regarding which the fairness hearing is sought are otherwise exempt from the registration provisions of this Chapter: (1) the Administrator shall have until 45 days after the filing of the application and supporting documents to hold a hearing on the application for approval; and (2) the hearing on the application shall not be held until at least 10 business days after the filing of the application.

(c) Within 10 business days after holding the hearing under subsection (a), the Administrator shall issue his approval or a statement that his approval will not be forthcoming.

(d) The Administrator's authority under this section shall extend to the issuance or the delivery of securities or other consideration:

(1) By any entity organized under the laws of this State; or

(2) In any transaction which is subject to the registration or qualification requirements of this Chapter or which would be so subject except for the availability of an exemption under G.S. 78A-16 or G.S. 78A-17, or by reason that the security is a security covered under federal law.

(e) The provisions of this section shall be permissive only and no request for approval, failure to request approval, withdrawal of a request for approval, or denial of approval by the Administrator shall affect the availability of any exemption from the registration or qualification requirements other than the exemption available under G.S. 78A-17(16), and shall not be admissible as evidence in any legal or administrative proceeding.

(f) This section is intended to provide for a fairness hearing before the Administrator with respect to transactions which, if approved by the

Administrator, would be exempt from the registration requirements of the federal securities laws under section 3(a)(10) of the Securities Act of 1933, or any section comparable thereto which may subsequently be enacted.

(g)   The Administrator shall charge a fee for a fairness hearing that the Administrator holds under this section. The Administrator shall set the fee based upon the time and expenses incurred by the Administrator. The fee may not be less than five hundred dollars ($500.00), and it may not exceed five thousand dollars ($5,000). (1979, c. 647, ss. 2, 3; 1987, c. 849, s. 8; 1997-419, s. 8; 1998-212, s. 29A.9(c); 2001-201, s. 14.)

§ 78A-31. Notice filings for securities covered under federal law.

(a)   The Administrator, by rule or order, may require the filing of any of the following documents with regard to a security (i) issued by an investment company that is registered or has filed a registration statement under the Investment Company Act of 1940 and (ii) covered under section 18(b)(2) of the Securities Act of 1933 (15 U.S.C. § 77r(b)(2)):

(1)   Prior to the initial offer of the security in this State, all documents that are part of a federal registration statement filed with the Securities and Exchange Commission under the Securities Act of 1933, or, in lieu thereof, a form prescribed by the Administrator, together with a consent to service of process signed by the issuer and with the payment of a notice filing fee equal to the sum of one thousand seven hundred twenty-five dollars ($1,725) and two hundred seventy-five dollars ($275.00) for each series, fund, or portfolio offered in this State and listed in the federal registration statement.

(2)   After the initial offer of the security in this State, all documents that are part of an amendment to a federal registration statement filed with the Securities and Exchange Commission under the Securities Act of 1933, or, in lieu thereof, a form prescribed by the Administrator, which shall be filed concurrently with the Administrator.

(3)   A report of the value of securities covered under federal law that are offered or sold in this State.

(4)   A notice filing pursuant to this section shall expire on December 31 of each year or some other date not more than one year from its effective date as

the Administrator may by rule or order provide. A notice filing of the offer of securities covered under federal law that are to be offered for a period in excess of one year shall be renewed annually by payment of a renewal fee equal to the sum of one thousand seven hundred twenty-five dollars ($1,725) and two hundred seventy-five dollars ($275.00) for each series, fund, or portfolio offered in this State and listed in the federal registration statement and by filing any documents and reports that the Administrator may by rule or order require consistent with this section. The renewal shall be effective upon the expiration of the prior notice period.

(5) A notice filed in accordance with this section may be amended after its effective date to increase the securities specified as proposed to be offered. An amendment becomes effective upon receipt by the Administrator. Every person submitting an amended notice filing shall pay a filing fee of fifty dollars ($50.00) with respect to the additional securities proposed to be offered.

(b) With regard to any security that is covered under section 18(b)(4)(D) of the Securities Act of 1933 (15 U.S.C. § 77r(b)(4)(d)), the Administrator, by rule or order, may require the issuer to file a notice on SEC Form D (17 C.F.R. § 239.500) and a consent to service of process signed by the issuer no later than 15 days after the first sale of the security in this State. There is established a fee of three hundred fifty dollars ($350.00) to recover costs for filing required by this section.

(c) The Administrator, by rule or order, may require the filing of any document filed with the Securities and Exchange Commission under the Securities Act of 1933, with respect to a security covered under section 18(b)(3) or (4) of the Securities Act of 1933 (15 U.S.C. § 77r(b)(3) or (4)). The Administrator may, by rule, establish a fee to recover costs for any filing required under this section, not to exceed one hundred fifty dollars ($150.00).

(d) The Administrator may suspend the offer and sale of a covered security, except a covered security under section 18(b)(1) of the Securities Act of 1933 (15 U.S.C. § 77r(b)(1)), if the Administrator finds that (i) the order is in the public interest, and (ii) there is a failure to comply with any condition established under this section.

(e) The Administrator, by rule or order, may waive any of the requirements set by this section. (1997-419, s. 9; 1998-212, s. 29A.9(d); 2002-126, ss. 29A.24, 29A.37; 2002-189, s. 4; 2003-284, s. 35B.2(a); 2008-107, s. 29.3(a); 2011-145, s. 31.27A(a).)

§§ 78A-32 through 78A-35. Reserved for future codification purposes.

Article 5.

Registration of Dealers and Salesmen.

§ 78A-36. Registration requirement.

(a) It is unlawful for any person to transact business in this State as a dealer or salesman unless he is registered under this Chapter. No dealer shall be eligible for registration under this Chapter, or for renewal of registration hereunder, unless such dealer is at the time registered as a dealer with the Securities and Exchange Commission under the Securities Exchange Act of 1934.

(b) It is unlawful for any dealer to employ a salesman unless the salesman is registered. The registration of a salesman is not effective during any period when he is not associated with a particular dealer registered under this Chapter. When a salesman begins or terminates those activities which make him a salesman, the salesman as well as the dealer shall promptly notify the Administrator.

The Administrator may by rule or order require the return of a salesman's license upon the termination of those activities which make him a salesman or, if such return is impossible, require a bond or evidence satisfactory to the Administrator of such impossibility. No salesman may be registered with more than one dealer.

(c) Every registration expires on the thirty-first day of March of each year (or such other date not more than one year from its effective date as the Administrator may by rule or order provide) unless renewed. (1925, c. 190, s. 19; 1927, c. 149, s. 19; 1955, c. 436, s. 9; 1959, c. 1122; 1971, c. 831, s. 1; 1973, c. 1380; 1975, c. 144, s. 2; 1979, 2nd Sess., c. 1148, s. 2; 1981, c. 624, s. 4; 1983, c. 817, s. 8; 2001-182, s. 1.)

§ 78A-36.1. Limited registration of Canadian dealers and salesmen.

(a) A dealer that is a resident of Canada and that has no office or other physical presence in this State may effect transactions in securities with or for, or induce or attempt to induce the purchase or sale of any security by:

(1) A person from Canada who is residing in this State temporarily and with whom the Canadian dealer had a bona fide dealer-client relationship before the person entered the United States; or

(2) A person from Canada who is a resident of this State and whose transactions are in a self-directed tax advantaged retirement plan in Canada of which the person is the holder or contributor.

This subsection only applies to dealers that are registered in accordance with this section.

(b) A salesman who will be representing a Canadian dealer registered under this section may effect transactions in securities in this State as permitted for the dealer in subsection (a) of this section, only if the salesman is registered in accordance with this section.

(c) A Canadian dealer may register under this section provided that it meets all of the following conditions:

(1) The dealer files an application in the form required by the jurisdiction in which it has its head office.

(2) The dealer files a consent to service of process.

(3) The dealer is registered as a dealer in good standing in the jurisdiction from which it is effecting transactions into this State and files evidence thereof.

(4) The dealer is a member of a self-regulatory organization, the Bureau des services financiers or a stock exchange in Canada.

(d) A salesman who will be representing a Canadian dealer registered under this section in effecting transactions in securities in this State may register under this section provided that the salesman meets all of the following conditions:

(1) The salesman files an application in the form required by the jurisdiction in which the dealer has its head office.

(2) The salesman files a consent to service of process.

(3) The salesman is registered in good standing in the jurisdiction from which the salesman is effecting transactions into this State and files evidence thereof.

(e) If no denial order is in effect and no proceeding is pending under G.S. 78A-39, registration becomes effective on the thirtieth day after an application is filed, unless the registration is made effective earlier.

(f) A Canadian dealer registered under this section shall meet all of the following conditions:

(1) The dealer maintains its provincial or territorial registration and its membership in a self-regulatory organization, the Bureau des services financiers or a stock exchange in good standing.

(2) The dealer provides the Administrator, upon request, with its books and records relating to its business in this State as a dealer.

(3) The dealer informs the Administrator forthwith of any criminal action taken against it or of any finding or sanction imposed on the dealer as a result of any self-regulatory or regulatory action involving fraud, theft, deceit, misrepresentation, or similar conduct.

(4) The dealer discloses to its clients in this State that the dealer and its agents are not subject to the full regulatory requirements under this Article.

(g) A salesman of a Canadian dealer registered under this section shall meet all of the following conditions:

(1) The salesman maintains the salesman's provincial or territorial registration in good standing.

(2) The salesman informs the Administrator forthwith of any criminal action taken against the salesman or of any finding or sanction imposed on the salesman as a result of any self-regulatory or regulatory action involving fraud, theft, deceit, misrepresentation, or similar conduct.

(h) Renewal applications for Canadian dealers and salesmen under this section shall be filed before December 31 of each year and may be made by filing the most recent renewal application, if any, filed in the jurisdiction in which the dealer has its head office, or if no such renewal application is required, the most recent application filed pursuant to subdivision (c)(1) of this section or subdivision (d)(1) of this section, as applicable.

(i) Every applicant for registration or renewal of registration under this section shall pay the fee for dealers and salesmen as required in this Chapter.

(j) Every Canadian dealer or salesman registered under this section may effect transactions in this State only:

(1) As permitted in subsection (a) or (b) of this section, and

(2) With or through:

a. The issuers of the securities involved in the transactions;

b. Other dealers; and

c. Banks, savings institutions, trust companies, insurance companies, investment companies, as defined in the Investment Company Act of 1940, pension or profit-sharing trusts, or other financial institutions or institutional buyers, whether acting for themselves or as trustees.

(k) Article 2 of this Chapter applies to Canadian dealers and salesmen registered under this section.

(l) Except as otherwise provided in this section, Canadian dealers or salesmen registered under this section and acting in accordance with the limitations set out in subsection (j) of this section are exempt from all of the requirements of this Chapter. A registration under this section may be denied, suspended, or revoked pursuant to G.S. 78A-39 only for a breach of Article 2 of this Chapter or this section. (2001-225, s. 1.)

§ 78A-37. Registration procedure.

(a) A dealer or salesman may obtain an initial or renewal registration by filing with the Administrator an application together with a consent to service of process pursuant to G.S. 78A-63(f). The application shall contain whatever information the Administrator by rule requires concerning such matters as (i) the applicant's form and place of organization; (ii) the applicant's proposed method of doing business; (iii) the qualifications and business history of the applicant; in the case of a dealer, the qualifications and business history of any partner, officer, or director, any person occupying a similar status or performing similar functions, or any person directly or indirectly controlling the dealer, and a representation that the applicant dealer is duly registered as a dealer under the Securities Exchange Act of 1934; (iv) any injunction or administrative order or conviction of a misdemeanor involving a security or any aspect of the securities business and any conviction of a felony; and (v) the applicant's financial condition and history. If no denial order is in effect and no proceeding is pending under G.S. 78A-39, registration becomes effective at noon of the thirtieth day after an application is filed. The Administrator may by rule or order specify an earlier effective date and may by order defer the effective date until noon of the thirtieth day after the filing of any amendment. Registration of a dealer automatically constitutes registration of any salesman who is a partner, executive officer, or director, or a person occupying a similar status or performing similar functions. After the Administrator institutes a proceeding under G.S. 78A-39 to postpone or deny an application for registration, withdrawal of the application shall be allowed only at such time and under such conditions as the Administrator may by order determine.

(b) Every applicant for initial or renewal registration shall pay a filing fee of three hundred dollars ($300.00) in the case of a dealer and one hundred twenty-five dollars ($125.00) in the case of a salesman. The Administrator may by rule reduce the registration fee proportionately when the registration will be in effect for less than a full year.

(c) A registered dealer may file an application for registration of a successor, whether or not the successor is then in existence, for the unexpired portion of the year. There shall be no filing fee.

(d) The Administrator may by rule require registered dealers to post surety bonds in amounts up to one hundred thousand dollars ($100,000) and salesmen to post surety bonds in amounts up to ten thousand dollars ($10,000), and may determine their conditions. Any appropriate deposit of cash or securities shall be accepted in lieu of any bond so required. No bond may be required of any registrant whose net capital, which may be defined by rule, exceeds one hundred thousand dollars ($100,000). Every bond shall provide for suit thereon by any person who has a cause of action under G.S. 78A-56 and, if the Administrator by rule or order requires, by any person who has a cause of action not arising under this Chapter. Every bond shall provide that no suit may be maintained to enforce any liability on the bond unless brought within two years after the sale or other act upon which it is based. (1925, c. 190, s. 19; 1927, c. 149, s. 19; 1955, c. 436, s. 9; 1959, c. 1122; 1971, c. 831, s. 1; 1973, c. 1380; 1983, c. 713, s. 48; c. 817, ss. 9, 10; 1987, c. 566, s. 1; 1991 (Reg. Sess., 1992), c. 965, s. 2; 2002-126, s. 29A.34; 2003-413, s. 3; 2009-451, s. 24.1(a).)

§ 78A-38. Post-registration provisions.

(a) Every registered dealer shall make and keep such accounts, correspondence, memoranda, papers, books, and other records as the Administrator by rule prescribes, subject to the limitations of section 15 of the Securities Exchange Act of 1934 (15 U.S.C. § 78o).

(b) Every registered dealer shall file such financial reports as the Administrator by rule prescribes, subject to the limitations of section 15 of the Securities Exchange Act of 1934 (15 U.S.C. § 78o).

(c) If the information contained in any document filed with the Administrator is or becomes inaccurate or incomplete in any material respect, the registrant shall promptly file a correcting amendment unless notification of the correction has been given under G.S. 78A-36(b).

(d) All the records referred to in subsection (a) of this section are subject at any time or from time to time to such reasonable periodic, special, or other examinations by representatives of the Administrator, within or without this State, as the Administrator deems necessary or appropriate in the public interest or for the protection of investors. For the purpose of avoiding unnecessary duplication of examinations, the Administrator, insofar as he deems it practicable in administering this subsection, may cooperate with the securities administrators of other states, the Securities and Exchange Commission, and any national securities exchange or national securities association registered under the Securities Exchange Act of 1934. (1925, c. 190, ss. 14, 15; 1927, c. 149, ss. 14, 15; 1973, c. 1380; 1997-419, s. 10.)

§ 78A-39. Denial, revocation, suspension, censure, cancellation, and withdrawal of registration.

(a) The Administrator may by order deny, suspend, or revoke any registration in whole or in part or restrict or limit as to any person, office, function, or activity or censure the registrant if he finds

(1) That the order is in the public interest and

(2) That the applicant or registrant or, in the case of a dealer, any partner, officer, or director, any person occupying a similar status or performing similar functions, or any person directly or indirectly controlling the dealer:

a. Has filed an application for registration which as of its effective date, or as of any date after filing in the case of an order denying effectiveness, was incomplete in any material respect or contained any statement which was, in light of the circumstances under which it was made, false or misleading with respect to any material fact; or

b. Has willfully violated or willfully failed to comply with any provision of this Chapter or a predecessor law or any rule or order under this Chapter or a predecessor law or any provision of the Securities Act of 1933, the Securities Exchange Act of 1934, the Investment Advisors Act of 1940, or the Commodity Exchange Act; or

c. Has been convicted, within the past 10 years, of any misdemeanor involving a security or any aspect of the securities business, or any felony; or

d. Is permanently or temporarily enjoined by any court of competent jurisdiction from engaging in or continuing any conduct or practice involving any aspect of the securities business; or

e. Is the subject of an order of the Administrator denying, suspending, or revoking registration as a dealer or salesman; or

f. Is the subject of an order entered within the past five years by the securities administrator of any state or by the Securities and Exchange Commission denying or revoking registration as a dealer or salesman, or the substantial equivalent of those terms as defined in this Chapter, or is the subject of a final order suspending or expelling him from a national securities exchange or national securities association registered under the Securities Exchange Act of 1934, or is the subject of a United States post office fraud order; but (i) the Administrator may not institute a revocation or suspension proceeding under subdivision (2)f of subsection (a) more than one year from the date of the order relied on, and (ii) the Administrator may not enter an order under subdivision (2)f of subsection (a) on the basis of an order under another state act unless that order was based on facts which would currently constitute a ground for an order under this section; or

g. Has engaged in dishonest or unethical practices in the securities business; or

h. Is insolvent, either in the sense that his liabilities exceed his assets or in the sense that he cannot meet his obligations as they mature; but the Administrator may not enter an order against a dealer under this paragraph without a finding of insolvency as to the dealer; or

i. Is not qualified on the basis of such factors as training, experience, and knowledge of the securities business, except as otherwise provided in subsection (b).

(a1) The Administrator may by order deny, suspend, or revoke any registration in whole or in part or restrict or limit as to any person, office, function, or activity or censure the registrant if he finds

(1) That the order is in the public interest and

(2) That the applicant or registrant:

a. Has failed reasonably to supervise his salesmen if he is a dealer; or

b. Has failed to pay the proper filing fee; but the Administrator may enter only a denial order under this clause, and he shall vacate any such order when the deficiency has been corrected.

The Administrator may not institute a suspension or revocation proceeding on the basis of a fact or transaction known to him when registration became effective unless the proceeding is instituted within the next 120 days.

(b) The following provisions govern the application of G.S. 78A-39(a)(2)i:

(1) The Administrator may not enter an order against a dealer on the basis of the lack of qualification of any person other than (i) the dealer himself if he is an individual or (ii) a salesman of the dealer.

(2) The Administrator may not enter an order solely on the basis of lack of experience if the applicant or registrant is qualified by training or knowledge or both or, in the case of a dealer if he is registered and in good standing under the Securities Exchange Act of 1934.

(3) The Administrator shall consider that a salesman who will work under the supervision of a registered dealer need not have the same qualifications as a dealer.

(4) The Administrator may by rule provide for an examination which may be written or oral or both, to be taken by any class of or all applicants.

(c) The Administrator may by order summarily postpone or suspend registration pending final determination of any proceeding under this section. Upon the entry of the order, the Administrator shall promptly notify the applicant or registrant, as well as the employer or prospective employer if the applicant or registrant is a salesman, that it has been entered and of the reasons therefor and that within 20 days after the receipt of a written request the matter will be scheduled for hearing in accordance with Chapter 150B of the General Statutes. If no request for a hearing, other responsive pleading, or submission is received by the Administrator within 30 business days of receipt of service of notice of the order upon the applicant or registrant and no hearing is ordered by the Administrator, the order shall become final and remain in effect unless it is modified or vacated by the Administrator. If a hearing is requested or ordered, the Administrator, after notice of and opportunity for hearing, may modify or vacate the order or extend it until final determination.

(d) If the Administrator finds that any registrant or applicant for registration is no longer in existence or has ceased to do business as a dealer or salesman, or is subject to an adjudication of mental incompetence or to the control of a committee, conservator, or guardian, or cannot be located after reasonable search, the Administrator may by order cancel the registration or application.

(e) Withdrawal from registration as a dealer or salesman becomes effective 90 days after receipt of an application to withdraw or within such shorter period of time as the Administrator may determine, unless a revocation or suspension proceeding is pending when the application is filed or a proceeding to revoke or suspend or to impose conditions upon the withdrawal is instituted within 90 days after the application is filed. If a proceeding is pending or instituted, withdrawal becomes effective at such time and upon such conditions as the Administrator by order determines. If no proceeding is pending or instituted and withdrawal automatically becomes effective, the Administrator may nevertheless institute a revocation or suspension proceeding under G.S. 78A-39(a)(2)b within one year after withdrawal became effective and enter a revocation or suspension order as of the last date on which registration was effective.

(f) No order may be entered under any part of this section except the first sentence of subsection (c) without (i) appropriate prior notice to the applicant or registrant (as well as the employer or prospective employer if the applicant or registrant is a salesman), (ii) opportunity for hearing, and (iii) written findings of fact and conclusions of law. (1925, c. 190, s. 19; 1927, c. 149, s. 19; 1955, c. 436, s. 9; 1959, c. 1122; 1971, c. 831, s. 1; 1973, c. 1380; 1983, c. 817, ss. 11-15; 1997-456, s. 27; 1997-462, ss. 1, 2; 2001-126, s. 3.)

§ 78A-40. Alternative methods of registration.

(a) The Administrator may by rule or order provide an alternative method of registration by which any dealer or salesman acting in that capacity or as a principal may satisfy the requirements of this Article by furnishing the information otherwise required to be filed pursuant to this Article. The Administrator may provide for, among other things, alternative filing periods for dealers or salesmen, elimination of the issuance of a paper license and alternative methods for the payment and collection of initial or renewal filing fees, which shall be known as "alternative filing fees". The alternative filing fees shall be the same as provided in G.S. 78A-37(b).

(b) The Administrator may not adopt an alternative method of registration unless its purpose is to facilitate a central registration depository whereby dealers or salesmen can centrally or simultaneously register and pay fees for all states in which they plan to transact business that require registration. The Administrator may enter into an agreement with or otherwise facilitate an alternative method of registration with any national securities association registered with the Securities and Exchange Commission pursuant to Section 15A of the Securities Exchange Act of 1934, any national securities exchange registered under the Securities Exchange Act of 1934, or any national association of state securities Administrators or similar association to effectuate the provisions of this section.

(c) Nothing in this section shall be construed to prevent the exercise of the authority of the Administrator as provided in G.S. 78A-39. (1981, c. 624, s. 5; 1983, c. 817, s. 16; 1987, c. 849, s. 3.)

§§ 78A-41 through 78A-44. Reserved for future codification purposes.

Article 6.

Administration and Review.

§ 78A-45. Administration of Chapter.

(a) This Chapter shall be administered by the Secretary of State. The Secretary of State as Administrator may delegate all or part of the authority under this Chapter to the Deputy Securities Administrator including, but not limited to, the authority to conduct hearings, make, execute and issue final agency orders and decisions. The Secretary of State may appoint such clerks and other assistants as may from time to time be needed. The Secretary of State may designate one or more hearing officers for the purpose of conducting administrative hearings.

(b) It is unlawful for the Administrator or any of his officers or employees to use for personal benefit any information which is filed with or obtained by the Administrator and which is not made public. No provision of this Chapter authorizes the Administrator or any of his officers or employees to disclose any such information except among themselves or when necessary or appropriate in a proceeding or investigation under this Chapter. No provision of this Chapter either creates or derogates from any privilege which exists at common law or otherwise when documentary or other evidence is sought under a subpoena directed to the Administrator or any of his officers or employees.

(c) All fees provided for under this Chapter shall be collected by the Administrator and shall be paid over to the State Treasurer to go into the general fund. (1925, c. 190, ss. 20, 21; 1927, c. 149, ss. 20, 21; 1973, c. 1380; 1983, c. 817, s. 17; 2001-126, s. 9.)

§ 78A-46. Investigations and subpoenas.

(a) The Administrator in his discretion

(1) May make any investigation within or outside of this State as the Administrator deems necessary to determine whether any person has violated or is about to violate any provision of this Chapter or any rule or order hereunder, or to aid in the enforcement of this Chapter or in the prescribing of rules and forms hereunder,

(2) May require or permit any person to file a statement in writing, under oath or otherwise as the Administrator determines, as to all the facts and circumstances concerning the matter to be investigated,

(3) May publish information concerning any violation of this Chapter or any rule or order hereunder, and

(4) May appoint employees of the Securities Division as securities law enforcement agents and as other enforcement personnel.

a. Subject matter jurisdiction - The responsibility of an agent shall be enforcement of this Chapter and Chapters 78C and 78D of the General Statutes.

b. Territorial jurisdiction - A securities law enforcement agent is a State officer with jurisdiction throughout the State.

c. Service of orders of the Administrator - Securities law enforcement agents may serve and execute notices, orders, or demands issued by the Administrator for the surrender of registrations or relating to any administrative proceeding. While serving and executing such notices, orders, or demands, securities law enforcement agents shall have all the power and authority possessed by a law enforcement officer.

(b) For the purpose of any investigation or proceeding under this Chapter, the Administrator or any officer designated by him may administer oaths and affirmations, subpoena witnesses, compel their attendance, take evidence and require the production of any books, papers, correspondence, memoranda, agreements, or other documents or records which the Administrator deems relevant or material to the inquiry.

(c)   In case of contumacy by, or refusal to obey a subpoena issued to any person, any court of competent jurisdiction, upon application by the Administrator, may issue to the person an order requiring him to appear before the Administrator, or the officer designated by him, there to produce documentary evidence if so ordered or to give evidence touching the matter under investigation or in question. Failure to obey the order of the court may be punished by the court as a contempt of court.

(d)   Repealed by Session Laws 1977, c. 610, s. 2.

(e)   The Administrator may act under subsection (b) or apply under subsection (c) to enforce subpoenas in this State at the request of a securities agency or administrator of any state if the alleged activities constituting a violation for which the information is sought would be a violation of this Chapter or any rule hereunder if the alleged activities had occurred in this State. (1925, c. 190, s. 16; 1927, c. 149, s. 16; 1973, c. 1380; 1977, c. 610, s. 2; 1987, c. 849, s. 4; 1991, c. 456, s. 2; 1997-462, s. 3.)

§ 78A-47. Injunctions; cease and desist orders.

(a)   Whenever it appears to the Administrator that any person has engaged or is about to engage in any act or practice constituting a violation of any provision of this Chapter or any rule or order hereunder, he may in his discretion bring an action in any court of competent jurisdiction to enjoin the acts or practices and to enforce compliance with this Chapter or any rule or order hereunder. Upon a proper showing a permanent or temporary injunction, restraining order, or writ of mandamus shall be granted and a receiver or conservator may be appointed for the defendant or the defendant's assets. In addition to any other remedies provided by this Chapter, the Administrator may apply to the court hearing this matter for an order of restitution whereby the defendant in such action shall be ordered to make restitution of those sums shown by the Administrator to have been obtained by him in violation of any of the provisions of this Chapter. Such restitution shall be payable, in the discretion of the court, to the Administrator or receiver appointed pursuant to this section for the benefit of those persons whose assets were obtained in violation of this Chapter, or directly to those persons. The court may not require the Administrator to post a bond.

(b)   (1)   If the Administrator determines after giving notice of and opportunity for a hearing, that any person has engaged in or is about to engage in, any act or practice constituting a violation of any provision of this Chapter or any rule or order hereunder, he may order such person to cease and desist from such unlawful act or practice and take such affirmative action as in the judgment of the Administrator will carry out the purposes of this Chapter.

(2)   If the Administrator makes written findings of fact that the public interest will be irreparably harmed by delay in issuing an order under G.S. 78A-47(b)(1), the Administrator may issue a temporary cease and desist order. Upon the entry of a temporary cease and desist order, the Administrator shall promptly notify in writing the person subject to the order that such order has been entered, the reasons therefor, and that within 20 days after the receipt of a written request from such person the matter shall be scheduled for hearing in accordance with Chapter 150B of the General Statutes to determine whether or not the order shall become permanent and final. If no request for a hearing, other responsive pleading, or submission is received by the Administrator within 30 business days of receipt of service of notice of the order upon the person subject to the order and no hearing is ordered by the Administrator, the order shall become final and remain in effect unless it is modified or vacated by the Administrator. If a hearing is requested or ordered, the Administrator, after giving notice of an opportunity for a hearing to the person subject to the order, shall by written findings of fact and conclusion of law, vacate, modify, or make permanent the order.

(3)   No order under subsection (b), except an order issued pursuant to G.S. 78A-47(b)(2), may be entered without prior notice of an opportunity for hearing. The Administrator may vacate or modify an order under this subsection (b) upon his finding that the conditions which required such an order have changed and that it is in the public interest to so vacate or modify.

(4)   A final order issued pursuant to the provisions of subsection (b) shall be subject to review as provided in G.S. 78A-48.

(c)   The Administrator may issue an order against an applicant, registered person, or other person who willfully violates this Chapter or a rule or order of the Administrator under this Chapter:

(1)   Imposing a civil penalty of up to two thousand five hundred dollars ($2,500) for a single violation or of up to twenty-five thousand dollars ($25,000)

for multiple violations in a single proceeding or a series of related proceedings; and

(2)   Requiring reimbursement of the costs of investigation.

The clear proceeds of civil penalties imposed under this subsection shall be remitted to the Civil Penalty and Forfeiture Fund in accordance with G.S. 115C-457.2. Any reimbursement imposed under this subsection shall be paid into the General Fund. No order under this subsection may be entered without prior notice and an opportunity for a hearing conducted pursuant to Article 3 of Chapter 150B of the General Statutes. (1925, c. 190, s. 16; 1927, c. 149, s. 16; 1973, c. 1380; 1983, c. 817, s. 18; 1991, c. 456, ss. 3, 4; 1997-462, s. 4; 1998-215, s. 120; 2001-126, s. 4.)

§ 78A-48. Judicial review of orders.

(a)   Any person aggrieved by a final order of the Administrator may obtain a review of the order in the Superior Court of Wake County by filing in court, within 30 days after a written copy of the decision is served upon the person by personal service or by registered or certified mail, a written petition praying that the order be modified or set aside in whole or in part. A copy of the petition shall be forthwith served upon the Administrator, and thereupon the Administrator shall certify and file in court a copy of the filing and evidence upon which the order was entered. When these have been filed, the court has exclusive jurisdiction to affirm, modify, enforce, or set aside the order, in whole or in part. The findings of the Administrator as to the facts, if supported by competent, material and substantial evidence, are conclusive. If either party applies to the court for leave to adduce additional material evidence, and shows to the satisfaction of the court that there were reasonable grounds for failure to adduce the evidence in the hearings before the Administrator, the court may order the additional evidence to be taken before the Administrator and to be adduced upon the hearing in such manner and upon such conditions as the court considers proper. The Administrator may modify his findings and order by reason of the additional evidence and shall file in court the additional evidence together with any modified or new findings or order. The judgment of the court is final, subject to review by the Court of Appeals.

(b)   The commencement of proceedings under subsection (a) does not, unless specifically ordered by the court, operate as a stay of the Administrator's order. (1925, c. 190, s. 18; 1927, c. 149, s. 18; 1973, c. 1380; 1977, c. 610, s. 3; 1983, c. 817, s. 19; 1987, c. 849, s. 5.)

§ 78A-49. Rules, forms, orders, and hearings.

(a)   The Administrator may from time to time make, amend, and rescind such rules, forms, and orders as are necessary to carry out the provisions of this Chapter, including rules and forms governing registration statements, applications, and reports, and defining any terms, whether or not used in this Chapter, insofar as the definitions are not inconsistent with the provisions of this Chapter. For the purpose of rules and forms the Administrator may classify securities, persons, and matters within his jurisdiction, and prescribe different requirements for different classes. In order to protect the investing public, the Administrator may by rule or order prescribe suitability standards for investments in viatical settlement contracts.

(b)   No rule, form, or order may be made, amended, or rescinded unless the Administrator finds that the action is necessary or appropriate in the public interest or for the protection of investors and consistent with the purposes fairly intended by the policy and provisions of this Chapter. In prescribing rules and forms the Administrator may cooperate with the securities administrators of the other states and the Securities and Exchange Commission with a view to effectuating the policy of this statute to achieve maximum uniformity in the form and content of registration statements, applications, and reports wherever practicable.

(c)   The Administrator may by rule or order prescribe (i) the form and content of financial statements required under this Chapter, (ii) the circumstances under which consolidated financial statements shall be filed, and (iii) whether any required financial statements shall be certified by independent or certified public accountants. All financial statements required to be filed with the Administrator shall be audited and shall be prepared in accordance with generally accepted accounting principles, except where the Administrator may by rule or order provide otherwise. In determining whether to permit the filing of financial statements that have not been audited, the Administrator shall consider all of the following factors:

(1)   Whether lesser standards for financial statements will impair investor protection.

(2)   The cost of preparation of audited financial statements relative to the proposed offering amount.

(3)   Whether recently audited financial statements of the issuer are available in addition to current interim statements.

(4)   Whether the issuer has commenced significant business operations.

(5)   Any other factors that are relevant to the protection of the investing public.

(d)   The Administrator may by rule or order require the filing of any prospectus, pamphlet, circular, form letter, advertisement, or other sales literature or advertising communication addressed or intended for distribution to prospective investors, unless the security or transaction is exempted by G.S. 78A-16 or 78A-17 (except 78A-17(9), (17), and (19)) and such exemption has not been denied or revoked under G.S. 78A-18 or the security is a security covered under federal law or the transaction is with respect to a security covered under federal law.

(e)   All rules and forms of the Administrator shall be published.

(f)   No provision of this Chapter imposing any liability applies to any act done or omitted in good faith in conformity with any rule, form, or order of the Administrator, notwithstanding that the rule, form, or order may later be amended or rescinded or be determined by judicial or other authority to be invalid for any reason.

(g)   Every hearing in an administrative proceeding shall be public unless the Administrator in his discretion grants a request joined in by all the respondents that the hearing be conducted privately. (1925, c. 190, s. 11; 1927, c. 149, s. 11; 1973, c. 1380; 1987, c. 849, s. 6; 1997-419, s. 11; 2001-436, s. 10; 2003-413, s. 4.)

§ 78A-50.   Administrative files and opinions.

(a)   A document is filed when it is received by the Administrator.

(b) The Administrator shall keep a register of all applications for registration and registration statements which are or have been effective under this Chapter and all denial, suspension, or revocation orders which have been entered under this Chapter. The register shall be open for public inspection.

(c) The information contained in or filed with any registration statement, application, or report may be made available to the public under such rules as the Administrator prescribes.

(c1) The files and records of the Administrator relating to criminal investigations and enforcement proceedings undertaken pursuant to this Chapter are subject to the provisions of G.S. 132-1.4.

(c2) The files and records of the Administrator relating to noncriminal investigations and enforcement proceedings undertaken pursuant to this Chapter shall not be subject to inspection and examination pursuant to G.S. 132-6 until the investigations and proceedings are completed and cease to be active.

(c3) Any information obtained by the Administrator from any law enforcement agency, administrative agency, or regulatory organization on a confidential or otherwise restricted basis in the course of an investigation or proceeding undertaken pursuant to this Chapter shall be confidential and exempt from G.S 132-6 to the same extent that it is confidential in the possession of the providing agency or organization.

(d) Upon request and at such reasonable charges as the administrator prescribes, the Administrator shall furnish to any person photostatic or other copies (certified under the seal of office if requested) of any entry in the register or any document which is a matter of public record. In any proceeding or prosecution under this Chapter, any copy so certified is prima facie evidence of the contents of the entry or document certified.

(e) The Administrator may honor requests from interested persons for interpretative opinions. When an exemption is claimed in writing, cites the section relied upon, and is considered eligible upon the showing made, a "no action" letter will be furnished upon request and upon the payment of a fee of one hundred fifty dollars ($150.00). (1925, c. 190, s. 17; 1927, c. 149, s. 17; 1955, c. 436, s. 8; 1973, c. 1380; 1979, 2nd Sess., c. 1148, s. 3; 1987, c. 566, s. 2; 1997-462, s. 5.)

§§ 78A-51 through 78A-55. Reserved for future codification purposes.

Article 7.

Civil Liabilities and Criminal Penalties.

§ 78A-56. Civil liabilities.

(a) Any person who:

(1) Offers or sells a security in violation of G.S. 78A-8(1), 78A-8(3), 78A-10(b), 78A-13, 78A-14, 78A-24, or 78A-36(a), or of any rule or order under G.S. 78A-49(d) which requires the affirmative approval of sales literature before it is used, or of any condition imposed under G.S. 78A-27(d) or 78A-28(g), or

(2) Offers or sells a security by means of any untrue statement of a material fact or any omission to state a material fact necessary in order to make the statements made, in the light of the circumstances under which they were made, not misleading (the purchaser not knowing of the untruth or omission), and who does not sustain the burden of proof that he did not know, and in the exercise of reasonable care could not have known, of the untruth or omission,

is liable to the person purchasing the security from him, who may sue either at law or in equity to recover the consideration paid for the security, together with interest at the legal rate from the date of payment, costs, and reasonable attorneys' fees, less the amount of any income received on the security, upon the tender of the security, or for damages if the purchaser no longer owns the security. Damages are the amount that would be recoverable upon a tender less the value of the security when the purchaser disposed of it and interest at the legal rate as provided by G.S. 24-1 from the date of disposition.

(b) Any person who purchases a security by means of any untrue statement of a material fact or any omission to state a material fact necessary in order to make the statements made, in the light of the circumstances under which they are made, not misleading (the seller not knowing of the untruth or omission), and who does not sustain the burden of proof that the person did not know, and in the exercise of reasonable care could not have known, of the untruth or omission, shall be liable to the person selling the security to him, who may sue either at law or in equity to recover the security, plus any income received by the purchaser thereon, upon tender of the consideration received, or for damages if the purchaser no longer owns the security. Damages are the excess of the value of the security when the purchaser disposed of it, plus interest at the legal rate as provided by G.S. 24-1 from the date of disposition, over the consideration paid for the security.

(b1) A person who willfully violates G.S. 78A-12 is liable to a person who purchases or sells a security, other than a security traded on a national securities exchange or quoted on a national automated quotation system administered by a self-regulatory organization, at a price that was affected by the act or transaction for the damages sustained as a result of the act or transaction. Damages are the difference between the price at which the securities were purchased or sold and the value the securities would have had at the time of the person's purchase or sale in the absence of the act or transaction, plus interest at the legal rate as provided by G.S. 24-1 from the date of the purchase or sale, costs, and reasonable attorneys' fees determined by the court.

(c) (1) Every person who directly or indirectly controls a person liable under subsection (a), (b), or (b1) of this section, every partner, officer, or director of the person, every person occupying a similar status or performing similar functions, and every dealer or salesman who materially aids in the sale is also liable jointly and severally with and to the same extent as the person, unless able to sustain the burden of proof that the person did not know, and in the exercise of reasonable care could not have known, of the existence of the facts by reason of which the liability is alleged to exist.

(2) Unless liable under subdivision (1) of this subsection, every employee of a person liable under subsection (a), (b), or (b1) of this section who materially aids in the transaction giving rise to the liability and every other person who materially aids in the transaction giving rise to the liability is also liable jointly and severally with and to the same extent as the person if the employee or other person actually knew of the existence of the facts by reason of which the liability is alleged to exist.

(3) There is contribution among the several persons liable under subdivisions (1) and (2) of this subsection as provided among tort-feasors pursuant to Chapter 1B of the General Statutes.

(d) Any tender specified in this section may be made at any time before entry of judgment. Tender shall require only notice of willingness to exchange the security for the amount specified. Any notice may be given by service as in civil actions or by certified mail addressed to the last known address of the person liable.

(e) Every cause of action under this statute survives the death of any person who might have been a plaintiff or defendant.

(f) No person may sue under this section for a violation of G.S. 78A-24 or G.S. 78A-36 more than two years after the sale or contract of sale.

No person may sue under this section for any other violation of this Chapter more than three years after the person discovers facts constituting the violation, but in any case no later than five years after the sale or contract of sale, except that if a person who may be liable under this section engages in any fraudulent or deceitful act that conceals the violation or induces the person to forgo or postpone commencing an action based upon the violation, the suit may be commenced not later than three years after the person discovers or should have discovered that the act was fraudulent or deceitful.

(g) (1) No purchaser may sue under this section if, before suit is commenced, the purchaser has received a written offer stating the respect in which liability under this section may have arisen and fairly advising the purchaser of his rights; offering to repurchase the security for cash payable on delivery of the security equal to the consideration paid, together with interest at the legal rate as provided by G.S. 24-1 from the date of payment, less the amount of any income received on the security or, if the purchaser no longer owns the security, offering to pay the purchaser upon acceptance of the offer an amount in cash equal to the damages computed in accordance with subsection (a); and stating that the offer may be accepted by the purchaser at any time within 30 days of its receipt; and the purchaser has failed to accept such offer in writing within the specified period.

(2) No seller may sue under this section if, before suit is commenced, the seller has received a written offer stating the respect in which liability under this section may have arisen and fairly advising the seller of his rights; offering to return the security plus the amount of any income received thereon upon payment of the consideration received, or, if the purchaser no longer owns the security, offering to pay the seller upon acceptance of the offer an amount in cash equal to the damages computed in accordance with subsection (b); and providing that the offer may be accepted by the seller at any time within 30 days

of its receipt; and the seller has failed to accept such offer in writing within the specified period.

(3) Offers shall be in the form and contain the information the Administrator by rule prescribes. Every offer under subsection (g) of this section shall be delivered to the offeree or sent by certified mail addressed to the offeree at the offeree's last known address. The person making the offer shall file a copy of the rescission offer with the Administrator at least 10 days before delivering the offer to the offeree. If an offer is not performed in accordance with its terms, suit by the offeree under this section shall be permitted without regard to this subsection.

(h) No person who has made or engaged in the performance of any contract in violation of any provision of this Chapter or any rule or order hereunder, or who has acquired any purported right under any such contract with knowledge of the facts by reason of which its making or performance was in violation, may base any suit on the contract.

(i) Any condition, stipulation, or provision binding any person acquiring any security to waive compliance with any provision of this Chapter or any rule or order hereunder is void.

(j) The rights and remedies provided by this Chapter are in addition to any other rights or remedies that may exist at law or in equity, but this Chapter does not create any cause of action not specified in this section or G.S. 78A-37(d). If the requirements of Chapter 1D of the General Statutes are met, punitive damages are available to the extent provided in that Chapter.

(k) The purchaser of a viatical settlement contract may rescind or cancel the purchase agreement for any reason by providing written notice of rescission or cancellation to the issuer or the issuer's agent, by certified mail, return receipt requested, within 10 business days after each of the following: (i) the date on which the purchase agreement for the viatical settlement contract is signed by the purchaser, and (ii) the date of actual notice to the purchaser of the assignment, transfer, or sale of all or a portion of an insurance policy on which the viatical settlement contract is based. Notice of rescission is effective upon deposit in the United States mail. The notice of rescission need not take a particular form and is sufficient if it expresses the intention of the purchaser to rescind the transaction. For purposes of this subsection and subsection (k1) of this section only, the rescission period of 10 business days following the purchaser's signing of the purchase agreement shall also be known as the "initial 10-day rescission period."

(k1) Immediately upon receipt of any consideration by an issuer or its agent pursuant to a viatical settlement purchase agreement, the issuer or its agent shall deliver the consideration to a domestic independent escrow agent. For purposes of this section, "domestic independent escrow agent" means an escrow agent, located in this State, and not affiliated with the issuer, its affiliate, its officers or directors, or its promoter, or any agents thereof. The domestic independent escrow agent shall maintain the funds received, in their entirety, in an escrow account or trust account located in this State, for the initial 10-day rescission period following the signing of the purchase agreement, as provided in subsection (k) of this section, unless the domestic independent escrow agent, prior to the completion of the initial 10-day rescission period, receives notice of the purchaser's cancellation or rescission of the purchase agreement in accordance with this section. If the purchase agreement is rescinded or cancelled within the initial 10-day rescission period, the domestic independent escrow agent shall immediately deliver the funds, in their entirety along with any interest earned on the funds during the time in which the funds were held in escrow, to the purchaser upon receiving notice, by certified mail, from the issuer or its agent that the purchase agreement has been rescinded or cancelled by the purchaser. If the purchase agreement has not been rescinded or cancelled within the initial 10-day rescission period, the domestic independent escrow agent shall release the funds to the issuer or its agent in a manner to be determined by agreement between the issuer and the domestic independent escrow agent. Until the funds become available for release by the domestic independent escrow agent to the issuer upon the expiration of the initial 10-day rescission period without rescission or cancellation by the purchaser, the funds are not subject to claims by creditors of the issuer, its affiliates, or associates.

(l) Within 90 days after the sale or execution of a contract of sale for an investment of funds intended to be used to purchase a viatical settlement contract or contracts, the seller shall provide the purchaser with a rescission offer in accordance with rules prescribed by the Administrator, if, within that period, there has not been the identification of each and every viatical settlement contract acceptable to the purchaser which has been or shall be purchased for the investment. The purchaser may accept the rescission offer within 10 business days after receiving it. Acceptance of the rescission offer is effective upon compliance by the purchaser with the procedural requirements for notice of rescission or cancellation by a viatical settlement purchaser set forth in subsection (k) of this section. The seller shall keep a record of the rescission offer and its acceptance or rejection for at least three years after providing that offer and shall provide that record to the Administrator at the Administrator's request. For purposes of this subsection only, "purchaser" means a person who executes a contract of sale, with a seller, for an investment of funds to be used to purchase a viatical settlement contract or viatical settlement contracts when, at the time of execution of the contract, each and every viatical settlement contract to be purchased pursuant to the investment has not been identified. (1925, c. 190, s. 23; 1927, c. 149, s. 23; 1955, c. 436, s. 10; 1971, c. 572, s. 2; 1973, c. 1380; 1975, c. 19, s. 22; c. 144, s. 3; 1977, c. 781, s. 2; 1983, c. 817, ss. 20, 21; 1987, c. 282, s. 9; 1991, c. 456, s. 5; 2001-183, s. 1; 2001-436, s. 11; 2003-413, ss. 5-10.)

§ 78A-57. Criminal penalties.

(a) Any person who willfully violates any provision of this Chapter except G.S. 78A-8, 78A-9, 78A-11, 78A-12, 78A-13, or 78A-14 is guilty of a Class I felony.

(a1) Any person who willfully violates any rule or order under this Chapter is guilty of a Class I felony. No person may be imprisoned for the violation of any rule if the person proves that the person had no knowledge of the rule. It is an affirmative defense to a charge of violating an order under this Chapter that the person had no knowledge of the order.

(a2) Any person who willfully violates G.S. 78A-8, 78A-11, 78A-13, or 78A-14 is guilty of a felony. If the losses caused by a single act or a series of related acts in a common scheme or plan are one hundred thousand dollars ($100,000) or more, the person is guilty of a Class C felony. If the losses caused by a single act or a series of related acts in a common scheme or plan are less than one hundred thousand dollars ($100,000), the person is guilty of a Class H felony.

(a3) Any person who willfully violates G.S. 78A-9 knowing the statement made to be false or misleading in any material respect is guilty of a Class H felony. Any other willful violation of G.S. 78A-9 constitutes a Class 2 misdemeanor.

(a4) Any person who willfully violates G.S. 78A-12 is guilty of a Class H felony.

(b) The Administrator may refer such evidence as is available concerning violations of this Chapter or of any rule or order hereunder to the proper district attorney, who may, with or without such a reference, institute the appropriate criminal proceedings under this Chapter. Upon receipt of a reference, the district attorney may request that a duly employed attorney of the Administrator prosecute or assist in the prosecution of the violation or violations on behalf of the State. Upon approval of the Administrator, the employee may be appointed a special prosecutor for the district attorney to prosecute or assist in the prosecution of the violations without receiving compensation from the district attorney. Such a special prosecutor shall have all the powers and duties prescribed by law for district attorneys and such other powers and duties as are lawfully delegated to the special prosecutor by the district attorney for violations of this Chapter.

(c) Nothing in this Chapter limits the power of the State to punish any person for any conduct which constitutes a crime by statute or at common law. (1925, c. 190, s. 23; 1927, c. 149, s. 23; 1955, c. 436, s. 10; 1971, c. 572, s. 2; 1973, c. 47, s. 2; c. 1380; 1987, c. 849, s. 7; 1991, c. 456, s. 6; 2001-436, s. 12; 2003-413, s. 11.)

§ 78A-58. Obstruction of investigation.

A person is guilty of a Class H felony if the person willfully does any of the following for the purpose of interfering with the performance of any audit, examination, or investigation by the Administrator under this Chapter:

(1) Makes or causes to be made to the Administrator or the Administrator's designated representative any false or misleading oral or written statement.

(2) Creates, causes to be made, or delivers any record, report, or document knowing that it is false or misleading in any material respect.

(3) Destroys or alters any record, report, or document.

(4) Conceals or secretes any record, report, or document. (2003-413, s. 12.)

§§ 78A-59 through 78A-62. Reserved for future codification purposes.

Article 8.

Miscellaneous Provisions.

§ 78A-63. Scope of the Chapter; service of process.

(a) G.S. 78A-8, 78A-10, 78A-13, 78A-14, 78A-24, 78A-31, 78A-36(a), and 78A-56 apply to persons who sell or offer to sell when (i) an offer to sell is made in this State, or (ii) an offer to buy is made and accepted in this State.

(b) G.S. 78A-8, 78A-10, 78A-36(a) and 78A-56(b) apply to persons who buy or offer to buy when (i) an offer to buy is made in this State, or (ii) an offer to sell is made and accepted in this State.

(b1) G.S. 78A-12 applies when any act instrumental to effecting prohibited conduct is done in this State.

(c) For the purpose of this section, an offer to sell or to buy is made in this State, whether or not either party is then present in this State, when the offer (i) originates from this State or (ii) is directed by the offeror to this State and received at the place to which it is directed (or at any post office in this State in the case of a mailed offer).

(d) For the purpose of this section, an offer to buy or to sell is accepted in this State when acceptance (i) is communicated to the offeror in this State and (ii) has not previously been communicated to the offeror, orally, or in writing, outside this State; and acceptance is communicated to the offeror in this State, whether or not either party is then present in this State when the offeree directs it to the offeror in this State reasonably believing the offeror to be in this State and it is received at the place to which it is directed (or at any post office in this State in the case of a mailed acceptance).

(e) An offer to sell or to buy is not made in this State when (i) the publisher circulates or there is circulated on his behalf in this State any bona fide newspaper or other publication of general, regular, and paid circulation which is not published in this State, or which is published in this State but has had more than two thirds of its circulation outside this State during the past 12 months, or

(ii) a radio or television program originating outside this State is received in this State.

(f) Every applicant for registration under this Chapter and every issuer who proposes to offer a security in this State through any person acting on an agency basis in the common-law sense shall file with the Administrator, in such form as he by rule prescribes, an irrevocable consent appointing the Administrator or his successor in office to be his attorney to receive service of any lawful process in any noncriminal suit, action or proceeding against him or his successor, executor or administrator which arises under this Chapter or any rule or order hereunder after the consent has been filed, with the same force and validity as if served personally on the person filing the consent. A person who has filed such a consent in connection with a previous registration or notice filing need not file another. Service may be made by leaving a copy of the process in the office of the Administrator, but it is not effective unless (i) the plaintiff, who may be the Administrator in a suit, action, or proceeding instituted by him, forthwith sends notice of the service and a copy of the process by registered mail to the defendant or respondent at his address on file with the Administrator, and (ii) the plaintiff's affidavit of compliance with the subsection is filed in the case on or before the return day of the process, if any, or within such further time as the court allows.

(g) When any person, including any nonresident of this State, engages in conduct prohibited or made actionable by this Chapter or any rule or order hereunder, and he has not filed a consent to service of process under subsection (f) and personal jurisdiction over him cannot otherwise be obtained in this State, that conduct shall be considered equivalent to his appointment of the Administrator or his successor in office to be his attorney to receive service of any lawful process in any noncriminal suit, action, or proceeding against him or his successor executor or administrator which grows out of that conduct and which is brought under this Chapter or any rule or order hereunder with the same force and validity as if served on him personally. Service may be made by leaving a copy of the process in the office of the Administrator, and it is not effective unless (i) the plaintiff, who may be the Administrator in a suit, action, or proceeding instituted by him, forthwith sends notice of the service and a copy of the process by registered mail to the defendant or respondent at his last known address or takes other steps which are reasonably calculated to give actual notice, and (ii) the plaintiff's affidavit of compliance with this subsection is filed in the case on or before the return day of the process, if any, or within such further time as the court allows.

(h) When process is served under this section, the court, or the Administrator in a proceeding before him, shall order such continuance as may be necessary to afford the defendant or respondent reasonable opportunity to defend.

(i) Interest charged by a broker or dealer registered under the Securities Exchange Act of 1934, as amended, or registered under this Chapter, as now or hereafter amended, on a debit balance in an account for a customer, shall be exempt from the provisions of Chapter 24 of the North Carolina General Statutes if such debit balance is payable at will without penalty and is secured by securities as defined in G.S. 25-8-102. (1927, c. 149, s. 24; 1955, c. 436, s. 10; 1973, c. 1380; 1975, c. 144, s. 4; 1997-181, s. 27; 1997-419, ss. 12, 13; 2001-436, s. 13; 2003-413, ss. 13-15.)

§ 78A-64. Statutory policy.

This Chapter shall be so construed as to effectuate its general purpose to make uniform the law of those states which enact it and to coordinate the interpretation and administration of this Chapter with the related federal regulation. (1973, c. 1380.)

§ 78A-65. Repeal and saving provisions.

(a) The Securities Law of the State of North Carolina, G.S. 78-1 through 78-25, is repealed except as saved in this section.

(b) Prior law exclusively governs all suits, actions, prosecution, or proceedings which are pending or may be initiated on the basis of facts or circumstances occurring before April 1, 1975, except that no civil suit or action may be maintained to enforce any liability under prior law unless brought within any period of limitation which applied when the cause of action accrued and in any event within two years after April 1, 1975.

(c) All effective registrations under prior law, all administrative orders relating to such registrations, and all conditions imposed upon such registrations remain in effect so long as they would have remained in effect if this Chapter had not been passed. They are considered to have been filed, entered, or imposed under this Chapter, but are governed by prior law.

(d) Prior law applies in respect to any offer or sale made within one year after the effective date of this Chapter pursuant to an offering begun in good faith before April 1, 1975, on the basis of an exemption available under prior law.

(e) Judicial review of all administrative orders as to which review proceedings have not been instituted by April 1, 1975, are governed by G.S. 78A-48, except that no review proceeding may be instituted unless the petition is filed within any period of limitation which applied to a review proceeding when the order was entered and in any event within 60 days after April 1, 1975. (1973, c. 1380.)

§ 78A-66. Jurisdictional limitations.

Nothing in this Chapter affects the Viatical Settlements Act or the jurisdiction of the North Carolina Department of Insurance. (2001-436, s. 14.)

Chapter 78B.

Tender Offer Disclosure Act.

§§ 78B-1 through 78B-11: Repealed by Session Laws 2001-201, s. 1, effective October 1, 2001.

Chapter 78C.

Investment Advisers.

Article 1.

Title and Definitions.

§ 78C-1. Title.

This Chapter shall be known and may be cited as the North Carolina Investment Advisers Act. (1987 (Reg. Sess., 1988), c. 1098, s. 1.)

§ 78C-2. Definitions.

When used in this Chapter, the definitions of G.S. 78A-2 shall apply along with the following, unless the context otherwise requires:

(1) "Investment adviser" means any person who, for compensation, engages in the business of advising others, either directly or through publications or writings, as to the value of securities or as to the advisability of investing in, purchasing, or selling securities, or who, for compensation and as part of a regular business, issues or promulgates analyses or reports concerning securities. "Investment adviser" also includes financial planners and other persons who, as an integral component of other financially related services, provide the foregoing investment advisory services to others for compensation and as a part of a business or who hold themselves out as providing the foregoing investment advisory services to others for compensation. "Investment adviser" does not include:

a. An investment adviser representative or a person excluded from the definition of investment adviser representative pursuant to G.S. 78C-2(3)c.

b. A bank, savings institution, or trust company.

c. A lawyer, accountant, engineer, or teacher whose performance of any such services is solely incidental to the practice of his profession.

d. A dealer or its salesman whose performance of these services is solely incidental to the conduct of its business as a dealer and who receives no special compensation for them.

e. A publisher of any newspaper, news column, newsletter, news magazine, or business or financial publication or service, whether communicated in hard copy form, or by electronic means, or otherwise, that does not consist of the rendering of advice on the basis of the specific investment situation of each client.

f. A person solely by virtue of such person's services to or on behalf of any "business development company" as defined in Section 202(a)(22) of the Investment Advisers Act of 1940 provided the business development company is not an "investment company" by reason of Section 3(c)(1) of the Investment Company Act of 1940, as both acts were in effect on June 1, 1988.

g. A personal representative of a decedent's estate, guardian, conservator, receiver, attorney in fact, trustee in bankruptcy, trustee of a testamentary trust, or a trustee of an inter vivos trust, not otherwise engaged in providing investment advisory services, and the performance of these services is not a part of a plan or scheme to evade registration or the substantive requirements of this Chapter.

h. A licensed real estate agent or broker whose only compensation is a commission on real estate sold.

i. An individual or company primarily engaged in acting as a business broker whose only compensation is a commission on the sale of a business.

j. An individual who, as an employee, officer or director of, or general partner in, another person and in the course of performance of his duties as such, provides investment advice to such other person, or to entities that are affiliates of such other person, or to employee benefit plans of such other person or its affiliated entities, or, with respect to such employee benefit plans, to employees of such other person or its affiliated entities.

k. Any person excepted from the definition of investment adviser under the Investment Advisers Act of 1940 or any rule or regulation promulgated under that act.

l. An employee of a person described in subdivision b., e., f., g., h., or j. of G.S. 78C-2(1) acting on behalf of such person within the scope of his employment.

l1. An investment adviser who is covered under federal law as defined in subdivision (4) of this section.

m. Such other persons not within the intent of this subsection as the Administrator may by rule or order designate.

(2) "Investment Advisers Act of 1940" means the federal statute of that name as amended before or after the effective date of this Chapter.

(3) "Investment adviser representative" means, with respect to any investment adviser registered under this Chapter, any partner, officer, director (or a person occupying a similar status or performing similar functions) or other individual employed by or associated with an investment adviser, except clerical or ministerial personnel, who:

a. Makes any recommendations or otherwise renders advice regarding securities directly to clients,

b. Manages accounts or portfolios of clients,

c. Determines which recommendations or advice regarding securities should be given; provided, however if there are more than five such persons employed by or associated with an investment adviser, who do not otherwise come within the meaning of G.S. 78C-2(3) a., b., d., or e., then only the direct supervisors of such persons are deemed to be investment adviser representatives under G.S. 78C-2(3) c.,

d. Solicits, offers or negotiates for the sale of or sells investment advisory services, unless such person is a dealer or salesman registered under Chapter 78A of the General Statutes and the person would not be an investment adviser representative except for the performance of the activities described in G.S. 78C-2(3) d., or

e. Directly supervises investment adviser representatives as defined in G.S. 78C-2(3) a., b., c. (unless such investment adviser representatives are already required to register due to their role as supervisors by operation of G.S. 78C-2(3) c.), or d. in the performance of the foregoing activities.

Notwithstanding this subdivision, the term "investment adviser representative" as used in this Chapter and as applied to a person who is employed by, or associated with, an investment adviser covered under federal law only includes an individual who (i) has a "place of business" in the State, as that term is defined in rules or regulations adopted or promulgated under section 203A of the Investment Advisers Act of 1940 by the United States Securities and Exchange Commission and (ii) either:

a. Is an "investment adviser representative" as that term is defined in rules or regulations adopted or promulgated under section 203A of the Investment Advisers Act of 1940 by the United States Securities and Exchange Commission; or

b. Is not a "supervised person" as that term is defined in rules or regulations adopted or promulgated under the Investment Advisers Act of 1940 by the United States Securities and Exchange Commission and who solicits, offers, or negotiates for the sale of, or who sells, investment advisory services on behalf of an adviser covered under federal law.

(4) "Investment adviser covered under federal law" means any adviser who is registered with the Securities and Exchange Commission under section 203 of the Investment Advisers Act of 1940 (15 U.S.C. § 80b-3).

(5) "Person" means an individual, a corporation, a partnership, an association, a joint-stock company, a trust where the interests of the beneficiaries are evidenced by a security, an unincorporated organization, a government, or a political subdivision of a government. (1987 (Reg. Sess., 1988), c. 1098, s. 1; 1989, c. 770, s. 12(a)-(c); 1997-419, s. 14; 1997-462, s. 6; 2001-273, s. 1; 2003-413, s. 16; 2013-91, s. 3(f).)

§§ 78C-3 through 78C-7: Reserved for future codification purposes.

Article 2.

Fraudulent and Prohibited Practices.

§ 78C-8. Advisory activities.

(a) It is unlawful for any person who receives, directly or indirectly, any consideration from another person for advising the other person as to the value of securities or their purchase or sale, whether through the issuance of analyses or reports or otherwise,

(1) To employ any device, scheme, or artifice to defraud the other person,

(2) To engage in any act, practice, or course of business which operates or would operate as a fraud or deceit upon the other person, or

(3) Acting as principal for his own account, knowingly to sell any security to or purchase any security from a client, or acting as broker for a person other than such client, knowingly to effect any sale or purchase of any security for the account of such client, without disclosing to such client in writing before the completion of such transaction the capacity in which he is acting and obtaining the consent of the client to such transaction. The prohibitions of this subdivision shall not apply to any transaction with a customer of a dealer if such dealer is not acting as an investment adviser in relation to such transaction.

(b) In the solicitation of advisory clients, it is unlawful for any person to make any untrue statement of a material fact, or omit to state a material fact necessary in order to make the statements made, in light of the circumstances under which they are made, not misleading.

(c) Except as may be permitted by rule or order of the Administrator, it is unlawful for any investment adviser to enter into, extend, or renew any investment advisory contract unless it provides in writing:

(1) That the investment adviser shall not be compensated on the basis of a share of capital gains upon or capital appreciation of the funds or any portion of the funds of the client (unless otherwise provided by subsection (d) or (f) below);

(2) That no assignment of the contract may be made by the investment adviser without the consent of the other party to the contract; and

(3) That the investment adviser, if a partnership, shall notify the other party to the contract of any change in the membership of the partnership within a reasonable time after the change.

(d) Subdivision (c)(1) does not apply to any person who is exempt from registration under G.S. 78C-16(a)(4) or to the performance, renewal, or extension of any advisory contract entered into by an investment advisor at a time when such investment advisor was exempt from registration under G.S. 78C-16(a)(4). Subdivision (c)(1) does not prohibit an investment advisory contract which provides for compensation based upon the total value of a fund averaged over a definite period, or as of definite dates or taken as of a definite date. "Assignment," as used in subdivision (c)(2), includes any direct or indirect transfer or hypothecation of an investment advisory contract by the assignor or of a controlling block of the assignor's outstanding voting securities by a security holder of the assignor; but, if the investment adviser is a partnership, no assignment of an investment advisory contract is considered to result from the death or withdrawal of a minority of the members of the investment adviser having only a minority interest in the business of the investment adviser, or from the admission to the investment adviser of one or more members who, after admission, will be only a minority of the members and will have only a minority interest in the business.

(e) It is unlawful for any investment adviser to take or have custody of any securities or funds of any client in contravention of any rule or order of the Administrator prohibiting, limiting or regulating such custody.

(f) The Administrator may by rule or order adopt exemptions from subdivision (a)(3) and subdivisions (c)(1), (c)(2) and (c)(3) where such exemptions are consistent with the public interest and within the purposes fairly intended by the policy and provisions of this Chapter. (1987 (Reg. Sess., 1988), c. 1098, s. 1; 2013-91, s. 3(g).)

§ 78C-9. Misleading filings.

It is unlawful for any person to make or cause to be made, in any document filed with the Administrator or in any proceeding under this Chapter, any statement which is, at the time and in the light of the circumstances under which it is made, false or misleading in any material respect. (1987 (Reg. Sess., 1988), c. 1098, s. 1.)

§ 78C-10. Unlawful representations concerning registration or exemption.

(a) Neither (i) the fact that an application for registration under Article 3 of this Chapter has been filed nor (ii) the fact that a person is effectively registered constitutes a finding by the Administrator that any document filed under this Chapter is true, complete, and not misleading. Neither any such fact nor the fact that an exemption or exception is available means that the Administrator has passed in any way upon the merits or qualifications of, or recommended, or given approval to any person.

(b)   It is unlawful to make, or cause to be made, to any prospective customer, or client, any representation inconsistent with subsection (a) of this section. (1987 (Reg. Sess., 1988), c. 1098, s. 1.)

§§ 78C-11 through 78C-15: Reserved for future codification purposes.

Article 3.

Registration and Notice Filing Procedures of Investment Advisers and Investment Adviser Representatives.

§ 78C-16. Registration and notice filing requirement.

(a)   It is unlawful for any person to transact business in this State as an investment adviser unless:

(1)   The person is registered under this Chapter;

(2)   The person's only clients in this State are investment companies as defined in the Investment Company Act of 1940, other investment advisers, investment advisers covered under federal law, dealers, banks, trust companies, savings institutions, savings and loan associations, insurance companies, employee benefit plans with assets of not less than one million dollars ($1,000,000), and governmental agencies or instrumentalities, whether acting for themselves or as trustees with investment control, or other institutional investors as are designated by rule or order of the Administrator;

(3)   The person has no place of business in this State, and during the preceding 12-month period has had not more than five clients, other than those specified in subdivision (2) of this subsection, who are residents of the State; or

(4) The person, during the course of the preceding 12 months, has had fewer than 15 clients, and neither holds himself or herself out generally to the public as an investment adviser nor acts as an investment adviser to any investment company registered under the Investment Company Act of 1940, or a company that has elected to be a business development company pursuant to section 54 of the Investment Company Act of 1940.

(a1) It is unlawful for any person to transact business in this State as an investment adviser representative unless:

(1) The person is registered under this Chapter; or

(2) The person is an investment adviser representative employed by or associated with an investment adviser exempt from registration under subdivision (2), (3), or (4) of subsection (a) of this section; or

(3) The person is an investment adviser representative employed by or associated with an investment adviser covered under federal law that is exempt from the notice filing requirements of G.S. 78C-17(a1).

(b) It is unlawful for any person required to be registered as an investment adviser under this Chapter to employ an investment adviser representative unless the investment adviser representative is registered under this Chapter. The registration of an investment adviser representative is not effective during any period when the investment adviser representative is not employed by (i) an investment adviser registered under this Chapter; or (ii) an investment adviser covered under federal law who has made a notice filing pursuant to the provisions of G.S. 78C-17(a1). When an investment adviser representative begins or terminates employment or association with an investment adviser who is registered under this Chapter, the investment adviser shall notify promptly the Administrator. When an investment adviser representative begins or terminates employment or association with an investment adviser covered under federal law, the investment adviser representative shall, and the investment adviser may, notify promptly the Administrator.

(b1) No investment adviser representative may be registered with more than one investment adviser registered under this Chapter or investment adviser covered under federal law unless each of the investment advisers which employs or associates the investment adviser representative is under common ownership or control.

(b2) Notwithstanding subsection (b1) of this section, an investment adviser representative may be registered with more than one investment adviser registered under this Chapter or investment adviser covered under federal law for the purposes of soliciting, offering, or negotiating for the sale of, or for selling investment advisory services for or on behalf of, those investment advisers. If an investment adviser representative is registered with more than one investment adviser pursuant to this subsection, the representative shall be registered separately with each investment adviser for whom the representative solicits business and shall provide in writing to each person solicited any information disclosing the terms of any compensation arrangement that is related to the representative's solicitation or referral activities and that is required by the Administrator pursuant to rule or order. The Administrator may, by rule or order, specify supervisory procedures consistent with regulations adopted by the United States Securities and Exchange Commission applicable to investment advisers who compensate persons for referrals of business.

(c) Every registration or notice filing expires December 31 of each year unless renewed.

(d) It is unlawful for any investment adviser covered under federal law to conduct advisory business in this State unless the investment adviser covered under federal law complies with the provisions of G.S. 78C-17(a1). (1987 (Reg. Sess., 1988), c. 1098, s. 1; 1997-419, ss. 15, 16; 1998-217, s. 9; 2001-273, s. 2; 2003-413, ss. 17, 18; 2013-91, s. 3(h).)

§ 78C-17. Registration and notice filing procedures.

(a) An investment adviser, or investment adviser representative may obtain an initial or renewal registration by filing with the Administrator or the Administrator's designee an application together with a consent to service of process pursuant to G.S. 78C-46(b) and paying any reasonable costs charged by the designee for processing the filings. The application shall contain whatever information the Administrator by rule requires concerning such matters as:

(1) The applicant's form and place of organization;

(2) The applicant's proposed method of doing business;

(3) The qualifications and business history of the applicant; in the case of an investment adviser, the qualifications and business history of any partner, officer, or director, any person occupying a similar status or performing similar functions, or any person directly or indirectly controlling the investment adviser;

(4) Any injunction or administrative order or conviction of a misdemeanor involving a security or any aspect of the securities business and any conviction of a felony;

(5) The applicant's financial condition and history; and

(6) Any information to be furnished or disseminated to any client or prospective client.

If no denial order is in effect and no proceeding is pending under G.S. 78C-19, registration becomes effective at noon of the 30th day after an application is filed. The Administrator may by rule or order specify an earlier effective date and may by order defer the effective date until noon of the 30th day after the filing of any amendment. Registration of an investment adviser automatically constitutes registration of any investment adviser representative who is a partner, executive officer, or director, or a person occupying a similar status or performing similar functions. After the Administrator institutes a proceeding under G.S. 78C-19 to postpone or deny an application for registration, withdrawal of the application shall be allowed only at such time and under such conditions as the Administrator may by order determine.

(a1) The Administrator may require investment advisers covered under federal law to file with the Administrator any documentation filed with the Securities and Exchange Commission as a condition of doing business in this State. This subsection does not apply to (i) an investment adviser covered under federal law whose only clients are those described in G.S. 78C-16(a)(2), or (ii) an investment adviser covered under federal law who has no place of business in this State, and during the preceding 12-month period has had not more than five clients, other than those described in G.S. 78C-16(a)(2), who are residents of this State. A notice filing under this section may be renewed by (i) filing documents required by the Administrator and filed with the Securities and Exchange Commission, prior to the expiration of the notice filing, and (ii) paying the fee required under subsection (b1) of this section. A notice filed under this section may be terminated by the investment adviser by providing the Administrator notice of the termination, which shall be effective upon receipt by the Administrator.

(b) Every applicant for initial or renewal registration shall pay a filing fee of three hundred dollars ($300.00) in the case of an investment adviser, and seventy-five dollars ($75.00) in the case of an investment adviser representative. When an application is denied or withdrawn, the Administrator shall retain the fee.

(b1) Every person acting as an investment adviser covered under federal law in this State shall pay an initial filing fee of three hundred dollars ($300.00) and a renewal notice filing fee of three hundred dollars ($300.00).

(b2) Any person required to pay a fee under this section may transmit through any designee any fee required by this section or by the rules adopted pursuant to this section.

(c) A registered investment adviser may file an application for registration of a successor, whether or not the successor is then in existence, for the unexpired portion of the year. There shall be no filing fee.

(d) The Administrator may by rule establish minimum net capital requirements not to exceed one hundred thousand dollars ($100,000) for registered investment advisers, subject to the limitations of section 222 of the Investment Advisers Act of 1940 (15 U.S.C. § 80(b)-18a), which may include different requirements for those investment advisers who maintain custody of clients' funds or securities or who have discretionary authority over same and those investment advisers who do not.

(e) The Administrator may by rule require registered investment advisers who have custody of or discretionary authority over client funds or securities to post surety bonds in amounts up to one hundred thousand dollars ($100,000), subject to the limitations of section 222 of the Investment Advisers Act of 1940 (15 U.S.C. § 80(b)-18a), and may determine their conditions. Any appropriate deposit of cash or securities shall be accepted in lieu of any bond so required. No bond may be required of any investment adviser whose minimum net capital, which may be defined by rule, exceeds one hundred thousand dollars ($100,000). Every bond shall provide for suit thereon by any person who has a cause of action under G.S. 78C-38 and, if the Administrator by rule or order requires, by any person who has a cause of action not arising under this Chapter. Every bond shall provide that no suit may be maintained to enforce any liability on the bond unless brought within the time limitations of G.S. 78C-

38(d). (1987 (Reg. Sess., 1988), c. 1098, s. 1; 1997-419, s. 17; 2001-273, s. 3; 2002-126, s. 29A.35; 2002-189, ss. 2, 3; 2003-413, s. 19.)

§ 78C-18. Post-registration provisions.

(a) Every registered investment adviser shall make and keep such accounts, correspondence, memoranda, papers, books and records as the Administrator by rule prescribes, subject to the limitations of section 222 of the Investment Advisers Act of 1940 (15 U.S.C. § 80(b)-18a).

All records so required shall be preserved for three years unless the Administrator by rule prescribes otherwise for particular types of records.

(b) With respect to investment advisers, the Administrator may require that certain information be furnished or disseminated as necessary or appropriate in the public interest or for the protection of investors and advisory clients. To the extent determined by the Administrator in his discretion, information furnished to clients or prospective clients of an investment adviser pursuant to the Investment Advisers Act of 1940 and the rules thereunder may be used in whole or partial satisfaction of this requirement.

(c) Every registered investment adviser shall file such financial reports as the Administrator by rule prescribes, subject to the limitations of section 222 of the Investment Advisers Act of 1940 (15 U.S.C. § 80(b)-18a).

(d) If the information contained in any document filed with the Administrator is or becomes inaccurate or incomplete in any material respect, the registrant or an investment adviser covered under federal law shall promptly file a correcting amendment, if the document is filed with respect to a registrant or when the amendment is required to be filed with the Securities and Exchange Commission with respect to an investment adviser covered under federal law, unless notification of the correction has been given under G.S. 78C-16(b).

(e) All the records referred to in subsection (a) of this section are subject at any time or from time to time to such reasonable periodic, special, or other examinations by representatives of the Administrator, within or without this State, as the Administrator deems necessary or appropriate in the public interest or for the protection of investors. For the purpose of avoiding unnecessary duplication of examinations, the Administrator, insofar as he deems it practicable in administering this subsection, may cooperate with the securities administrators of other states, the Securities and Exchange Commission, and any national securities exchange or national securities association registered under the Securities Exchange Act of 1934. (1987 (Reg. Sess., 1988), c. 1098, s. 1; 1997-419, s. 18.)

§ 78C-19. Denial, revocation, suspension, bar, censure, cancellation, and withdrawal of registration.

(a) The Administrator may by order deny, suspend or revoke any registration, or bar or censure any registrant or any officer, director, partner or person occupying a similar status or performing similar functions for a registrant, from employment with a registered investment adviser, or restrict or limit a registrant as to any function or activity of the business for which registration is required in this State if he finds:

(1) That the order is in the public interest and;

(2) That the applicant or registrant or, in the case of an investment adviser, any partner, officer or director, any person occupying a similar status or performing similar functions, or any person directly or indirectly controlling the investment adviser;

a. Has filed an application for registration which as of its effective date, or as of any date after filing in the case of an order denying effectiveness, was incomplete in any material respect or contained any statement which was, in light of the circumstances under which it was made, false or misleading with respect to any material fact;

b. Has willfully violated or willfully failed to comply with any provision of this Chapter or Chapter 78A or any rule or order under this Chapter or Chapter 78A;

c. Has been convicted, within the past 10 years, of any misdemeanor involving a security or the financial services business, or any aspect of the securities business, or the financial services business, or any felony;

d. Is permanently or temporarily enjoined by any court of competent jurisdiction from engaging in or continuing any conduct or practice involving any aspect of the securities or financial services business;

e. Is the subject of an order of the Administrator denying, suspending, barring, revoking, restricting or limiting registration as a dealer, salesman, investment adviser or investment adviser representative;

f. Is the subject of an adjudication or determination within the past five years by a securities, commodities or other financial services regulatory agency or an administrator of such laws of another state or a court of competent jurisdiction that the person has violated the Securities Act of 1933, the Securities Exchange Act of 1934, the Investment Advisers Act of 1940, the Investment Company Act of 1940 or the Commodity Exchange Act, or the securities or commodities law of any other state or any other financial services regulatory laws as the Administrator may designate by rule;

g. Has engaged in dishonest or unethical practices in the securities or financial services business;

h. Is insolvent, either in the sense that his liabilities exceed his assets or in the sense that he cannot meet his obligations as they mature; but the Administrator may not enter an order against an investment adviser under this clause without a finding of insolvency as to the investment adviser;

i. Is not qualified on the basis of such factors as training, experience, and knowledge of the securities business, except as otherwise provided in subsection (b) of this section;

j. Has failed reasonably to supervise his salesmen or employees if he is a dealer or his investment adviser representatives or employees if he is an investment adviser to assure their compliance with this Chapter; or

k. Has failed to pay the proper filing fee; but the Administrator may enter only a denial order under this clause, and he shall vacate any such order when the deficiency has been corrected.

The Administrator may not institute a suspension or revocation proceeding on the basis of a fact or transaction known to him when registration became effective unless the proceeding is instituted within the next 120 days.

(b) The following provisions govern the application of G.S. 78C-19(a)(2)i:

(1) The Administrator may not enter an order against an investment adviser on the basis of the lack of qualification of any person other than (i) the investment adviser himself if he is an individual or (ii) an investment adviser representative.

(2) The Administrator may not enter an order solely on the basis of lack of experience if the applicant or registrant is qualified by training or knowledge or both.

(3) The Administrator shall consider that an investment adviser representative who will work under the supervision of a registered investment adviser need not have the same qualifications as an investment adviser.

(4) The Administrator shall consider that an investment adviser or investment adviser representative is not necessarily qualified solely on the basis of experience as a dealer or salesman.

(5) The Administrator may by rule provide for an examination, including an examination developed or approved by an organization of securities administrators, which examination may be written or oral or both, to be taken by any class of or all applicants. The Administrator may by rule or order waive the examination requirement as to a person or class of persons if the Administrator determines that the examination is not necessary for the protection of advisory clients.

(c) The Administrator may by order summarily postpone or suspend registration pending final determination of any proceeding under this section. Upon the entry of the order, the Administrator shall promptly notify the applicant or registrant, as well as the employer or prospective employer if the applicant or registrant is an investment adviser representative, that it has been entered and of the reasons therefor and that within 20 days after the receipt of a written request the matter will be scheduled for hearing in accordance with Chapter 150B of the General Statutes. If no request for a hearing, other responsive pleading, or submission is received by the Administrator within 30 business days of receipt of service of notice of the order upon the applicant or registrant and no hearing is ordered by the Administrator, the order shall become final and remain in effect unless it is modified or vacated by the Administrator. If a hearing is requested or ordered, the Administrator, after notice of and opportunity for hearing, may modify or vacate the order or extend it until final determination.

(d) If the Administrator finds that any registrant or applicant for registration is no longer in existence or has ceased to do business as an investment adviser or investment adviser representative, or is subject to an adjudication of mental incompetence or to the control of a committee, conservator, or guardian, or cannot be located after reasonable search, the Administrator may by order cancel the registration or application.

(e) Withdrawal from registration as an investment adviser or investment adviser representative becomes effective 90 days after receipt of an application to withdraw or within such shorter period of time as the Administrator may determine, unless a revocation or suspension proceeding is pending when the application is filed or a proceeding to revoke or suspend or to impose conditions upon the withdrawal is instituted within 90 days after the application is filed. If a proceeding is pending or instituted, withdrawal becomes effective at such time and upon such conditions as the Administrator by order determines. If no proceeding is pending or instituted and withdrawal automatically becomes effective, the Administrator may nevertheless institute a revocation or suspension proceeding under G.S. 78C-19(a)(2)b within one year after withdrawal became effective and enter a revocation or suspension order as of the last date on which registration was effective.

(f) No order may be entered under any part of this section except the first sentence of subsection (c) of this section without (i) appropriate prior notice to the applicant or registrant (as well as the employer or prospective employer if the applicant or registrant is an investment adviser representative), (ii) opportunity for hearing, and (iii) written findings of fact and conclusions of law. (1987 (Reg. Sess., 1988), c. 1098, s. 1; 1997-462, s. 7; 2001-126, s. 5.)

§ 78C-20. Methods of registration.

(a) All applications for initial and renewal registrations or notice filings required under G.S. 78C-17 shall be filed with the Investment Adviser Registration Depository (IARD) operated by the National Association of Securities Dealers.

(b) Repealed by Session Laws 2001-273, s. 4, effective October 1, 2001.

(c) Nothing in this section shall be construed to prevent the exercise of the authority of the Administrator as provided in G.S. 78C-19. (1987 (Reg. Sess., 1988), c. 1098, s. 1; 2001-273, s. 4; 2002-159, s. 16.)

§§ 78C-21 through 78C-25: Reserved for future codification purposes.

Article 4.

Administration and Review.

§ 78C-26. Administration of Chapter.

(a) This Chapter shall be administered by the Secretary of State. The Secretary of State as Administrator may delegate all or part of the authority under this Chapter to the Deputy Securities Administrator including, but not limited to, the authority to conduct hearings, and make, execute and issue final agency orders and decisions. The Secretary of State may appoint such clerks and other assistants as may from time to time be needed. The Secretary of State may designate one or more hearing officers for the purpose of conducting administrative hearings.

(b) It is unlawful for the Administrator or any of his officers or employees to use for personal benefit any information which is filed with or obtained by the Administrator and which is not made public. No provision of this Chapter authorizes the Administrator or any of his officers or employees to disclose any such information except among themselves or when necessary or appropriate in a proceeding or investigation under this Chapter. No provision of this Chapter either creates or derogates from any privilege which exists at common law or otherwise when documentary or other evidence is sought under a subpoena directed to the Administrator or any of his officers or employees.

(c) All fees provided for under this Chapter shall be collected by the Administrator and shall be paid over to the State Treasurer to go into the General Fund. (1987 (Reg. Sess., 1988), c. 1098, s. 1; 2001-126, s. 10.)

§ 78C-27. Investigations and subpoenas.

(a) The Administrator in his discretion:

(1) May make any investigation within or outside of this State as the Administrator deems necessary to determine whether any person has violated or is about to violate any provision of this Chapter or any rule or order hereunder, or to aid in the enforcement of this Chapter or in the prescribing of rules and forms hereunder;

(2) May require or permit any person to file a statement in writing, under oath or otherwise as the Administrator determines, as to all the facts and circumstances concerning the matter to be investigated; and

(3) May publish information concerning any violation of this Chapter or any rule or order hereunder.

(b) For the purpose of any investigation or proceeding under this Chapter, the Administrator or any officer designated by him may administer oaths and affirmations, subpoena witnesses, compel their attendance, take evidence and require the production of any books, papers, correspondence, memoranda, agreements, or other documents or records which the Administrator deems relevant or material to the inquiry.

(c) In case of contumacy by, or refusal to obey a subpoena issued to any person, any court of competent jurisdiction, upon application by the Administrator, may issue to the person an order requiring him to appear before the Administrator, or the officer designated by him, there to produce documentary evidence if so ordered or to give evidence touching the matter under investigation or in question. Failure to obey the order of the court may be punished by the court as a contempt of court.

(d) The Administrator may act under subsection (b) of this section or apply under subsection (c) of this section to enforce subpoenas in this State at the request of a securities agency or administrator of any state if the alleged activities constituting a violation for which the information is sought would be a violation of this Chapter or any rule hereunder if the alleged activities had occurred in this State. (1987 (Reg. Sess., 1988), c. 1098, s. 1; 1997-462, s. 8.)

§ 78C-28. Injunctions; cease and desist orders; civil penalties.

(a) Whenever it appears to the Administrator that any person has engaged or is about to engage in any act or practice constituting a violation of any provision of this Chapter or any rule or order hereunder, he may in his discretion bring an action in any court of competent jurisdiction to enjoin the acts or practices and to enforce compliance with this Chapter or any rule or order hereunder. Upon a proper showing a permanent or temporary injunction, restraining order, or writ of mandamus shall be granted and a receiver or conservator may be appointed for the defendant or the defendant's assets. In addition to any other remedies provided by this Chapter, the Administrator may apply to the court hearing this matter for an order of restitution whereby the defendant in such action shall be ordered to make restitution of those sums shown by the Administrator to have been obtained by him in violation of any of the provisions of this Chapter. Such restitution shall be payable, in the discretion of the court, to the Administrator or receiver appointed pursuant to this section for the benefit of those persons whose assets were obtained in violation of this Chapter, or directly to those persons. The court may not require the Administrator to post a bond.

(b) (1) If the Administrator determines after giving notice of an opportunity for a hearing, that any person has engaged in, or is about to engage in, any act or practice constituting a violation of any provision of this Chapter or any rule or order hereunder, he may order such person to cease and desist from such unlawful act or practice and take such affirmative action as in the judgment of the Administrator will carry out the purposes of this Chapter.

(2) If the Administrator makes written findings of fact that the public interest will be irreparably harmed by delay in issuing an order under G.S. 78C-28(b)(1), the Administrator may issue a temporary cease and desist order. Upon the entry of a temporary cease and desist order, the Administrator shall promptly notify in writing the person subject to the order that such order has been entered, the reasons therefor, and that within 20 days after the receipt of a written request from such person the matter shall be scheduled for hearing in accordance with Chapter 150B of the General Statutes to determine whether or not the order shall become permanent and final. If no request for a hearing, other responsive pleading, or submission is received by the Administrator within 30 business days of receipt of service of notice of the order upon the person subject to the order and no hearing is ordered by the Administrator, the order shall become final and remain in effect unless it is modified or vacated by the Administrator. If a hearing is requested or ordered, the Administrator, after giving notice of an opportunity for a hearing to the person subject to the order, shall by written

findings of fact and conclusion of law, vacate, modify, or make permanent the order.

(3)   No order under subsection (b) of this section, except an order issued pursuant to G.S. 78C-28(b)(2), may be entered without prior notice or an opportunity for hearing. The Administrator may vacate or modify an order under subsection (b) of this section upon his finding that the conditions which required such an order have changed and that it is in the public interest to so vacate or modify.

(4)   A final order issued pursuant to the provisions of subsection (b) of this section shall be subject to review as provided in G.S. 78C-29.

(c)   The Administrator may issue an order against an applicant, registered person, or other person who willfully violates this Chapter or a rule or order of the Administrator under this Chapter:

(1)   Imposing a civil penalty of up to two thousand five hundred dollars ($2,500) for a single violation or of up to twenty-five thousand dollars ($25,000) for multiple violations in a single proceeding or a series of related proceedings; and

(2)   Requiring reimbursement of the costs of investigation.

The clear proceeds of civil penalties imposed under this subsection shall be remitted to the Civil Penalty and Forfeiture Fund in accordance with G.S. 115C-457.2. Any reimbursement imposed under this subsection shall be paid into the General Fund. No order authorized by this subsection may be entered without prior notice of an opportunity for a hearing conducted pursuant to Article 3 of Chapter 150B of the General Statutes. (1987 (Reg. Sess., 1988), c. 1098, s. 1; 1991, c. 456, s. 7; 1997-462, s. 9; 1998-215, s. 121; 2001-126, s. 6.)

§ 78C-29. Judicial review of orders.

(a)   Any person aggrieved by a final order of the Administrator may obtain a review of the order in the Superior Court of Wake County by filing in court, within 30 days after a written copy of the decision is served upon the person by personal service or by registered or certified mail, a written petition praying that the order be modified or set aside in whole or in part. A copy of the petition shall be forthwith served upon the Administrator, and thereupon the Administrator shall certify and file in court a copy of the filing and evidence upon which the order was entered. When these have been filed, the court has exclusive jurisdiction to affirm, modify, enforce, or set aside the order, in whole or in part. The findings of the Administrator as to the facts, if supported by competent, material and substantial evidence, are conclusive. If either party applies to the court for leave to adduce additional material evidence, and shows to the satisfaction of the court that there were reasonable grounds for failure to adduce the evidence in the hearings before the Administrator, the court may order the additional evidence to be taken before the Administrator and to be adduced upon the hearing in such manner and upon such conditions as the court considers proper. The Administrator may modify his findings and order by reason of the additional evidence and shall file in court the additional evidence together with any modified or new findings or order. The judgment of the court is final, subject to review by the Court of Appeals.

(b)   The commencement of proceedings under subsection (a) of this section does not, unless specifically ordered by the court, operate as a stay of the Administrator's order. (1987 (Reg. Sess., 1988), c. 1098, s. 1.)

§ 78C-30. Rules, forms, orders, and hearings.

(a)   The Administrator may from time to time make, amend, and rescind such rules, forms, and orders as are necessary to carry out the provisions of this Chapter, including rules and forms governing registration, applications, and reports, and defining any terms, whether or not used in this Chapter, insofar as the definitions are not inconsistent with the provisions of this Chapter. For the purpose of rules and forms the Administrator may classify persons, and matters within his jurisdiction, and prescribe different requirements for different classes.

(b)   No rule, form, or order may be made, amended, or rescinded unless the Administrator finds that the action is necessary or appropriate in the public interest or for the protection of investors and clients and consistent with the purposes fairly intended by the policy and provisions of this Chapter. In prescribing rules and forms the Administrator may cooperate with the securities administrators of the other states and the Securities and Exchange Commission with a view to effectuating the policy of this statute to achieve maximum uniformity in the form and content of registrations, applications, and reports wherever practicable.

(c) The Administrator may by rule or order prescribe (i) the form and content of financial statements required under this Chapter, (ii) the circumstances under which consolidated financial statements shall be filed, and (iii) whether any required financial statements shall be certified by independent or certified public accountants. All financial statements required to be filed with the Administrator shall be audited and shall be prepared in accordance with generally accepted accounting principles, except where the Administrator shall by rule or order provide otherwise.

(d) The Administrator may by rule or order require the filing of any prospectus, pamphlet, circular, form letter, advertisement, or other sales literature or advertising communication addressed or intended for distribution to prospective investors, including clients or prospective clients of an investment adviser.

(e) All rules and forms of the Administrator shall be published.

(f) No provision of this Chapter imposing any liability applies to any act done or omitted in good faith in conformity with any rule, form, or order of the Administrator, notwithstanding that the rule, form, or order may later be amended or rescinded or be determined by judicial or other authority to be invalid for any reason.

(g) Every hearing in an administrative proceeding shall be public unless the Administrator in his discretion grants a request joined in by all the respondents that the hearing be conducted privately. (1987 (Reg. Sess., 1988), c. 1098, s. 1; 2003-413, s. 20.)

§ 78C-31. Administrative files and opinions.

(a) A document is filed when it is received by the Administrator.

(b) The Administrator shall keep a register of all applications for registration which are or have been effective under this Chapter and all denial, suspension, or revocation orders or similar orders which have been entered under this Chapter. The register shall be open for public inspection.

(c) The information contained in or filed with any registration, application, or report may be made available to the public under such rules as the Administrator prescribes.

(c1) The files and records of the Administrator relating to criminal investigations and enforcement proceedings undertaken pursuant to this Chapter are subject to the provisions of G.S. 132-1.4.

(c2) The files and records of the Administrator relating to noncriminal investigations and enforcement proceedings undertaken pursuant to this Chapter shall not be subject to inspection and examination pursuant to G.S. 132-6 until the investigations and proceedings are completed and cease to be active.

(c3) Any information obtained by the Administrator from any law enforcement agency, administrative agency, or regulatory organization on a confidential or otherwise restricted basis in the course of an investigation or proceeding undertaken pursuant to this Chapter shall be confidential and exempt from G.S. 132-6 to the same extent that it is confidential in the possession of the providing agency or organization.

(d) Upon request and at such reasonable charges as the Administrator prescribes, the Administrator shall furnish to any person photostatic or other copies (certified under the seal of office if requested) of any entry in the register or any document which is a matter of public record. In any proceeding or prosecution under this Chapter, any copy so certified is prima facie evidence of the contents of the entry or document certified.

(e) The Administrator may honor requests from interested persons for interpretative opinions upon the payment of a fee of one hundred fifty dollars ($150.00). (1987 (Reg. Sess., 1988), c. 1098, s. 1; 1997-462, s. 10.)

§§ 78C-32 through 78C-37: Reserved for future codification purposes.

Article 5.

Civil Liabilities and Criminal Penalties.

§ 78C-38. Civil liabilities.

(a) Any person who:

(1) Engages in the business of advising others, for compensation, either directly or through publications or writings, as to the value of securities or as to the advisability of investing in, purchasing, or selling securities, or who, for compensation and as a part of a regular business, issues or promulgates analyses or reports concerning securities, in violation of G.S. 78C-8(b), G.S. 78C-16(a), (a1), or (b) (an action pursuant to a violation of G.S. 78C-16(b) may not be maintained except by those persons who directly received advice from the unregistered investment adviser representative), G.S. 78C-10(b), or of any rule or order under G.S. 78C-30(d) which requires the affirmative approval of sales literature before it is used, or

(2) Receives, directly or indirectly, any consideration from another person for advice as to the value of securities or their purchase or sale, whether through the issuance of analyses, reports or otherwise and employs any device, scheme, or artifice to defraud such other person or engages in any act, practice or course of business which operates or would operate as a fraud or deceit on such other person, in violation of G.S. 78C-8(a)(1) or (2),

is liable to any person who is given such advice in such violation, who may sue either at law or in equity to recover (i) the consideration paid for such advice together with interest thereon at the legal rate as provided in G.S. 24-1 from the date of payment of the consideration, plus (ii) the actual damages to such person proximately caused by such violation, plus (iii) costs of the action and reasonable attorneys' fees. An action based on violation of G.S. 78C-8(b) may not prevail where the person accused of the violation sustains the burden of proof that he did not know, and in the exercise of reasonable care could not have known of the existence of the facts by reason of which the liability is alleged to exist.

(b) (1) Every person who directly or indirectly controls a person liable under subsection (a) of this section, including every partner, officer, or director of the person, every person occupying a similar status or performing similar functions, and every dealer or salesman who materially aids in the conduct giving rise to the liability is liable jointly and severally with and to the same extent as the person, unless able to sustain the burden of proof that the person did not know, and in the exercise of reasonable care could not have known, of the existence of the facts by reason of which the liability is alleged to exist.

(2) Unless liable under subdivision (1) of this subsection, every employee or associate of a person liable under subsection (a) of this section who materially aids in the conduct giving rise to the liability and every other person who materially aids in the conduct giving rise to the liability is liable jointly and severally with and to the same extent as the person if the employee or associate or other person actually knew of the existence of the facts by reason of which the liability is alleged to exist.

(3) There is contribution among the several persons liable under subdivisions (1) and (2) of this subsection as provided among tort-feasors pursuant to Chapter 1B of the General Statutes.

(c) Every cause of action under this statute survives the death of any person who might have been a plaintiff or defendant.

(d) No person may sue under this section more than three years after the rendering of investment advice in violation of G.S. 78C-16.

No person may sue under this section for any other violation of this Chapter more than three years after the person discovers facts constituting the violation, but in any case no later than five years after the rendering of investment advice, except that if a person who may be liable under this section engages in any fraudulent or deceitful act that conceals the violation or induces the person to forgo or postpone commencing an action based upon the violation, the suit may be commenced not later than three years after the person discovers or should have discovered that the act was fraudulent or deceitful.

(e) No person who has made or engaged in the performance of any contract in violation of any provision of this Chapter or any rule or order hereunder, or who has acquired any purported right under such contract with knowledge of the facts by reason of which its making or performance was in violation, may base any suit on the contract.

(f) Any condition, stipulation, or provision binding any person receiving any investment advice to waive compliance with any provision of this Chapter or any rule or order hereunder is void.

(g) The rights and remedies provided by this Chapter are in addition to any other rights or remedies that may exist at law or in equity, but this Chapter does not create any cause of action not specified in this section or G.S. 78C-17(e). If the requirements of Chapter 1D of the General Statutes are met, punitive damages are available to the extent provided in that Chapter. (1987 (Reg. Sess., 1988), c. 1098, s. 1; 1991, c. 456, s. 8; 2003-413, ss. 21-24.)

§ 78C-39. Criminal penalties.

(a) Any person who willfully violates any provision of this Chapter except G.S. 78C-8(a)(1), 78C-8(a)(2), 78C-8(b), or 78C-9 is guilty of a Class I felony.

(a1) Any person who willfully violates any rule or order under this Chapter is guilty of a Class I felony. No person may be imprisoned for the violation of any rule if the person proves that the person had no knowledge of the rule. It is an affirmative defense to a charge of violating an order under this Chapter that the person had no knowledge of the order.

(a2) Any person who willfully violates G.S. 78C-8(a)(1), 78C-8(a)(2), or 78C-8(b) is guilty of a felony. If the losses caused, directly or indirectly, by the violator for a single act or for a series of related acts in a common scheme or plan is one hundred thousand dollars ($100,000) or more, the person is guilty of a Class C felony. If the losses caused, directly or indirectly, by the violator for a single act or for a series of related acts in a common scheme or plan is less than one hundred thousand dollars ($100,000), the person is guilty of a Class H felony.

(a3) Any person who willfully violates G.S. 78C-9 knowing the statement made to be false or misleading in any material respect is guilty of a Class H felony. Any other willful violation of G.S. 78C-9 constitutes a Class 2 misdemeanor.

(a4) A person is guilty of a Class H felony if the person willfully does any of the following for the purpose of interfering with the performance of any audit, examination, or investigation by the Administrator under this Chapter:

(1) Makes or causes to be made to the Administrator or the Administrator's designated representative any false or misleading oral or written statement.

(2) Creates, causes to be made, or delivers any record, report, or document knowing that it is false or misleading in any material respect.

(3) Destroys or alters any record, report, or document.

(4) Conceals or secretes any record, report, or document.

(b) The Administrator may refer such evidence as is available concerning violations of this Chapter or of any rule or order hereunder to the proper district attorney, who may, with or without such a reference, institute the appropriate criminal proceedings under this Chapter. Upon receipt of a reference, the district attorney may request that a duly employed attorney of the Administrator prosecute or assist in the prosecution of the violation or violations on behalf of the State. Upon approval of the Administrator, the employee may be appointed a special prosecutor for the district attorney to prosecute or assist in the prosecution of the violations without receiving compensation from the district attorney. Such a special prosecutor shall have all the powers and duties prescribed by law for district attorneys and such other powers and duties as are lawfully delegated to the special prosecutor by the district attorney for violations of this Chapter.

(c) Nothing in this Chapter limits the power of the State to punish any person for any conduct which constitutes a crime by statute or at common law. (1987 (Reg. Sess., 1988), c. 1098, s. 1; 1991, c. 456, s. 9; 2003-413, s. 25.)

§ 78C-40. Burden of proof.

In a civil or administrative proceeding brought under this Chapter, the burden of proving an exemption or an exception from a definition is upon the person claiming it. In a criminal proceeding brought under this Chapter, the State has no initial burden of producing evidence to show that the defendant's actions do not fall within the exemption or exceptions; however, once the defendant introduces evidence to show that his conduct is within the exemption or exception, the burden of persuading the trier of fact that the exemption or exception does not apply falls upon the State. (1987 (Reg. Sess., 1988), c. 1098, s. 1.)

§§ 78C-41 through 78C-45: Reserved for future codification purposes.

Article 6.

Miscellaneous Provisions.

§ 78C-46. Scope of the Chapter; service of process.

(a) G.S. 78C-8, 78C-16(a) and (b), 78C-10, and 78C-38 apply when any act instrumental in effecting prohibited conduct is done in this State, whether or not either party is then present in this State.

(b) Every applicant for registration under this Chapter shall file with the Administrator, in such form as he by rule prescribes, an irrevocable consent appointing the Administrator or his successor in office to be his attorney to receive service of any lawful process in any noncriminal suit, action or proceeding against him or his successor, executor or administrator which arises under this Chapter or any rule or order hereunder after the consent has been filed, with the same force and validity as if served personally on the person filing the consent. A person who has filed such a consent in connection with a previous registration or notice filing need not file another. Service may be made by leaving a copy of the process in the office of the Administrator, but it is not effective unless (i) the plaintiff, who may be the Administrator in a suit, action, or proceeding instituted by him, forthwith sends notice of the service and a copy of the process by registered or certified mail to the defendant or respondent at his last address on file with the Administrator, and (ii) the plaintiff's affidavit of compliance with the subsection is filed in the case on or before the return day of the process, if any, or within such further time as the court allows.

(c) When any person, including any nonresident of this State, engages in conduct prohibited or made actionable by this Chapter or any rule or order hereunder, and he has not filed a consent to service of process under subsection (b) of this section and personal jurisdiction over him cannot otherwise be obtained in this State, that conduct shall be considered equivalent to his appointment of the Administrator or his successor in office to be his attorney to receive service of any lawful process in any noncriminal suit, action, or proceeding against him or his successor, executor or administrator which grows out of that conduct and which is brought under this Chapter or any rule or order hereunder with the same force and validity as if served on him personally. Service may be made by leaving a copy of the process in the office of the Administrator, and it is not effective unless (i) the plaintiff, who may be the Administrator in a suit, action, or proceeding instituted by him, forthwith sends notice of the service and a copy of the process by registered or certified mail to the defendant or respondent at his last known address or takes other steps which are reasonably calculated to give actual notice, and (ii) the plaintiff's affidavit of compliance with this subsection is filed in the case on or before the return day of the process, if any, or within such further time as the court allows.

(d) When process is served under this section, the court, or the Administrator in a proceeding before him, shall order such continuance as may be necessary to afford the defendant or respondent reasonable opportunity to defend. (1987 (Reg. Sess., 1988), c. 1098, s. 1; 1997-419, s. 19.)

§ 78C-47. Statutory policy.

This Chapter shall be so construed as to effectuate its general purpose to make uniform the law of those states which enact it and to coordinate the interpretation and administration of this Chapter with the related federal regulation. Nothing in this Chapter shall be construed to limit or preclude the applicability of any provision of Chapters 78A or 150B of the General Statutes. (1987 (Reg. Sess., 1988), c. 1098, s. 1.)

§ 78C-48. Severability of provisions.

If any provision of this Chapter or the application thereof to any person or circumstance is held invalid, the invalidity shall not affect other provisions or applications of the Chapter which can be given effect without the invalid provision or application, and to this end the provisions of this Chapter are severable. (1987 (Reg. Sess., 1988), c. 1098, s. 1.)

§§ 78C-49 through 78C-59. Reserved for future codification purposes.

Article 7.

Sports Agents.

§§ 78C-60 through 78C-62: Expired.

§§ 78C-63 through 78C-70. Reserved for future codification purposes.

Article 8.

Regulation of Athlete Agents.

§§ 78C-71 through 78C-81: Repealed by Session Laws 2003-375, s. 1, effective August 1, 2003.

§§ 78C-82 through 78C-84. Reserved for future codification purposes.

Article 9.

Uniform Athlete Agents Act.

§ 78C-85. Title.

This Article may be cited as the "Uniform Athlete Agents Act". (2003-375, s. 2.)

§ 78C-86. Definitions.

The following definitions apply in this Article:

(1) Agency contract. - An agreement in which a student-athlete authorizes a person to negotiate or solicit on behalf of the student-athlete a professional-sports-services contract or an endorsement contract.

(2) Athlete agent. - An individual who enters into an agency contract with a student-athlete or, directly or indirectly, recruits or solicits a student-athlete to enter into an agency contract. The term includes an individual who represents to the public that the individual is an athlete agent. The term does not include a spouse, parent, sibling, or guardian of the student-athlete or an individual acting solely on behalf of a professional sports team or professional sports organization.

(3) Athletic director. - An individual responsible for administering the overall athletic program of an educational institution or, if an educational institution has separately administered athletic programs for male students and female students, the athletic program for males or the athletic program for females, as appropriate.

(4) Contact. - A communication, direct or indirect, between an athlete agent and a student-athlete to recruit or solicit the student-athlete to enter into an agency contract.

(5) Endorsement contract. - An agreement under which a student-athlete is employed or receives consideration to use on behalf of the other party any value that the student-athlete may have because of publicity, reputation, following, or fame obtained because of athletic ability or performance.

(6) Intercollegiate sport. - A sport played at the collegiate level for which eligibility requirements for participation by a student-athlete are established by a national association for the promotion or regulation of collegiate athletics.

(7) Person. - An individual, company, corporation, partnership, association, or any other legal or commercial entity.

(8) Professional-sports-services contract. - An agreement under which an individual is employed or agrees to render services as a player on a professional sports team, with a professional sports organization, or as a professional athlete.

(9) Record. - Information that is inscribed on a tangible medium or that is stored in an electronic or other medium and is retrievable in perceivable form.

(10) Registration. - A certificate issued by the Secretary of State evidencing that a person has satisfied the requirements of an athlete agent pursuant to this Article.

(11) Student-athlete. - An individual who engages in, is eligible to engage in, or may be eligible in the future to engage in any intercollegiate sport. If an individual is permanently ineligible to participate in a particular intercollegiate sport, the individual is not a student-athlete for purposes of that sport. (2003-375, s. 2.)

§ 78C-87. Service of process; subpoenas.

(a) By acting as an athlete agent in this State, a nonresident individual appoints the Secretary of State as the individual's agent for service of process in any civil action in this State related to the individual's acting as an athlete agent in this State.

(b) The Secretary of State may issue subpoenas for any material that is relevant to the administration of this Article. (2003-375, s. 2.)

§ 78C-88. Athlete agents; registration required; exceptions; void contracts.

(a) Except as otherwise provided in this section, an individual may not act as an athlete agent in this State without holding a certificate of registration under G.S. 78C-90 or G.S. 78C-92.

(b) Before being issued a certificate of registration, an individual may act as an athlete agent in this State for all purposes except signing an agency contract if: (i) a student-athlete or another person acting on behalf of the student-athlete initiates communication with the individual; and (ii) within seven days after an initial act as an athlete agent, the individual submits an application for registration as an athlete agent in this State.

(c) A North Carolina licensed and resident attorney may act as an athlete agent in this State for all purposes without registering pursuant to this section if the attorney neither advertises directly for, nor solicits, any student-athlete by representing to any person that the attorney has special experience or qualifications with regard to representing student-athletes and represents no more than two student-athletes.

(d) An agency contract resulting from conduct in violation of this section is void, and the athlete agent shall return any consideration received under the contract. (2003-375, s. 2.)

§ 78C-89. Registration as athlete agent; form; requirements.

(a) An individual seeking registration as an athlete agent shall submit an application for registration to the Secretary of State in a form prescribed by the Secretary of State. The application must be in the name of an individual and, except as otherwise provided in subsection (b) of this section, signed or otherwise authenticated by the applicant under penalty of perjury and must state or contain the following:

(1) The name of the applicant and the address of the applicant's principal place of business.

(2) The name of the applicant's business or employer, if applicable.

(3) Any business or occupation engaged in by the applicant for the five years immediately preceding the date of submission of the application.

(4) A description of the applicant's:

a. Formal training as an athlete agent.

b. Practical experience as an athlete agent.

c. Educational background relating to the applicant's activities as an athlete agent.

(5) The names and addresses of three individuals not related to the applicant who are willing to serve as references.

(6) The name, sport, and last known team for each individual for whom the applicant acted as an athlete agent during the five years immediately preceding the date of submission of the application.

(7) The names and addresses of all persons who are:

a. With respect to the athlete agent's business if it is not a corporation, the partners, members, officers, managers, associates, or profit-sharers of the business.

b. With respect to a corporation employing the athlete agent, the officers, directors, and any shareholder of the corporation having an interest of five percent (5%) or greater.

(8) Whether the applicant or any person named under subdivision (7) of this subsection has been convicted of a crime that, if committed in this State, would be a crime involving moral turpitude or a felony and identify the crime.

(9) Whether there has been any administrative or judicial determination that the applicant or any person named under subdivision (7) of this subsection has made a false, misleading, deceptive, or fraudulent representation.

(10) Any instance in which the conduct of the applicant or any person named under subdivision (7) of this subsection resulted in the imposition of a sanction, suspension, or declaration of ineligibility to participate in an interscholastic or intercollegiate athletic event on a student-athlete or educational institution.

(11) Any sanction, suspension, or disciplinary action taken against the applicant or any person named under subdivision (7) of this subsection arising out of occupational or professional conduct.

(12) Whether there has been any denial of an application for, suspension or revocation of, or refusal to renew the registration or licensure of the applicant or any person named under subdivision (7) of this subsection as an athlete agent in any state.

(b) An individual who has submitted an application for registration or licensure as an athlete agent in another state or who holds a certificate of registration or licensure as an athlete agent in another state may submit a copy of the application and certificate in lieu of submitting an application in the form prescribed pursuant to subsection (a) of this section. The Secretary of State shall accept the application and the certificate from the other state as an application for registration in this State if the application to the other state satisfied all of the following criteria:

(1) Was submitted in the other state within six months immediately preceding the submission of the application in this State and the applicant certifies that the information contained in the application is current.

(2) Contains information substantially similar to or more comprehensive than that required in an application submitted in this State.

(3) Was signed by the applicant under penalty of perjury.

(c) An application filed under this section is a "public record" within the meaning of Chapter 132 of the General Statutes. (2003-375, s. 2.)

§ 78C-90. Certificate of registration; issuance or denial; renewal.

(a) Except as otherwise provided in subsection (b) of this section, the Secretary of State shall issue a certificate of registration to an individual who complies with G.S. 78C-89(a) or whose application has been accepted under G.S. 78C-89(b).

(b) The Secretary of State may refuse to issue a certificate of registration if the Secretary of State determines that the applicant has engaged in conduct that has a significant adverse effect on the applicant's fitness to act as an athlete agent. In making the determination, the Secretary of State may consider whether the applicant has:

(1) Been convicted of a crime that, if committed in this State, would be a crime involving moral turpitude or a felony.

(2) Made a materially false, misleading, deceptive, or fraudulent representation in the application or as an athlete agent.

(3) Engaged in conduct that would disqualify the applicant from serving in a fiduciary capacity.

(4) Engaged in conduct prohibited by G.S. 78C-98.

(5) Had a registration or licensure as an athlete agent suspended, revoked, or denied or been refused renewal of registration or licensure as an athlete agent in any state.

(6)   Engaged in conduct the consequence of which was that a sanction, suspension, or declaration of ineligibility to participate in an interscholastic or intercollegiate athletic event was imposed on a student-athlete or educational institution.

(7)   Engaged in conduct that significantly adversely reflects on the applicant's credibility, honesty, or integrity.

(c)   In making a determination under subsection (b) of this section, the Secretary of State shall consider: (i) how recently the conduct occurred; (ii) the nature of the conduct and the context in which it occurred; and (iii) any other relevant conduct of the applicant.

(d)   An athlete agent may apply to renew a registration by submitting an application for renewal in a form prescribed by the Secretary of State. The application for renewal must be signed by the applicant under penalty of perjury and must contain current information on all matters required in an original registration.

(e)   An individual who has submitted an application for renewal of registration or licensure in another state, in lieu of submitting an application for renewal in the form prescribed pursuant to subsection (d) of this section, may file a copy of the application for renewal and a valid certificate of registration or licensure from the other state. The Secretary of State shall accept the application for renewal from the other state as an application for renewal in this State if the application to the other state satisfied the following:

(1)   Was submitted in the other state within six months immediately preceding the filing in this State and the applicant certifies the information contained in the application for renewal is current.

(2)   Contains information substantially similar to or more comprehensive than that required in an application for renewal submitted in this State.

(3)   Was signed by the applicant under penalty of perjury.

(f)   A certificate of registration or a renewal of a registration is valid for one year.

(g) An application filed under this section is a "public record" within the meaning of Chapter 132 of the General Statutes. (2003-375, s. 2.)

§ 78C-91. Suspension; revocation; refusal to renew registration.

(a) The Secretary of State may suspend, revoke, or refuse to renew a registration for conduct that would have justified denial of registration under G.S. 78C-90(b).

(b) The Secretary of State may deny, suspend, revoke, or refuse to renew a certificate of registration or licensure only after proper notice and an opportunity for a hearing in accordance with the Administrative Procedures Act pursuant to Article 3 of Chapter 150B of the General Statutes. (2003-375, s. 2.)

§ 78C-92. Temporary registration.

The Secretary of State may issue a temporary certificate of registration while an application for registration or renewal of registration is pending. (2003-375, s. 2.)

§ 78C-93. Registration; renewal of fees.

An application for registration or renewal of registration must be accompanied by a fee in the following amount:

(1)....... Application for registration... $200.00

(2)....... Application for registration based upon a certificate of

.... registration or licensure issued by another state.................................. 200.00

(3)....... Application for renewal of registration... 200.00

(4)....... Application for renewal of registration based upon an

.... application for renewal of registration or licensure

.... submitted in another state..
200.00.

(2003-375, s. 2.)

§ 78C-94. Required form of contract.

(a)   An agency contract must be in a record, signed or otherwise authenticated by the parties.

(b)   An agency contract must state or contain the following:

(1)   The amount and method of calculating the consideration to be paid by the student-athlete for services to be provided by the athlete agent under the contract and any other consideration the athlete agent has received or will receive from any other source for entering into the contract or for providing the services.

(2)   The name of any person not listed in the application for registration or renewal of registration who will be compensated because the student-athlete signed the agency contract.

(3)   A description of any expenses that the student-athlete agrees to reimburse.

(4)   A description of the services to be provided to the student-athlete.

(5)   The duration of the contract.

(6)   The date of execution.

(c)   An agency contract must contain, in close proximity to the signature of the student-athlete, a conspicuous notice in boldface type in capital letters stating:

WARNING TO STUDENT-ATHLETE

IF YOU SIGN THIS CONTRACT:

(1) YOU SHALL LOSE YOUR ELIGIBILITY TO COMPETE AS A STUDENT-ATHLETE IN YOUR SPORT;

(2) IF YOU HAVE AN ATHLETIC DIRECTOR, WITHIN 72 HOURS AFTER ENTERING INTO THIS CONTRACT, BOTH YOU AND YOUR ATHLETE AGENT MUST NOTIFY YOUR ATHLETIC DIRECTOR;

(3) YOU WAIVE YOUR ATTORNEY-CLIENT PRIVILEGE WITH RESPECT TO THIS CONTRACT AND CERTAIN INFORMATION RELATED TO IT; AND

(4) YOU MAY CANCEL THIS CONTRACT WITHIN 14 DAYS AFTER SIGNING IT. CANCELLATION OF THIS CONTRACT SHALL NOT REINSTATE YOUR ELIGIBILITY.

(d) An agency contract that does not conform to this section is voidable by the student-athlete. If a student-athlete voids an agency contract, the student-athlete is not required to pay any consideration under the contract or to return any consideration received from the athlete agent to induce the student-athlete to enter into the contract.

(e) The athlete agent shall give a record of the signed or otherwise authenticated agency contract to the student-athlete at the time of execution.

(f) The waiver of attorney-client privilege does not affect those privileges between client and attorney when the attorney is not an athlete agent. (2003-375, s. 2.)

§ 78C-95. Notice to educational institution.

(a) Within 72 hours after entering into an agency contract or before the next scheduled athletic event in which the student-athlete may participate, whichever occurs first, the athlete agent shall give notice in a record of the existence of the contract to the athletic director of the educational institution at which the student-athlete is enrolled or the athlete agent has reasonable grounds to believe the student-athlete intends to enroll.

(b) Within 72 hours after entering into an agency contract or before the next athletic event in which the student-athlete may participate, whichever occurs first, the student-athlete shall inform the athletic director of the educational institution at which the student-athlete is enrolled that he or she has entered into an agency contract. (2003-375, s. 2.)

§ 78C-96. Student-athlete's right to cancel.

(a) A student-athlete may cancel an agency contract by giving notice of the cancellation to the athlete agent in a record within 14 days after the contract is signed.

(b) A student-athlete may not waive the right to cancel an agency contract.

(c) If a student-athlete cancels an agency contract, the student-athlete is not required to pay any consideration under the contract or to return any consideration received from the athlete agent to induce the student-athlete to enter into the contract. (2003-375, s. 2.)

§ 78C-97. Required records; waiver of attorney-client privilege.

(a) An athlete agent shall retain the following records for a period of five years:

(1) The name and address of each individual represented by the athlete agent.

(2) Any agency contract entered into by the athlete agent.

(3) Any direct costs incurred by the athlete agent in the recruitment or solicitation of a student-athlete to enter into an agency contract.

(b) Records required to be retained by subsection (a) of this section are open to inspection by the Secretary of State during normal business hours.

(c) Where a student-athlete enters into an agency contract regulated under this Article, the student-athlete will be deemed to waive the attorney-client privilege with respect to records required to be retained by subsection (a) of this section, subject to G.S. 78C-94(f). (2003-375, s. 2.)

§ 78C-98. Prohibited conduct.

(a) An athlete agent, with the intent to induce a student-athlete to enter into an agency contract, shall not:

(1) Give any materially false or misleading information or make a materially false promise or representation.

(2) Furnish anything of value to a student-athlete before the student-athlete enters into the agency contract.

(3) Furnish anything of value to any individual other than the student-athlete or another registered athlete agent.

(b) An athlete agent shall not intentionally:

(1) Initiate contact with a student-athlete unless the athlete agent is registered under this Article.

(2) Refuse or fail to retain or permit inspection of the records required to be retained by G.S. 78C-97.

(3) Fail to register as required by G.S. 78C-88.

(4) Provide materially false or misleading information in an application for registration or renewal of registration.

(5) Predate or postdate an agency contract.

(6) Fail to notify a student-athlete before the student-athlete signs or otherwise authenticates an agency contract for a particular sport that the signing or authentication shall make the student-athlete ineligible to participate as a student-athlete in that sport. (2003-375, s. 2.)

§ 78C-99. Criminal penalties.

An athlete agent who violates any provision under G.S. 78C-98(a) is guilty of a Class I felony. (2003-375, s. 2.)

§ 78C-100. Civil remedies.

(a)   An educational institution has a right of action against an athlete agent or a former student-athlete for damages caused by a violation of this Article. In an action under this section, the court may award costs and reasonable attorneys' fees to the prevailing party.

(b)   Damages suffered by an educational institution under subsection (a) of this section include losses and expenses incurred because, as a result of the conduct of an athlete agent or former student-athlete, the educational institution was injured by a violation of this Article or was penalized, disqualified, or suspended from participation in athletics by: (i) a national association for the promotion and regulation of athletics; (ii) an athletic conference; or (iii) reasonable self-imposed disciplinary action taken to mitigate sanctions likely to be imposed by an athletic organization.

(c)   A right of action under this section does not accrue until the educational institution discovers, or by the exercise of reasonable diligence would have discovered, the violation by the athlete agent or former student-athlete.

(d)   Any liability of the athlete agent or the former student-athlete under this section is several and not joint.

(e)   This Article does not restrict rights, remedies, or defenses of any person under law or equity. (2003-375, s. 2.)

§ 78C-101. Administrative penalty.

The Secretary of State may assess a civil penalty against an athlete agent not to exceed twenty-five thousand dollars ($25,000) for a violation of this Article. (2003-375, s. 2.)

§ 78C-102. Uniformity of application and construction.

In applying and construing this Uniform Act, consideration must be given to the need to promote uniformity of the law with respect to its subject matter among states that enact it. (2003-375, s. 2.)

§ 78C-103. Electronic Signatures in Global and National Commerce Act.

The provisions of this Article governing the legal effect, validity, or enforceability of electronic records or signatures, and of contracts formed or performed with the use of those records or signatures, conform to the requirements of section 102 of the Electronic Signatures in Global and National Commerce Act, Pub. L. 106-229, 114 Stat. 464 (2000), and supersede, modify, and limit the Electronic Signatures in Global and National Commerce Act. (2003-375, s. 2.)

§ 78C-104. Severability.

If any provision of this Article or its application to any person or circumstance is held invalid, the invalidity does not affect other provisions or applications of this Article which can be given effect without the invalid provision or application, and to this end the provisions of this Article are severable. (2003-375, s. 2.)

§ 78C-105. Rules.

The Secretary of State may, in accordance with Chapter 150B of the General Statutes, adopt rules necessary to carry out the provisions of this Article. (2003-375, s. 2.)

Chapter 78D.

Commodities Act.

Article 1.

Scope.

§ 78D-1. Definitions.

(1) "Administrator" means the Secretary of State.

(2) "Board of Trade" means any person or group of persons engaged in buying or selling any commodity or receiving the same for sale on consignment, whether such person or group of persons is characterized as a board of trade, exchange or other form of marketplace.

(3) "CFTC Rule" means any rule, regulation or order of the Commodity Futures Trading Commission in effect on October 1, 1989, and all subsequent amendments, additions or other revisions thereto, unless the Administrator, within 10 days following the effective date of any such amendment, addition or revision, disallows the application thereof to this Part or to any provision thereof by rule, regulation or order.

(4) "Commodity" means, except as otherwise specified by the Administrator by rule, regulation or order, any agricultural, grain or livestock product or by-product, any metal or mineral (including a precious metal set forth in subdivision (13) of this section), any gem or gemstone (whether characterized as precious, semi-precious or otherwise), any fuel (whether liquid, gaseous or otherwise), any foreign currency, and all other goods, articles, products or items of any kind; provided that the term commodity shall not include (i) a numismatic coin whose fair market value is at least fifteen percent (15%) higher than the value of the metal it contains, (ii) real property or any timber, agricultural or livestock product grown or raised on real property and offered or sold by the owner or lessee of such real property or (iii) any work of art offered or sold by art dealers, at public auction or offered or sold through a private sale by the owner thereof.

(5) "Commodity Contract" means any account, agreement or contract for the purchase or sale, primarily for speculation or investment purposes and not for use or consumption by the offeree or purchaser, of one or more commodities, whether for immediate or subsequent delivery or whether delivery is intended by the parties, and whether characterized as a cash contract, deferred shipment or deferred delivery contract, forward contract, futures contract, installment or margin contract, leverage contract or otherwise. Any commodity contract offered or sold shall, in the absence of evidence to the contrary, be presumed to be offered or sold for speculation or investment purposes. A commodity contract shall not include any contract or agreement

which requires, and under which the purchaser receives, within 28 calendar days from the payment in good funds of any portion of the purchase price, physical delivery of the total amount of each commodity to be purchased under the contract or agreement.

(6) "Commodity Exchange Act" means the act of Congress known as the Commodity Exchange Act, as amended to October 1, 1989, codified at 7 U.S.C. § 1, et seq. and all subsequent amendments, additions or other revisions thereto, unless the Administrator, within 10 days following the effective date of any such amendment, addition or revision, disallows the application thereof to this Part or to any provision thereof by rule, regulation or order.

(7) "Commodity Futures Trading Commission" means the independent regulatory agency established by Congress to administer the Commodity Exchange Act.

(8) "Commodity Merchant" means any of the following as defined or described in the Commodity Exchange Act or by CFTC Rule:

a. Futures commission merchant;

b. Commodity pool operator;

c. Commodity trading advisor;

d. Introducing broker;

e. Leverage transaction merchant;

f. An associated person of any of the foregoing;

g. Floor broker; and

h. Any other person (other than a futures association) required to register with the Commodity Futures Trading Commission.

(9) "Commodity Option" means any account, agreement or contract giving a party thereto the right but not the obligation to purchase or sell one or more commodities and/or one or more commodity contracts, whether characterized as an option, privilege, indemnity, bid, offer, put, call, advance guaranty, decline guaranty or otherwise, but shall not include an option traded on a national

securities exchange registered with the United States Securities and Exchange Commission.

(10) "Financial Institution" means a bank, savings institution or trust company organized under, or supervised pursuant to, the laws of the United States or of any state.

(11) "Offer" includes every offer to sell, offer to purchase, or offer to enter into a commodity contract or commodity option.

(12) "Person" means an individual, a corporation, a partnership, association, a joint-stock company, a trust where the interests of the beneficiaries are evidenced by a security, an unincorporated organization, a government, or a political subdivision of a government, but shall not include a contract market designated by the Commodity Futures Trading Commission or any clearinghouse thereof or a national securities exchange registered with the Securities and Exchange Commission (or any employee, officer or director of such contract market, clearinghouse or exchange acting solely in that capacity).

(13) "Precious Metal" means the following in either coin, bullion or other form:

a. Silver;

b. Gold;

c. Platinum;

d. Palladium;

e. Copper; and

f. Such other items as the Administrator may specify by rule.

(14) "Sale" or "sell" includes every sale, contract of sale, contract to sell, or disposition, for value. (1989, c. 634, s. 1.)

§ 78D-2. Unlawful commodity transactions.

Except as otherwise provided in G.S. 78D-3 or G.S. 78D-4, no person shall sell or purchase or offer to sell or purchase any commodity under any commodity contract or under any commodity option or offer to enter into or enter into as seller or purchaser any commodity contract or any commodity option. (1989, c. 634, s. 1.)

§ 78D-3. Exempt person transactions.

The prohibitions in G.S. 78D-2 shall not apply to any transaction offered by and in which any of the following persons (or any employee, officer or director thereof acting solely in that capacity) is the purchaser or seller:

(1)   A person registered with the Commodity Futures Trading Commission as a futures commission merchant or as a leverage transaction merchant whose activities require such registration;

(2)   A person registered with the Securities and Exchange Commission as a broker-dealer whose activities require such registration;

(3)   A person affiliated with, and whose obligations and liabilities under the transaction are guaranteed by, a person referred to in subdivisions (1) or (2) of this section;

(4)   A person who is a member of a contract market designated by the Commodity Futures Trading Commission (or any clearinghouse thereof);

(5)   A financial institution; or

(6)   A person registered under the laws of this State as a securities broker-dealer whose activities require such registration.

The exemption provided by this section shall not apply to any transaction or activity which is prohibited by the Commodity Exchange Act or CFTC Rule. (1989, c. 634, s. 1.)

§ 78D-4. Exempt transactions.

(a) The prohibitions in G.S. 78D-2 shall not apply to the following:

(1) An account, agreement or transaction within the exclusive jurisdiction of the Commodity Futures Trading Commission as granted under the Commodity Exchange Act;

(2) A commodity contract for the purchase of one or more precious metals which requires, and under which the purchaser receives, within 28 calendar days from the payment in good funds of any portion of the purchase price, physical delivery of the quantity of the precious metals purchased by such payment, provided that, for purposes of this paragraph, physical delivery shall be deemed to have occurred if, within such twenty-eight-day period, such quantity of precious metals purchased by such payment is delivered (whether in specifically segregated or fungible bulk form) into the possession of a depository (other than the seller) which is either (i) a financial institution, (ii) a depository the warehouse receipts of which are recognized for delivery purposes for any commodity on a contract market designated by the Commodity Futures Trading Commission, (iii) a storage facility licensed or regulated by the United States or any agency thereof, or (iv) a depository designated by the Administrator, and such depository (or other person which itself qualifies as a depository as aforesaid) or a qualified seller issues and the purchaser receives, a certificate, document of title, confirmation or other instrument evidencing that such quantity of precious metals has been delivered to the depository and is being and will continue to be held by the depository on the purchaser's behalf, free and clear of all liens and encumbrances, other than liens of the purchaser, tax liens, liens agreed to by the purchaser, or liens of the depository for fees and expenses, which have previously been disclosed to the purchaser;

(3) A commodity contract solely between persons engaged in producing, processing, using commercially or handling as merchants, each commodity subject thereto, or any by-product thereof; or

(4) A commodity contract under which the offeree or the purchaser is a person referred to in G.S. 78D-3 of this Chapter, an insurance company, an investment company as defined in the Investment Company Act of 1940, or an employee pension and profit sharing or benefit plan (other than a self-employed individual retirement plan, or individual retirement account).

(b) For the purposes of G.S. 78D-4(a)(2), a qualified seller is a person who:

(1) Is a seller of precious metals and has a tangible net worth of at least $5,000,000 (or has an affiliate who has unconditionally guaranteed the obligations and liabilities of the seller and the affiliate has a tangible net worth of at least $5,000,000);

(2) Has stored precious metals with one or more depositories on behalf of customers for at least the previous three years;

(3) Prior to any offer, and annually thereafter, files with the Administrator a sworn notice of intent to act as a qualified seller under G.S. 78D-4(a)(2), containing:

a. The seller's name and address, names of its directors, officers, controlling shareholders, partners, principals, and other controlling persons;

b. The address of its principal place of business, state and date of incorporation or organization, and the name and address of seller's registered agent in this State;

c. A statement that the seller (or a person affiliated with the seller who has guaranteed the obligations and liabilities of the seller) has a tangible net worth of at least $5,000,000;

d. Depository information including:

1. The name and address of the depository or depositories that the seller intends to use;

2. The name and address of each and every depository where the seller has stored precious metals on behalf of customers for the previous three years; and

3. Independent verification from each and every depository named in (3)d2 of this section that the seller has in fact stored precious metals on behalf of the seller's customers for the previous three years and a statement of total deposits made during this period.

e. Financial statements for the seller (or the person affiliated with the seller who has guaranteed the obligations and liabilities of the seller) for the past three years, audited by an independent certified public accountant, together with the accountant's report;

f. A statement describing the details of all civil, criminal, or administrative proceedings currently pending or adversely resolved against the seller or its directors, officers, controlling shareholders, partners, principals, or other controlling persons during the past 10 years including: (i) civil litigation and administrative proceedings involving securities or commodities violations, or fraud, (ii) criminal proceedings, (iii) denials, suspensions or revocations of securities or commodities licenses or registrations, and (iv) suspensions or expulsions from membership in, or associations with, self-regulatory organizations registered under the Securities Exchange Act of 1934, or the Commodity Exchange Act; or (v) a statement that there were no such proceedings.

(4) Notifies the Administrator within 15 days of any material changes in the information provided in the notice of intent; and

(5) Annually furnishes to each purchaser for whom the seller is then storing precious metals, and to the Administrator, a report by an independent certified public accountant of the accountant's examination of the seller's precious metals storage program that includes a reconciliation of the total amount of depository confirmations issued by all depositories where the seller has stored precious metals to the total amount of all confirmations issued to customers by the seller.

(c) The Administrator may, upon request by the seller, waive any of the exemption requirements in G.S. 78D-4(b), conditionally or unconditionally.

(d) The Administrator may, by order, deny, suspend, revoke or place limitations on the authority to engage in business as a qualified seller under G.S. 78D-4(a)(2) if the Administrator finds that the order is in the public interest and that the person, the person's officers, directors, partners, agents, servants or employees, any person occupying a similar status or performing similar functions, any person who directly or indirectly controls or is controlled by the seller, or any of them, the seller's affiliates or subsidiaries:

(1) Has filed a notice of intention under G.S. 78D-4(c) with the Administrator or the designee of the Administrator which was incomplete in any material respect or contained any statement which was, in light of the circumstances under which it was made, false or misleading with respect to any material fact;

(2) Has, within the last 10 years, pled guilty or nolo contendere to, or been convicted of any crime indicating a lack of fitness to engage in the investment commodity business;

(3) Has been permanently or temporarily enjoined by any court of competent jurisdiction from engaging in, or continuing, any conduct or practice which injunction indicates a lack of fitness to engage in the investment commodities business;

(4) Is the subject of an order of the Administrator denying, suspending, or revoking the person's license as a securities broker-dealer, sales representative, or investment adviser;

(5) Is the subject of any of the following orders which are currently effective and which were issued within the last five years:

a. An order by the securities agency or Administrator of another state, Canadian province or territory, the Securities and Exchange Commission, or the Commodity Futures Trading Commission, entered after notice and opportunity for hearing, denying, suspending, or revoking the person's registration as a futures commission merchant, leverage transaction merchant, introducing broker, commodity trading adviser, commodity pool operator, securities broker-dealer, sales representative, or investment adviser, or the substantial equivalent of those terms;

b. Suspension or expulsion from membership in, or association with, a self-regulatory organization registered under the Securities Exchange Act of 1934 or the Commodity Exchange Act;

c. A United States Postal Service fraud order;

d. A cease and desist order entered after notice and opportunity of hearing by the Administrator or the securities agency or Administrator of any other state, Canadian province or territory, the Securities and Exchange Commission, or the Commodity Futures Trading Commission;

e. An order entered by the Commodity Futures Trading Commission denying, suspending or revoking registration under the Commodity Exchange Act.

(6) Has engaged in an unethical or dishonest act or practice in the investment commodities or securities business; or

(7) Has failed reasonably to supervise sales representatives or employees.

(e) If the public interest or the protection of investors so requires, the Administrator may, by order, summarily deny or suspend the exemption for a qualified seller. Upon the entry of the order, the Administrator shall promptly notify the person claiming said status that an order has been entered and the reasons therefor and that within 20 days after the receipt of a written request the matter will be scheduled for hearing. The provisions of G.S. 78D-30 shall apply with respect to all subsequent proceedings.

(f) If the Administrator finds that any applicant or qualified seller is no longer in existence or has ceased to do business or is subject to an adjudication of mental incompetence or to the control of a committee, conservator, or guardian, or cannot be located after reasonable search, the Administrator may, by order, deny or revoke the exemption for a qualified seller.

(g) The Administrator may issue rules or orders prescribing the terms and conditions of all transactions and contracts covered by the provisions of this Chapter which are not within the exclusive jurisdiction of the Commodity Futures Trading Commission as granted by the Commodity Exchange Act, exempting any person or transaction from any provision of this Chapter conditionally or unconditionally and otherwise implementing the provisions of this Chapter for the protection of purchasers and sellers of commodities. (1989, c. 634, s. 1; 2001-126, s. 7.)

§ 78D-5. Unlawful commodity activities.

(a) No person shall engage in a trade or business or otherwise act as a commodity merchant unless such person (i) is registered or temporarily licensed with the Commodity Futures Trading Commission for each activity constituting such person as a commodity merchant and such registration or temporary license shall not have expired, nor been suspended nor revoked; or (ii) is exempt from such registration by virtue of the Commodity Exchange Act or of a CFTC rule.

(b) No board of trade shall trade, or provide a place for the trading of, any commodity contract or commodity option required to be traded on or subject to the rules of a contract market designated by the Commodity Futures Trading Commission unless such board of trade has been so designated for such commodity contract or commodity option and such designation shall not have been vacated, nor suspended nor revoked. (1989, c. 634, s. 1.)

§ 78D-6. Fraudulent conduct.

No person, shall directly or indirectly:

(1) Cheat or defraud, or attempt to cheat or defraud, any other person or employ any device, scheme or artifice to defraud any other person;

(2) Make any false report, enter any false record, or make any untrue statement of a material fact or omit to state a material fact necessary in order to make the statements made, in the light of the circumstances under which they were made, not misleading;

(3) Engage in any transaction, act, practice or course of business, including, without limitation, any form of advertising or solicitation, which operates or would operate as a fraud or deceit upon any person; or

(4) Misappropriate or convert the funds, security or property of any other person;

in or in connection with the purchase or sale of, the offer to sell, the offer to purchase, the offer to enter into, or the entry into of, any commodity contract or commodity option subject to the provisions of G.S. 78D-2, 78D-3, 78D-4(a)(2) or G.S. 78D-4(a)(4) of this Chapter. (1989, c. 634, s. 1.)

§ 78D-7. Liability of principals, controlling persons and others.

(a) The act, omission, or failure of any official, agent, or other person acting for any individual, association, partnership, corporation, or trust within the scope of his employment or office shall be deemed the act, omission, or failure of such individual, association, partnership, corporation, or trust, as well as of such official, agent, or other person.

(b) Every person who directly or indirectly controls another person liable under any provision of this Chapter, every partner, officer, or director of such other person, every person occupying a similar status or performing similar functions, every employee of such other person who materially aids in the violation is also liable jointly and severally with and to the same extent as such other person, unless the person who is also liable by virtue of this provision sustains the burden of proof that he did not know, and in exercise of reasonable care could not have known, of the existence of the facts by reason of which the liability is alleged to exist. (1989, c. 634, s. 1.)

§ 78D-8. Securities and laws unaffected.

Nothing in this Chapter shall impair, derogate or otherwise affect the authority or powers of the Administrator under Chapters 78A or 78C of the General Statutes or the application of any provision thereof to any person or transaction subject thereto. (1989, c. 634, s. 1.)

§ 78D-9. Purpose.

This Chapter may be construed and implemented to effectuate its general purpose to protect investors, to prevent and prosecute illegal and fraudulent schemes involving commodity contracts and to maximize coordination with federal and other states' laws and the administration and enforcement thereof. This Chapter is not intended to create any rights or remedies upon which actions may be brought by private persons against persons who violate the provisions of this Chapter. (1989, c. 634, s. 1.)

§§ 78D-10 through 78D-20. Reserved for future codification purposes.

Article 2.

Administration and Enforcement.

§ 78D-21. Investigations.

(a) The Administrator may make investigations, within or without this State, as it finds necessary or appropriate to:

(1) Determine whether any person has violated, or is about to violate, any provision of this Chapter or any rule or order of the Administrator; or

(2) Aid in enforcement of this Chapter.

(b) The Administrator may publish information concerning any violation of this Chapter or any rule or order of the Administrator.

(c) For purposes of any investigation or proceeding under this Chapter, the Administrator or any officer or employee designated by rule or order, may administer oaths and affirmations, subpoena witnesses, compel their attendance, take evidence, and require the production of any books, papers, correspondence, memoranda, agreements, or other documents or records which the Administrator finds to be relevant or material to the inquiry.

(d) (1) If a person does not give testimony or produce the documents required by the Administrator or a designated employee pursuant to an administrative subpoena, the Administrator or designated employee may apply for a court order compelling compliance with the subpoena or the giving of the required testimony.

(2) The request for order of compliance may be addressed to either:

a. The Superior Court of Wake County where service may be obtained on the person refusing to testify or produce, if the person is within this State; or

b. The appropriate court of the State having jurisdiction over the person refusing to testify or produce, if the person is outside this State.

(e) The Administrator in his discretion may appoint commodities law enforcement agents and other enforcement personnel.

(1) Subject Matter Jurisdiction. - The responsibility of an agent shall be enforcement of this Chapter.

(2) Territorial Jurisdiction. - A commodities law enforcement agent is a State officer with jurisdiction throughout the State.

(3) Service of Orders of the Administrator. - Commodities law enforcement agents may serve and execute notices, orders, or demands issued by the Administrator for the surrender of registrations or relating to any administrative proceeding. While serving and executing such notices, orders, or demands, commodities law enforcement agents shall have all the power and authority

possessed by law enforcement officers when executing an arrest warrant. (1989, c. 634, s. 1.)

§ 78D-22. Enforcement of Chapter.

(a)   If the Administrator believes, whether or not based upon an investigation conducted under G.S. 78D-21 that any person has engaged or is about to engage in any act or practice constituting a violation of any provision of this Chapter or any rule or order hereunder, the Administrator may:

(1)   Issue a cease and desist order;

(2)   Issue an order imposing a civil penalty in an amount which may not exceed twenty-five thousand dollars ($25,000) for any single violation or five hundred thousand dollars ($500,000) for multiple violations in a single proceeding or a series of related proceedings;

(3)   Issue an order requiring reimbursement of the costs of investigation; or

(4)   Initiate any of the actions specified in subsection (b) of this section.

The clear proceeds of civil penalties imposed pursuant to this subsection shall be remitted to the Civil Penalty and Forfeiture Fund in accordance with G.S. 115C-457.2. Any reimbursement of costs imposed by this subsection shall be paid to the General Fund.

(b)   The Administrator may institute any of the following actions in the appropriate courts of this State, or in the appropriate courts of another state, in addition to any legal or equitable remedies otherwise available:

(1)   A declaratory judgment;

(2)   An action for a prohibitory or mandatory injunction to enjoin the violation and to ensure compliance with this Chapter or any rule or order of the Administrator;

(3)   An action for disgorgement; or

(4) An action for appointment of a receiver or conservator for the defendant or the defendant's assets. (1989, c. 634, s. 1; 1998-215, s. 123.)

§ 78D-23. Power of court to grant relief.

(a) (1) Upon a proper showing by the Administrator that a person has violated, or is about to violate, any provision of this Chapter or any rule or order of the Administrator, any court of competent jurisdiction may grant appropriate legal or equitable remedies.

(2) Upon showing of violation of this Chapter or a rule or order of the Administrator, the court, in addition to traditional legal and equitable remedies, including temporary restraining orders, permanent or temporary prohibitory or mandatory injunctions, and writs of prohibition or mandamus, may grant the following special remedies:

a. Imposition of a civil penalty in an amount which may not exceed twenty-five thousand dollars ($25,000) for any single violation or five hundred thousand dollars ($500,000) for multiple violations in a single proceeding or a series of related proceedings;

b. Disgorgement;

c. Declaratory judgment;

d. Restitution to investors wishing restitution; and

e. Appointment of a receiver or conservator for the defendant or the defendant's assets.

(3) Appropriate remedies when the defendant is shown only about to violate this Chapter or a rule or order of the Administrator shall be limited to:

a. A temporary restraining order;

b. A temporary or permanent injunction;

c. A writ of prohibition or mandamus; or

d. An order appointing a receiver or conservator for the defendant or the defendant's assets.

The clear proceeds of civil penalties imposed pursuant to this subsection shall be remitted to the Civil Penalty and Forfeiture Fund in accordance with G.S. 115C-457.2.

(b) The court shall not require the Administrator to post a bond in any official action under this Chapter.

(c) (1) Upon a proper showing by the administrator or securities or commodity agency of another state that a person (other than a government or governmental agency or instrumentality) has violated, or is about to violate, any provision of the commodity code of that state or any rule or order of the administrator or securities or commodity agency of that state, the Superior Court of Wake County may grant appropriate legal and equitable remedies.

(2) Upon showing of a violation of the securities or commodity act of the foreign state or a rule or order of the administrator or securities or commodity agency of the foreign state, the court, in addition to traditional legal or equitable remedies including temporary restraining orders, permanent or temporary prohibitory or mandatory injunctions and writs of prohibition or mandamus, may grant the following special remedies:

a. Disgorgement; and

b. Appointment of a receiver, conservator, or ancillary receiver or conservator for the defendant or the defendant's assets located in this State.

(3) Appropriate remedies when the defendant is shown only about to violate the securities or commodity act of the foreign state or a rule or order of the administrator or securities or commodity agency of the foreign state shall be limited to:

a. A temporary restraining order;

b. A temporary or permanent injunction;

c. A writ of prohibition or mandamus; or

d. An order appointing a receiver, conservator, or ancillary receiver or conservator for the defendant or the defendant's assets located in this State. (1989, c. 634, s. 1; 1998-215, s. 124.)

§ 78D-24. Criminal penalties.

(a) Any person who willfully violates any provision of this Chapter is guilty of a felony. If the losses caused by the violation or violations are one hundred thousand dollars ($100,000) or more, the person is guilty of a Class C felony. If the losses caused by the violation or violations are less than one hundred thousand dollars ($100,000), the person is guilty of a Class H felony.

(b) Any person convicted of violating a rule or order under this Chapter may be fined, but may not be imprisoned, if the person proves he had no knowledge of the rule or order.

(c) In lieu of a fine otherwise authorized by law, a person who has been convicted of or who has pleaded guilty or no contest to having engaged in conduct in violation of the provisions of this Chapter may be sentenced to pay a fine that does not exceed the greater of three times the gross value gained or three times the gross loss caused by such conduct, plus court costs and the costs of investigation and prosecution, reasonably incurred.

(d) The Administrator may refer such evidence as is available concerning violations of this Chapter or any rule or order of the Administrator to the Attorney General or the proper district attorney, who may, with or without such a reference from the Administrator, institute the appropriate criminal proceedings under this Chapter. Upon receipt of such reference, the Attorney General or the district attorney may request that a duly employed attorney of the Administrator prosecute or assist in the prosecution of such violation or violations on behalf of the State. Upon approval of the Administrator, such employee shall be appointed a special prosecutor for the Attorney General or the district attorney to serve without compensation from the Attorney General or district attorney. Such special prosecutor shall have all the powers and duties prescribed by law for Assistant Attorneys General or district attorneys and such other powers and duties as are lawfully delegated to such special prosecutor by the Attorney General or the district attorney.

(e) Nothing in this Chapter limits the power of the State to punish any person for any conduct which constitutes a crime by statute or at common law. (1989, c. 634, s. 1; 2003-413, s. 26.)

§ 78D-25. Administration of Chapter.

(a) This Chapter shall be administered by the Secretary of State. The Secretary of State as Administrator may delegate all or part of the authority under this Chapter to the Deputy Securities Administrator including, but not limited to, the authority to conduct hearings, make, execute and issue final agency orders and decisions. The Secretary of State may appoint such clerks and other assistants as may from time to time be needed. The Secretary of State may designate one or more hearing officers for the purpose of conducting administrative hearings.

(b) Neither the Administrator nor any employees of the Administrator shall use any information which is filed with or obtained by the Administrator which is not public information for personal gain or benefit, nor shall the Administrator nor any employees of the Administrator conduct any securities or commodity dealings whatsoever based upon any such information, even though public, if there has not been a sufficient period of time for the securities or commodity markets to assimilate such information.

(c) (1) Except as provided in subdivision (2) of this subsection, all information collected, assembled or maintained by the Administrator is public information and is available for the examination of the public as provided by Chapter 132 of the General Statutes.

(2) The following are exceptions to subdivision (1) which are deemed to be confidential:

a. Information obtained in private investigations pursuant to G.S. 78D-21 of this Chapter;

b. Information made confidential by the provisions of Chapter 132 of the General Statutes;

c. Information obtained from federal agencies which may not be disclosed under federal law.

(3) The Administrator in his discretion may disclose any information made confidential under subsection (2)a. to persons identified in G.S. 78D-26(a).

(4) No provision of this Chapter either creates or derogates any privilege which exists at common law, by statute or otherwise when any documentary or other evidence is sought under subpoena directed to the Administrator or any employee of the Administrator. (1989, c. 634, s. 1; 2001-126, s. 11.)

§ 78D-26. Cooperation with other agencies.

(a) To encourage uniform application and interpretation of this Chapter and securities regulation and enforcement in general, the Administrator and the employees of the Administrator may cooperate, including bearing the expense of the cooperation, with the securities agencies or administrator of another jurisdiction, Canadian province or territory or such other agencies administering this Chapter, the Commodity Futures Trading Commission, the Securities and Exchange Commission, any self-regulatory organization established under the Commodity Exchange Act or the Securities Exchange Act of 1934, any national or international organization of commodities or securities officials or agencies, and any governmental law enforcement agency.

(b) The cooperation authorized by subsection (a) shall include, but need not be limited to, the following:

(1) Making joint examinations or investigations;

(2) Holding joint administrative hearings;

(3) Filing and prosecuting joint litigation;

(4) Sharing and exchanging personnel;

(5) Sharing and exchanging information and documents;

(6) Formulating and adopting mutual regulations, statements of policy, guidelines, proposed statutory changes and releases; and

(7) Issuing and enforcing subpoenas at the request of the agency administering this Chapter in another jurisdiction, the securities agency of

another jurisdiction, the Commodity Futures Trading Commission or the Securities and Exchange Commission if the information sought would also be subject to lawful subpoena for conduct occurring in this State. (1989, c. 634, s. 1.)

§ 78D-27. General authority to adopt rules, forms, and orders.

(a)   In addition to specific authority granted elsewhere in this Chapter, the Administrator may make, amend, and rescind rules, forms, and orders as are necessary to carry out the provisions of this Chapter. Such rules or forms shall include, but need not be limited to, the following:

(1)   Rules defining any terms, whether or not used in this Chapter, insofar as the definitions are not inconsistent with the provisions of this Chapter. For the purpose of rules or forms, the Administrator may classify commodities and commodity contracts, persons, and matters within the Administrator's jurisdiction.

(2)   Reserved.

(b)   Unless specifically provided in this Chapter, no rule, form, or order may be adopted, amended or rescinded unless the Administrator finds that the action is:

(1)   Necessary or appropriate in the public interest or for the protection of investors; and

(2)   Consistent with the purposes fairly intended by the policy and provisions of this Chapter.

(c)   All rules and forms of the Administrator shall be published.

(d)   No provision of this Chapter imposing any liability applies to any act done or omitted in good faith in conformity with a rule, order, or form adopted by the Administrator, notwithstanding that the rule, order, or form may later be amended, or rescinded, or be determined by judicial or other authority to be invalid for any reason. (1989, c. 634, s. 1.)

§ 78D-28. Consent to service of process.

When a person, including a nonresident of this State, engages in conduct prohibited or made actionable by the Chapter or any rule or order of the Administrator, the engaging in the conduct shall constitute the appointment of the Administrator as the person's attorney to receive service of any lawful process in a noncriminal proceeding against the person, a successor, or personal representative, which grows out of that conduct and which is brought under the Chapter or any rule or order of the Administrator with the same force and validity as if served personally. (1989, c. 634, s. 1.)

§ 78D-29. Scope of the Chapter.

(a)   G.S. 78D-2, 78D-5 and 78D-6 apply to persons who sell or offer to sell when:

(1)   An offer to sell is made in this State, or

(2)   An offer to buy is made and accepted in this State.

(b)   G.S. 78D-2, 78D-5 and 78D-6 apply to persons who buy or offer to buy when:

(1)   An offer to buy is made in this State, or

(2)   An offer to sell is made and accepted in this State.

(c)   For the purpose of this section, an offer to sell or to buy is made in this State, whether or not either party is then present in this State, when the offer:

(1)   Originates from this State, or

(2)   Is directed by the offeror to this State and received at the place to which it is directed (or at any post office in this State in the case of a mailed offer).

(d)   For the purpose of this section, an offer to buy or to sell is accepted in this State when acceptance:

(1) Is communicated to the offeror in this State, and

(2) Has not previously been communicated to the offeror, orally or in writing, outside this State; and acceptance is communicated to the offeror in this State, whether or not either party is then present in this State, when the offeree directs it to the offeror in this State, reasonably believing the offeror to be in this State and it is received at the place to which it is directed (or at any post office in this State in the case of a mailed acceptance).

(e) An offer to sell or to buy is not made in this State when:

(1) The publisher circulates or there is circulated on his behalf in this State any bona fide newspaper or other publication of general, regular, and paid circulation which is not published in this State, or which is published in this State but has had more than two-thirds of its circulation outside this State during the past 12 months, or

(2) A radio or television program originating outside this State is received in this State. (1989, c. 634, s. 1.)

§ 78D-30. Procedure for entry of an order.

(a) The Administrator shall commence an administrative proceeding under this Chapter, by entering either a notice of intent to do a contemplated act or a summary order. The notice of intent or summary order may be entered without notice, without opportunity for hearing, and need not be supported by findings of fact or conclusions of law, but must be in writing.

(b) Upon entry of a notice of intent or summary order, the Administrator shall promptly notify all interested parties that the notice or summary order has been entered and the reasons therefor. If the proceeding is pursuant to a notice of intent, the Administrator shall inform all interested parties of the dates, time, and place set for the hearing on the notice. If the proceeding is pursuant to a summary order, the Administrator shall inform all interested parties that they have 30 business days from the entry of the order to file a written request for a hearing on the matter with the Administrator and that the hearing will be scheduled within 20 days after the receipt of the written request.

(c) If the proceeding is pursuant to a summary order, the Administrator, whether or not a written request for a hearing is received from any interested party, may schedule the matter for hearing on the Administrator's own motion.

(d) If no request for a hearing, other responsive pleading, or submission is received by the Administrator within 30 business days of receipt of service of notice of summary order under subsection (b) of this section and no hearing is ordered by the Administrator, the summary order will automatically become a final order after 30 business days from the date service of the notice of summary order was received.

(e) If a hearing is requested or ordered, the Administrator, after notice of, and opportunity for, hearing to all interested persons, may modify or vacate the order or extend it until final determination.

(f) No final order or order after hearing may be returned without:

(1) Appropriate notice to all interested persons;

(2) Opportunity for hearing by all interested persons; and

(3) Entry of written findings of fact and conclusions of law.

Every hearing in an administrative proceeding under this Chapter shall be public unless the Administrator grants a request joined in by all the respondents that the hearing be conducted privately. (1989, c. 634, s. 1; 1998-196, s. 1; 2001-126, s. 8.)

§ 78D-31. Judicial review of orders.

(a) Any person aggrieved by a final order of the Administrator may obtain a review of the order in the Superior Court of Wake County by filing in court, within 30 days after a written copy of the decision is served upon the person by personal service or by registered or certified mail, a written petition praying that the order be modified or set aside in whole or in part. A copy of the petition shall be forthwith served upon the Administrator, and thereupon the Administrator shall certify and file in court a copy of the filing and evidence upon which the order was entered. When these have been filed, the court has exclusive jurisdiction to affirm, modify, enforce, or set aside the order, in whole or in part. The findings of the Administrator as to the facts, if supported by competent, material and substantial evidence, are conclusive. If either party applies to the court for leave to adduce additional material evidence, and shows to the satisfaction of the court that there were reasonable grounds for failure to adduce the evidence in the hearing before the Administrator, the court may order the additional evidence to be taken before the Administrator and to be adduced upon the hearing in such manner and upon such conditions as the court considers proper. The Administrator may modify his findings and order by reason of the additional evidence and shall file in court the additional evidence together with any modified or new findings or order. The judgment of the court is final, subject to review by the Court of Appeals.

(b) The commencement of proceedings under subsection (a) does not, unless specifically ordered by the court, operate as a stay of the Administrator's order. (1989, c. 634, s. 1.)

§ 78D-32. Pleading exemptions.

It shall not be necessary to negative any of the exemptions of this Chapter in any complaint, information or indictment, or any writ or proceeding brought under this chapter; and the burden of proof of any such exemption shall be upon the party claiming the same. (1989, c. 634, s. 1.)

§ 78D-33. Affirmative defense.

It shall be a defense in any complaint, information, indictment, any writ or proceeding brought under this Chapter alleging a violation of G.S. 78D-2 based solely on the failure in an individual case to make physical delivery within the applicable time period under G.S. 78D-1(5) or G.S. 78D-4(a)(2) if the party asserting the defense sustains the burden of proof that:

(1) Failure to make physical delivery was due solely to factors beyond the control of the seller, the seller's officers, directors, partners, agents, servants or employees, every person occupying a similar status or performing similar functions, every person who directly or indirectly controls or is controlled by the seller, or any of them, the seller's affiliates, subsidiaries or successors; and

(2) Physical delivery was completed within a reasonable time under the applicable circumstances. (1989, c. 634, s. 1.)

Chapter 79.

Strays

§§ 79-1 through 79-4: Repealed by Session Laws 1991, c. 472, s. 1.

Vision Books Order Form

Fax Orders:	1-704-921-9271
Phone Orders:	1-704-921-9271
E-mail Orders:	www.visionbooks.org
Mail Orders:	Vision Books P.O. Box 42406 Charlotte, NC 28215

Shipp To:
Name_____
Address_____
City_____State_____Zip_____
Phone_____Fax_____
Email_____@_____

Bill To: We can bill a third party on your behalf.
Name_____
Address_____
City_____State_____Zip_____
Phone____(_____)_____Fax_____
Email_____@_____

Pamphlet Number ($15.00 Each)	Qty	Total Cost
_____	_____	_____
_____	_____	_____
_____	_____	_____
_____	_____	_____
_____	_____	_____
_____	_____	_____
_____	_____	_____
<u>Full Volume Set 1-92</u>	<u>92 Pamphlets</u>	<u>1,380.00</u>

Free Shipping Shipping & Handling on Full Volume Orders
Add $1.00 Shipping & Handling per pamphlet $_____

Total Cost $_____

DID YOU ENJOY THIS BOOK?

Vision Books, LLC would like to hear from you! If you or someone you know has been fasely imprisoned, we would like to hear your story. If the 'North Carolina Criminal Law and Procedure' has had an effect in your life or if you have suggestions, we would like to hear from you. Send your letters to:

Vision Books, LLC
Attn: Staff Writers
P.O. Box 42406
Charlotte, NC 28215
Email: staff@visionbooks.org

Order Additional Copies:

Fax Orders:	1-704-921-9271
Phone Orders:	1-704-921-9271
E-mail Orders:	www.visionbooks.org
Mail Orders:	Vision Books P.O. Box 42406 Charlotte, NC 28215

www.ingramcontent.com/pod-product-compliance
Lightning Source LLC
Chambersburg PA
CBHW051627170526
45167CB00001B/96